Verdi's *Aida*

ALSO BY CLYDE T. MCCANTS

American Opera Singers and Their Recordings:
Critical Commentaries and Discographies
(McFarland, 2004)

Opera for Libraries: A Guide to Core Works, Audio and
Video Recordings, Books and Serials
(McFarland, 2003)

Verdi's *Aida*

*A Record of the Life of the Opera
On and Off the Stage*

CLYDE T. MCCANTS

McFarland & Company, Inc., Publishers
Jefferson, North Carolina, and London

LIBRARY OF CONGRESS CATALOGUING-IN-PUBLICATION DATA

McCants, Clyde T.
Verdi's Aida : a record of the life of the opera
on and off the stage / Clyde T. McCants.
p.   cm.
Includes discography (p.   ), videography (p.   ), and index.

ISBN 0-7864-2328-5 (softcover: 50# alkaline paper) ∞

1. Verdi, Giuseppe, 1813–1901. Aïda [sic].
2. Opera—19th century. I. Title.
ML410.V4M34   2006   782.1—dc22   2005030237

British Library cataloguing data are available

©2006 Clyde T. McCants. All rights reserved

*No part of this book may be reproduced or transmitted in any form
or by any means, electronic or mechanical, including photocopying
or recording, or by any information storage and retrieval system,
without permission in writing from the publisher.*

Cover photograph © 2005 Photo Disc

Manufactured in the United States of America

*McFarland & Company, Inc., Publishers
Box 611, Jefferson, North Carolina 28640
www.mcfarlandpub.com*

Table of Contents

Introduction . . . 1

1. The Winding Road to *Aida* . . . 7
2. From Story to Stage . . . 25
3. *Aida* for the World — and for the Ages . . . 45
4. Words and Music . . . 67
5. A Legacy in Sound . . . 103
6. Linking Sight to Sound . . . 151

Appendix I — Discography . . . 173
Appendix II — Videography . . . 179
Appendix III — Additional Resources . . . 183
Index . . . 189

Introduction

Why a book about Verdi's *Aida*?

Let me begin by confessing that *Aida* is my favorite opera, and I can still say that even after the intensive review of fifty or more sound and video recordings. It may not be the best opera ever composed. I'd probably place Bizet's *Carmen*, Mozart's *Le Nozze di Figaro,* and certainly Verdi's *Otello* ahead of *Aida* on my personal list of the greatest operas. In *Aida*, however, are all the elements of opera wrapped up in one neat package — fascinating characters engaged in an interesting plot with intense personal encounters; the music of a master at his mature best; impressive staging possibilities; dancers, stage extras, and maybe even a horse or two; and six roles that challenge the greatest singers to deliver the vocal and dramatic goods. It is the quintessential opera, a work that truly defines the genre for scores of opera lovers.

So why *not* a book about *Aida*?

I encountered *Aida* relatively early in my childhood. I was studying piano and just beginning to look outside the Kinsella method primers for something a bit more exciting than "The March of the Wee Folk" and "Gertrude's Dream Waltz." It was a copy of what I believe was titled *Everybody's Favorite Opera* purchased at a local five-and-dime that started me picking out the themes of the "Triumphal March" and "Celeste Aida" on the piano keyboard. Here was something about which I wanted to know more, and our public library provided precisely the right source: the ninth edition of the ubiquitous and irreplaceable *Victor Book of the Opera*. I looked at the pictures of the impressively solid sets designed by A. Pasquali, the strange, exotic, old-fashioned Consecration scene from the Metropolitan Opera in the early twentieth century; and the character portraits of Martinelli, Caruso, Rethberg, and Aureliano Pertile and they whetted my appetite for the real thing. Then I read the story, and it was impossible to resist a work that promised "Egyptian troops ... preceded by musicians playing long, brazen trumpets ... dancing girls who execute their curious Egyptian steps before the King"* combined with a love

---

***The Victor Book of the Opera*, ninth edition, edited by Charles O'Connell (Camden, N.J.: RCA Manufacturing Company, 1936), p. 33.

story that ended as "the lovers, clasped in one final, passionate embrace, sing their farewell to earth and its sorrows and together await Eternity."*

All that was missing now was the opportunity to hear the opera and then to see it actually performed on stage. The Saturday afternoon Metropolitan Opera broadcasts took care of the hearing. Perhaps I had tuned in to an earlier broadcast, but the first one that I recall took place on the afternoon of February 19, 1949, when Emil Cooper conducted Ljuba Welitsch, Frederic Jagel, Margaret Harshaw, Frank Guarrera, Jerome Hines, and Philip Kinsman.

Frankly, I was disappointed. I probably wanted something from the title character that Welitsch didn't offer—a rounder, broader, more velvety tone, something more like the only recording of "Ritorna vincitor" that I knew, the version by an unlikely Helen Traubel. Recently, I listened to some selections from that 1949 performance on compact disc, and the experience opened my ears to Welitsch's firm, silvery, cleanly focused voice and her keen dramatic awareness. In 1949, however, I was sixteen years old, and there was a lot of listening and learning ahead for me.

It was 1956 before I had an opportunity to encounter *Aida* on the stage, although I had seen the 1953 film version at a local theatre and been duly impressed and somewhat confused by it. It was Thanksgiving break during my second year of teaching and my first trip to New York City in 1956. The old Met at Broadway and 39th Street seemed incredibly beautiful, crowded, dirty, and wonderful to me. The stage settings—they were the product of Rudolf Bing's second season as general manager in 1951—had seen too many trips in and out of the opera house and too much exposure to New York's winter weather, and the walls of ancient Egypt fluttered at the slightest movement on stage. But this was *Aida* and this was the Met, and that was enough for me. The heroine was Antonietta Stella—I remember particularly her beautiful *piano* at the end of her first act aria—and Amneris was Nell Rankin, who made an impressively big sound and maneuvered the long stairway adroitly in the Judgment scene. Otherwise the cast was competent but hardly memorable. They didn't quite erase the memory of the Maria Callas *Norma* I had heard two evenings before, but they certainly didn't dampen my enthusiasm for *Aida*.

Since then there have been many *Aidas*, on stage, on television, on radio, and on recordings, and I have found something to enjoy in all of them, even the bad ones. It's out of that background that I write this book about the opera that I like best and know best. My personal collection of compact discs includes more than fifty complete recordings of the opera, a large number of highlights discs, and countless versions of the individual arias and ensembles. Over the years I have read everything I could find about *Aida*, I have thought about the opera (when I probably should have been thinking about other things), and I have often spoken about

---

Ibid., p. 28.

it. Somehow, it just seemed inevitable that the time would come for me to write about *Aida*.

My aim has been to cover most, if not quite all, of the bases and offer a full-length picture of the opera. We begin at the beginning, with a chapter on the origins of *Aida*. An opera, at least the kind most of us are familiar with, must have a plot and the characters to fill it, and in the case of *Aida*, plot and characters came to exist in a rather unusual way and not without some mysteries that we will need to explore. Chapter 2 takes us into the complex process by which Verdi and Ghislanzoni, his librettist, shaped the actual words to be sung and the music to which they would be set, and then the convoluted pathway that led to the opera's premiere performance in Cairo, Egypt. From Egypt to the rest of the world is the subject of chapter 3 as we take the opera to Verdi's homeland in Italy and from there all around the globe. Among other things, we'll meet some interesting people and discover some of the strange things that have been done with *Aida* in the many years since its first performance. Chapter 4 is designed to help the reader approach the opera wisely and well with an analysis of what to listen for and how it fits into the story. Chapter 5, the longest in the book, presents a critical survey of officially issued recordings — thirty-three more or less complete and three abridged versions of the opera. Finally, there is a chapter on film and video presentations of *Aida*, not only what we can hear but also what we can see. Three appendices give a detailed discography of officially issued complete recordings, a videography of those versions generally available for viewing, and a brief annotated guide to lead the reader to some helpful sources for additional information and interpretation. The Index will guide readers to pertinent references to proper names and titles within the basic text of the book.

When it comes to the audio and video recordings, I have tried to limit my choices to those that are "official issues." By the term "official issues," I mean performances that have been sanctioned for release by the artists or the performing companies involved. Unfortunately, the information printed on the packaging or in the enclosed booklets does not ordinarily tell us who, if anyone, approved the issue of the performance, and in a few cases I may have misjudged. The fact that a given audio or visual recording is not included, however, is not meant to suggest that I believe it has been illegally produced and distributed. Many "unofficial" versions are in no sense "pirate" recordings, and some of the unofficial issues are extremely valuable in documenting performances of individual artists at different points in their careers. For this reason, at a few places in this book I have commented on some of these unofficial recordings. There are many available from various dealers who specialize in such material, well over 100 audio recordings and almost as many videos. We should note that the Metropolitan Opera does not sanction the sale of recordings of their performances in the United States other than those that have been either officially issued or approved for release by the Met.

Introduction

Although I don't like to think of myself as a critic, obviously it's in the nature of things that much of what I have written in this book reflects my personal critical perspective of the opera and its performers. Any artist who makes a sincere, honest effort to interpret a great musical and dramatic work deserves credit and respect, but it is also clear that some do it better than others and some, unfortunately, do it poorly. It would be less than honest not to call the shots as I hear and see them, and that I have attempted to do.

It's also true that critics do not always agree about the quality of what they have seen and heard, and occasionally we may even differ about precisely what it is we have seen and heard. As a matter of fact, we sometimes don't agree with ourselves from one day to the next. A handful of my personal opinions and standards, however, may help you to weigh my judgments against your own and those of other critics.

First of all, just what am I looking for in a performance of *Aida*, or any other opera for that matter? Let me confess to a basic kind of operatic conservatism that leads me, for one thing, to place the composer's wishes, as we find them in the score of the opera, above all else. It seems to me that a good performance must inevitably follow that score in every detail as much as it's humanly possible to do so. I would much prefer to have the entire opera performed with no cuts, and I appreciate particularly conductors and singers who follow Verdi's relatively detailed dynamic, tempo, and phrase markings. I do know that some of the best performers bend the rules a bit from time to time. I'm not above cutting them a little slack if their misbehavior produces a truly effective result, but conductors and cast members need to realize that their revisions are always open to challenge and criticism. Verdi's score is not.

I'm also an operatic conservative when it comes to the quality of the performance itself. I assuredly want an excellent conductor who has a sure grasp of the score, who can keep the performance dramatically alive and meaningful, and who can provide the kind of support that the artists on stage need to do their very best. I also want an orchestra that plays in tune (some don't), that follows the conductor to maintain a firm ensemble, and that responds sensitively to their conductor's demands. Ahead of everything else, I want singers who really sing the notes without approximating them; who have the technical competence to maintain a firm, secure Verdian line; who have voices adequate in size and of the proper type for their roles; who can and will vary the volume level from top to bottom of their ranges; who use their voices dramatically and musically at the same time; and who sound good while they're doing it. Good singers can sometimes save a performance in spite of a sleepy conductor and a sloppy orchestra, but no amount of skill and artistry on the podium and in the orchestra pit can rescue an evening filled with bad singing.

One caveat, however, needs to be emphasized. There is an unfortunate tendency among inveterate opera lovers to be disappointed with anything less than a perfect performance, and that means that we are bound to be unhappy every time we hear or see an opera. There are no perfect performances! Those of us who know our opera more from recorded versions than from live performances in an opera house are especially at risk. We encounter a new recording or performance of *Aida* with our aural memories filled with the sound of a Milanov *pianissimo*, a Corelli climax, a Toscanini turbulence in the orchestra, the glory of Rethberg's phrasing in "O patria mia," and the forbidding resonance of Tancredi Pasero in the Judgment scene, and the result may well be that nothing we hear nowadays lives up to the ideal. What I strive for, and occasionally manage to achieve, is an open mind, an open ear, and an open heart ready to delight in a "good" *Aida* that falls short of a "perfect" *Aida*. It also may be that we often need to battle our tendency to hear only the performance and not the opera itself. Too much attention to the trees can spoil our delight in the forest as a whole.

When it comes to *Aida* in the various visual formats on film, VHS, or DVD, I am rarely completely happy simultaneously with what I see and what I hear. Too often, the very best singers are not the best actors from the visual standpoint, and let's be honest and admit that many a top-flight Aida, Radamès, or Amneris doesn't really have the ideal *physique de rôle*. So what's a producer to do? Choose visual appeal over aural? Vice versa? I'm not certain what the ideal solution should be. Perhaps the answer is a film in which attractive, gifted actors play the roles while lip-synching a sound track recorded by the best singers available, but even then, as we shall see, there are multiple problems. The 1953 *Aida* film is the only attempt made in that fashion that I have seen, but it was far from the ideal. The jury is still out then on whether a lip-synched *Aida* in an excellent film version truly can bring the opera effectively to a motion picture or television screen near you.

One thing is certain from my viewpoint: An *Aida* designed to be seen, whether on stage, on film, or in a video format, should correctly reflect the intentions of the composer and the librettist. There is ample room for creative imagination within the rather broad boundaries of "Egypt in the time of the Pharaohs," and a producer and designer demonstrate nothing beyond the limits of their artistic creativity when they have to reset the opera in another time and place in the attempt to make it "relevant" to a contemporary audience. *Aida* cannot be made any more relevant than it already is, and one of the opera's great lessons to us is that the life of the human mind and heart can reach across all of the years and bind us in an unbroken unity with all times and all places. It is thus relevant to us precisely because Verdi — along with those who worked with him on *Aida*— has set the opera firmly in the distant past of ancient Egypt and in the process has shown us that what mattered most in that distant yesterday still matters today.

In writing my book I have enjoyed the help and advice of many friends, and I have drawn on a number of printed materials. There are many published sources for information about the life of Verdi and those associated with him in the creation and early history of *Aida*. Some of the material that has been particularly helpful to me and may be of interest to those who want to pursue our subject further is listed in Appendix III, and many other useful sources are referenced in the annotations. Any writer concerned with Verdi in general and *Aida* in particular, however, must acknowledge special gratitude for Hans Busch's *Verdi's Aida: The History of an Opera*; Julian Budden's *The Operas of Verdi: From* Don Carlos *to* Falstaff; and Mary Jane Phillips-Matz's *Verdi: A Biography*. They are models of scholarship and critical perception, and without their volumes, and those of many other authors, I could not have written my book. I have tried to use these and all other resources responsibly and to acknowledge carefully my quotations from them in the annotations. If I have failed at any point, it is certainly not from a lack of gratitude for those who have loved Verdi's operas enough to devote years to the study of his life and works. I appreciate particularly the permission of the University of Minnesota Press to use numerous quotations from Busch's *Verdi's Aida* and the Oxford University Press for similar permission to use quotations from Budden's *The Operas of Verdi*.

My sincere aim is that my book will enhance your appreciation of the opera. I hope that after reading you will come to *Aida* for the first time or return to it with an appreciation of the beauty of the opera and of Verdi's profound understanding of the human heart and his brilliant ability to convey that understanding in music. I hope you will love Verdi and *Aida* as much as I do.

Notes on Style

In referring to the various scenes in *Aida*, I have used traditional titles for certain sections of the score: Act 1, Scene 2 — the Consecration scene; Act 2, Scene 2 — the Triumphal scene; Act 3 — the Nile scene; and Act 4, Scene 1— the Judgment scene, including the opening duet with Radamès.

A question may arise about the form in which the name of the character and the corresponding title of the opera appear. Should it be *Aïda* with a diaeresis over the second letter or *Aida* with no such marking? The opera originated in a synopsis in French by Auguste Mariette, which gave birth to a detailed scenario, also in French, prepared by Verdi's friend Camille Du Locle. The actual libretto was, of course, written in Italian by Antonio Ghislanzoni and Verdi. The diaeresis was necessary in French to ensure that the two opening vowels would both be pronounced, but Italian needs no diaeresis and thus as a formality the Italian opera title (and character) has none, although many earlier writers maintained it. The three scores that I have seen include the diaeresis, but I suspect that they all originate in a much earlier Italian edition. A few writers may hold on to this form, but most contemporary English language works omit the diaeresis, and that is the practice followed in this book.

1

The Winding Road to *Aida*

Operas are not born overnight, not even with composers like Rossini and Donizetti, who were known for the speed with which they could put notes to paper. There must first be a libretto and a plot to base it on, and along with the music, a performance venue, a conductor, a cast, a designer, a director, and a thousand and one other details. It's true even for the simplest of them, and for a complex grand opera like *Aida*, the hurdles to be leaped are multiplied. In fact, with *Aida*, the arduous path from idea to realization was uncommonly complicated, involving, as it did, the politics of nations; warfare between them; and a full assortment of interesting, volatile, and occasionally obstreperous personalities with decided and individual opinions of their own. There were even a few side roads of doubtful origin and destination to confuse the traveler. As a result, to trace the complicated history of this opera, we must begin at a non-operatic moment in history, with what was happening in the 1860s in one of the great nations of Africa—Egypt, that is.

Egypt was on a roll!

For more years than most people could count the nation had languished. The vivid reminders of the glory days of the Pharaohs still dotted the landscape in masterpieces of artistic and architectural splendor from the massive pyramids, eighty or more of them still standing, to the majestic statues of Ramses II guarding the temple at Abu Simbel. Egypt was—and still is—a treasure chest of ancient monuments, but the land itself had long ago lost its powerful, influential place among the mighty nations of the world. The Persians, then the Greeks and the Romans dominated Egypt, to be followed by the Persians again, the Arabians, and representatives of the Byzantine and eventually the Ottoman Empires. More recently, although still part of the Ottoman realm, Egypt had become a pawn in the struggle of the French and British for supremacy.

The first half of the nineteenth century brought periods of progress under Muhammad Ali, Viceroy of Egypt from 1805 to 1848. Nominally under the control of the Ottoman Empire, Muhammad Ali was nonetheless able to assert his own authority in the attempt to bring Egypt out of the past and into the modern era. Before the major European nations stripped much of his power from him in 1841, he managed to modernize the military forces, the education system, industry, and agriculture (it was during this century that Egypt became a major producer of cotton, in part a result of the American Civil War). Unfortunately, his two immediate successors were unable or unwilling to continue his reforms, but with the accession to power of Ismail Pasha in 1863, the wheels of progress began to turn again in Egypt, and it appeared, at least for a few exhilarating years, that Egypt would move at last into the mainstream of nineteenth-century life.

By 1869, Egypt truly was "on a roll," and nothing pointed to continued success and progress so strongly as the opening of the Suez Canal in 1869. The Pharaohs had managed some thirty-eight hundred years earlier to connect the Nile and the Red Sea, but after repeated destruction and reconstruction, the canal finally ceased to function in the eighth century A.D. Now, more than a thousand years later, a new and spectacularly successful attempt had been made to join the Mediterranean Sea with the Red Sea. It had taken more than a decade of incredibly trying engineering and troublesome political difficulties, but the project begun under Ismail's predecessor was at last successfully concluded and the Suez Canal opened to traffic on November 17, 1869. It's worth noting, however, that it had needed a bit of political arm-twisting by Emperor Napoleon III of France to persuade Ismail, the Khedive, to continue the project begun by his predecessor in power. Needless to say, by November 1869, he was glad he had yielded to the Emperor's persuasion.

It was an occasion for celebration, and celebrate they surely did. The rich and famous, led by the Empress Eugènie of France, turned out in number, the flags waved, and the bands played. It was a triumph for Egypt and Ismail; for Ferdinand de Lesseps, who had spearheaded the canal; for the engineers, who achieved it; and for the French, who were vitally involved from the beginning of the project.

In many ways and for many people, however, the triumph was short lived. Within a year, the Franco-Prussian War had brought an end to the reign of Napoleon III and his Empress, and the French were facing humiliating defeat at the hands of the Germans. In 1875, under an overwhelming financial burden, Ismail sold the Egyptian interest in the Suez Canal to the British. Ten years later he was forced into exile. By 1894, when poor de Lesseps died, he, his son, and their company were in disgrace as a result of financial fraud during their abortive attempt to construct a similar canal across Panama.

In 1869, however, the problems were all in the future, and the present was bright with promise and fulfillment. Along with the political, agricultural, industrial, and technological advances, Egypt's modernization was clearly intended by the adventurous Khedive to bring a new artistic initiative. As part of his preparation for the formal opening of the canal, he and his advisors planned a full program of musical celebration, and Ismail Pasha had decreed that the occasion would be marked with a beautiful new opera house for Cairo. This jewel box of a theatre seating only eight hundred fifty opened November 1, 1869, with a performance of Guiseppe Verdi's opera *Rigoletto* conducted by the composer's trusted friend, Emmanuelle Muzio. It was a fitting prelude for the inauguration of the canal seventeen days later and for the premiere of Verdi's *Aida* two years later, the event that would enshrine the Khedive's opera house permanently in the annals of spectacular operatic "firsts."

Just who was this man, Ismail Pasha, the Khedive of Egypt under the Ottoman regime? He was born in Cairo in 1830, the son of a Turkish nobleman, and like many others from the Egyptian ruling class, he was sent to Paris for his education. As a young man, he won official favor both as the commander of a large army sent to the Sudan to suppress a rebellion among the slaves there and in a series of diplomatic assignments. When his uncle, Said Pasha, died in 1863, he replaced him as Viceroy of Egypt. A small man, inclined to corpulence, he was described favorably by a contemporary Italian music critic: "His face is alert, gentle, with tiny eyes that do not stare, but speak volumes."* Some aspects of his life had not yielded to European influence, and he included in his retinue fourteen wives and a large harem of concubines, but he was wise enough to surround himself with an accomplished group of advisors, many of them French.

Perhaps it was his early exposure to Continental life and culture during his education and later diplomatic travels that inspired him to renew and continue the efforts of Muhammad Ali to bring to Egypt the advances and advantages that he saw in nineteenth-century Europe. That was clearly his mission in life, and he is said to have commented on one occasion, "My country is no longer Africa. I have made it part of Europe."† It was certainly a project to which he was fully committed, even to the point of bringing his nation to the brink of bankruptcy in order to pay for his programs. Financial excesses would spell his eventual downfall. Large foreign loans led to ultimate disaster and brought about the humiliating control of Egypt's monetary resources by a combined French and British commission. When in 1879 Ismail sought to free Egypt from this control, he was removed from office and remanded to exile in Turkey, where he died in 1895.

His may have been the tragic story of a man who, in reaching for the best for his people, exceeded by far his financial grasp and failed both himself and his nation. During the exciting years from 1869 to 1871, however, there was hardly a hint of the dark days ahead for Ismail and Egypt. When it came to the arts — and the art of music in particular — the Khedive surely wanted the best for his nation and set out with his lieutenants to find it. Those who gathered for the opening of the Suez

---

*Fillipo Filippi, quoted in Hans Busch, *Verdi's Aida: The History of an Opera in Letters and Documents* (Minneapolis: University of Minnesota Press, 1978), p. 6. (The description of Ismail Pasha derives primarily from this volume, hereinafter annotated as Busch, *Verdi's Aida*.)
†Quoted in Busch, *Verdi's Aida*, p. 6.

Canal were serenaded by a concert conducted by Emmanuele Muzio, and there was the performance of a grand anthem, the *Hymn for the Celebration of Ismaila*, composed especially for the occasion by Temistocle Solera.

Both Solera and Muzio play significant roles in the life story of Verdi, the composer whose opera is the subject of this book. Emmanuele Muzio was born in 1821 in a small town close to Verdi's own birthplace. As a young man, he came to Milan to study with Verdi. The composer took him under his wing, encouraged him, found work for him to do, and in general taught him not only the art of musical composition but also the intricacies involved in seeing an opera from the manuscript pages to actual performance. The result was a friendship that lasted until Muzio's death in 1890. With Verdi's encouragement Muzio composed, conducted, taught, and worked in operatic administration in a number of settings, including Italy, of course, but also London, Brussels, Paris, New York, Havana, and obviously Egypt. One of Muzio's students was the most famous of nineteenth-century sopranos, Adelina Patti, and for a time he was artistic director of the Théâtre Italien in Paris. Beginning with the initial *Rigoletto*, Muzio conducted performances during the 1869–70 season at the new Cairo Opera House, an experience that he was not eager to repeat. "There are many employees in the administration of the theatre," he complained, "but no order whatever."* He, however, did manage to reassure Verdi about the quality of the company that performed opera in Cairo, a point that may have encouraged the composer's eventual agreement to write *Aida* for the theatre there.

Muzio's devotion to his friend Verdi never wavered, and close to the end of his life he wrote a moving reminder of his affection for both Verdi and his wife, Giuseppina. "Soon I shall leave for the next world, full of affection and friendship for you and for your good and dear wife. I have loved you both; remember that, since 1844, my faithful friendship has never wavered."†

Muzio was a man of sterling qualities. He was faithful, committed, honest, and dependable — just the opposite of Temistocle Solera. After running away with a circus, he settled down to his studies. It was, however, a temporary "settling" in a life filled with adventures, including the leadership of more than one Italian police force, the operation of an antique dealership, and a rumored affair with Queen Isabella of Spain. He wrote poetry, composed librettos, and supplied his own music for two of them. For Verdi, he wrote the librettos for *Oberto, Conte di San Bonifacio*, Verdi's first opera to reach the stage; *Nabucco*, his first resounding success; and two more of his early operas. In 1845, however, after completing the text of the first three acts of Verdi's *Attila*, Solera packed his bags and left for Spain with his

---

*Muzio to Giulio Riccordi, March 3, 1870 (in Busch, *Verdi's Aida*, p. 8).
†Quoted in Charles Osborne, *Verdi: A Life in the Theatre* (New York: Fromm International, 1989), p. 297.

wife. Verdi was forced to seek out Francesco Maria Piave to fill in the blanks in the final act, and it hardly bears mentioning that the composer was not happy. There were no further collaborations with Solera, but to the credit of Verdi's generosity, we should record that in 1860, when Solera was facing true poverty, the composer sent an anonymous contribution for his relief.

Among his other adventures, Solera had found his way into the service of the Khedive, Ismail Pasha, and there in 1869, he held a position in the official Egyptian security force and was also charged with the responsibility of planning the music for the opening of the canal. In August 1869, Verdi had politely declined the invitation conveyed to him by Paul Draneht, who was charged with management of the new opera house in Cairo, to compose the anthem for the big celebration. The task fell instead to Solera, thus his *Hymn for the Celebrations at Ismaila* mentioned earlier. In her biography of Verdi, Mary Jane Phillips-Matz suggests that Solera's *Hymn* might possibly be a source for the tune that for many years was Egypt's national anthem, often, though inaccurately, attributed to Verdi.*

The possibility of a Verdi premiere for Egypt, however, was not forgotten. If it could not be arranged as part of the celebrations surrounding the opening of the Suez Canal, then why not look to the future and to an exciting premiere for the new Cairo Opera House? Ismail Pasha was eager to focus the worldwide artistic spotlight on his new theatre. His advisers and their associates, as we shall see, were prepared to do all in their power to assist. Most important of all, Verdi was ready for the challenge of a new work.

At fifty-seven years of age, Verdi had achieved more than most composers of opera would have dared to dream. He was a national hero, a patriot in the long-fought battle for Italian unity, and an occasional servant in the government of his country. He was also a cultural icon, the shining light among all Italian creative artists. His works were performed in opera houses all over the world. *Ernani, Trovatore, Traviata, Rigoletto,* and *Ballo in Maschera* were at the center of the repertoire in Italy and many other nations, a position that in spite of occasional lapses they have continued to hold, and Verdi had made a fortune from them. He was a wealthy man by anyone's standard, a large landowner with a farm at St. Agata, his pride and joy in which he took a far more than passive interest. He had considered retiring as an active composer more than once, most seriously probably in the early days of his career and again at the end of the 1850s and the early 1860s, the years surrounding the completion of *Un Ballo in Maschera* and the beginning of *La Forza del Destino*.

The early years of his life and career offered a number of challenges. He was born October 9, 1813, in Le Roncole, a little village near Busetto in the Parma

---

*Mary Jane Phillips-Matz, *Verdi: A Biography* (Oxford and New York: Oxford University Press, 1993), p. 571.

province. In his later years, he apparently enjoyed painting a picture of an almost destitute youth. "Born poor," he wrote in 1890, "in a poor village. I hadn't the means of acquiring any education; they put a wretched spinet under my hands and some time after that I started writing notes."* Life was surely not easy for him and his family, but in fact he was given a solid education, both in general subjects and in music. Even the "wretched spinet" was a luxury that many homes would have been unable to afford. Through the good graces of the man who became his patron and his father-in-law, Antonio Barezzi, a well-to-do merchant in Busetto, he was sent to Milan to be trained at the conservatory there. He, however, was denied admission to the already crowded Milan Conservatory, in part because he was eighteen years of age, four years too old to meet the admission requirements. (It was a disappointment that rankled in Verdi's memory for the remainder of his life.) Barezzi, however, increased his support and financed lessons with Vincenzo Lavigna, studies that according to Verdi consisted primarily of counterpoint but that equipped the student well for the career that was ahead of him.

After three years of study, he returned to Busetto, assumed the position of music master for the town, and married his patron's daughter, Margherita. His first opera, *Rocester,* did not achieve performance and exists, if it exists at all, only in the music of *Oberto, Conte di Bonifacio*, which was premiered successfully at La Scala in Milan on November 17, 1839.

It might have been a period of joy and fulfillment, but tragedy struck Verdi and his wife, first with the death of their daughter, Virginia, in 1838, then little more than a year later, the death of Icilio, their son. Eight months later, Margherita herself died. In less than three months, Verdi's second opera for La Scala, the comic *Un Giorno di Regno,* failed miserably and was withdrawn after a single performance. It must have been the darkest period of Verdi's life, and like his rejection at the Milan Conservatory, the thought of those sad days haunted him. In later years, he compressed the memory of those three years into two tragic months that, he later said, led him to give up all hope of a career in music. After the success of *Oberto,* however, Verdi had agreed with Bartolomeo Merelli, the La Scala impresario, to provide three additional operas. With great wisdom and foresight, Merelli insisted that Verdi fulfill his contract, and his next opera, *Nabucco*, scored a triumph and assured Verdi's future as a leading Italian composer.

These were busy, often frustrating times for Verdi. During the twenty years from 1839 to 1859, he composed twenty-one operas and prepared major revisions of two of them. Along with most composers of the period, he participated in almost every aspect of their initial performances and some of their important revivals. Premieres of his works had kept him on the road to every important theatre in Italy

---

†Quoted in Julian Budden, *Verdi* (New York: Schirmer Books, 1996), p. 1.

and also to Paris and London. He had also fought battles with the regional Italian censors, who objected to the presentation on stage of profligate kings (*Rigoletto*), murdered kings (*Un Ballo in Maschera*), and forgiving pastors (*Stiffelio*), and he had struggled with librettists who didn't understand his approach to operatic drama and impresarios who provided inadequate casts and unconvincing productions. These were truly, as Verdi himself and his biographers have labeled them, his "years in the galleys." He wrote in 1858, "Ever since *Nabucco* I haven't known an hour's peace and quiet, sixteen years of hard labor."*

After *La Forza del Destino*, which had its premiere in St. Petersburg in 1862, Verdi surely deserved a rest. He settled into his home at St. Agata for a peaceful life with his second wife, Giuseppina Strepponi. She had been his mistress-companion since the mid 1840s and became his wife in 1859, a relationship that ended only with her death in 1897 and that was strong enough to weather Verdi's volatile mood changes and his suspected romantic interest in soprano Teresa Stolz. Inactivity for an extended period, however, was not to Verdi's liking, and in 1866 he was back again in Paris at work on a new opera, *Don Carlos*, for the Paris Opéra. The reception at the premiere in March 1867 was at best ambiguous, and there were suggestions from some critics that Verdi was becoming "Wagnerian," a criticism that the composer particularly resented. The Empress Eugénie, an avid supporter of the Roman Catholic party in France, displayed her displeasure by turning her back on the stage at the King's words to the Grand Inquisitor, "Tais-toi, prêtre" ("Be silent, priest"), and thus began the long-standing accusation that the opera is "anti-catholic."†

It was also a period of personal sadness and disappointment in Verdi's life. His father, Carlo, died in January 1867, to be followed five months later by his Busetto patron, Antonio Barezzi. The same year his frequent librettist, Francesco Maria Piave, author of the texts for ten of Verdi's operas and a man for whom the composer felt a great deal of affection, suffered a debilitating stroke that left him completely paralyzed until his death ten years later. What Verdi no doubt needed was something to lift him out of his depression and set his creative abilities to work on a new challenge.

It may well have been the remarkably successful revival of a revised *Forza del Destino* in February of 1869 that took care of that need and lifted Verdi's spirits so that he was once more eager to find a truly good, dramatically and musically satisfying libretto. In the process, he had the help and encouragement of Camille Du Locle.

---

*Quoted in Julian Budden, *Verdi*, p. 179.
†See George Martin, *Aspects of Verdi* (New York: Dodd, Mead 1987), pp. 101 and 270–271, n. 18. The accusation, which is hardly supported by the opera itself, was still around in 1950, when *Don Carlo*, the Italian version of the opera, opened the first season of Rudolf Bing's regime at the Metropolitan Opera.

Since Du Locle plays a significant role in the process that led to Aida, a few words about his relationship with Verdi are in order. He was almost twenty years Verdi's junior, still in his thirties when he first entered into collaboration with Verdi. Joseph Méry, the librettist, died in 1865 while he was at work on the text of *Don Carlos*, and the task of completing the libretto fell to Du Locle. At the time, he was assisting his father-in-law, Emile Perrin, at the Paris Opéra. He moved then to the Opéra-Comique, where he was the administrator first with Adolph de Leuven and then alone, from 1870 to 1876. It was during this period that Bizet's *Carmen* had its premiere there. While working together on *Don Carlos*, Du Locle and his wife, Marie, became close friends of Verdi and his wife, a friendship that continued after the opera was completed. In the years that followed, he almost literally bombarded Verdi with suggestions for operas and did so with the composer's encouragement. The suggested material covered the whole range from tragedy to comedy, lighter fare like Victorien Sardou's *Piccolino* and material of serious nature like the same writer's *Patrie*. Some of the ideas interested Verdi, but "not one of them," he wrote Du Locle, "is for me ... I want something more simple, *more in our style*."* Eventually, however, the idea for *Aida* made its way from Du Locle to Verdi, and then, of course, Verdi recognized something very much "in our style."

In later years, after the success of *Aida*, Verdi's friendship with Du Locle suffered a serious setback when debts to the composer were not repaid. Verdi, who was often a man of great generosity, was also a careful business man. He clearly expected those with whom he had dealings to follow suit, and Du Locle was not the only person whose financial dealings caused a strain on the relationship with Verdi. The composer eventually took this case to court, but the outcome of the suit is not known. Du Locle, however, went on to translate into French the librettos of *Forza del Destino* and *Aida* for performances in Paris. Eventually composer and librettist were reconciled, and Du Locle prepared the French libretto for Verdi's 1884 revision of *Don Carlos* and in 1894 worked with Arrigo Boito on the French language version of *Otello*.

How Du Locle came to be involved in what would become Verdi's *Aida* takes us first back to 1868 and across the Mediterranean Sea to Egypt, where Du Locle visited an old friend, Auguste Mariette, the distinguished Egyptologist and archaeologist in the service of the Khedive Ismail Pasha. (He is generally known as Mariette Bey, "Bey" being a title of respect granted by the Turkish authorities.) Precisely when during their conversations the idea for an Egyptian opera was introduced we cannot be certain, but it's likely that the subject was discussed either during the trip in 1868 or perhaps in 1867, when Mariette was in Paris for the great Exposition

---

*Quoted in Julian Budden, *The Operas of Verdi: From* Don Carlos *to* Falstaff (New York: Oxford University Press, 1981) p. 162 (hereinafter referred to as Budden, *The Operas of Verdi*, III.) Budden mentions a number of possibilities considered by Verdi (pp. 161–163).

1—The Winding Road to Aida

there. In response to a letter sent by Du Locle from Thebes, Verdi wrote his friend in February of 1868, "You must describe all the events of your voyage, the wonders you have seen, and the beauty and the ugliness of a country which once had a greatness and a civilization I have never been able to admire."* There is no indication, however, that at that early date, Du Locle was hinting at the possibility of an opera. In any case, during the opening months of 1868, Verdi was primarily occupied with watching over preparations for the first performances at La Scala of *Don Carlo* (as the Italian version of the French *Don Carlos* is known), an event that held his attention for several weeks although he had no intention of going to Milan for the occasion.

However, without Verdi's knowledge, *Aida* was already in the process of being born — and here the story of the origins of the opera is beset with mysteries and not a little confusion. The best we can offer is a studied possibility that at least attempts to account for the often conflicting versions of the tale. Somewhere at the root of the opera, however, there was Mariette Bey, Du Locle's Egyptologist friend, and he was precisely the man equipped to conceive a story based on life in ancient Egypt.

Mariette was born in France in 1821 and spent his early working years there and in Great Britain. As a young man he made a few false starts in other professions before he found the interest that would occupy him for the remainder of his life. He learned on his own to read hieroglyphics and Coptic, and in 1849 he assumed a position in the Egyptology Department of the Louvre Museum. In 1851, the Museum sent him to Egypt to search for Coptic, Ethiopic, and Syriac manuscripts, but Mariette soon discovered that archeology interested him far more than the manuscripts he had been sent to locate, and aside from occasional visits to the Continent, the rest of his life was spent in Egypt.

It was not an easy life. Digging in the desert sands of Egypt was often frustrating and always uncomfortable work, and his family suffered with him. Death claimed his wife and five of their eleven children, and in 1881, Mariette himself died in Egypt, which had certainly become his adopted country. By the time of his death, however, he had contributed significantly to the archeological study of ancient Egypt. He established his reputation among archeologists by his discovery of the Serapeum and continued with the direction of important work at Tanis, Abydos, Edfu, and Karnak. In 1858, the Khedive Said Pasha appointed him Director of Egyptian Monuments, and one of his first accomplishments was the permanent establishment of the institution that eventually became the Cairo Egyptian Museum, the world's greatest collection of the antiquities of Egypt. Perhaps his most significant gift to the study of archeology was his insistence that ancient Egypt was

---

*Verdi to Camille Du Locle, February 19, 1868 (in Busch, *Verdi's Aida*, p. 3).

not to be treated as a free-for-all supermarket of antiquities for individual collectors and the museums of other nations. Egypt honored Auguste Mariette for his service with the additional title of Pasha, and he is now buried beneath a statue at the Egyptian Museum.

Mariette's role in the drama that led to *Aida* was about to begin. The possibility of an opera for Cairo had already been suggested to Verdi by Du Locle, probably first during a visit to Verdi in Genoa at the end of 1869 or the beginning of 1870. Ismail Pasha and Paul Draneht, the manager of the Cairo Opera House, were eager to present the premiere of a major operatic work, preferably composed by Italy's leading musician, but Verdi wasn't interested. Du Locle, however, returned to the subject when Verdi talked with him again in France during the spring of 1870. One thing more was needed to capture Verdi's imagination — a good libretto, or at least a plot that would lead to one, and that is exactly what Auguste Mariette was prepared to deliver. The Khedive was intrigued and pleased with Mariette's suggested story. It took place in ancient Egypt, the right setting, needless to say, for a work to be premiered in Cairo, and without pinning down a specific period, it was set against events that made sense in the history of the nation. It offered ample opportunity for colorful costumes and spectacular scenic effects and, thus, the opportunity to display to an admiring public the facilities and possibilities of the new opera house. At the same time, the plot centered on strong human emotions and conflicts, the kind that could well challenge a gifted composer to musical flights of lyrical beauty and dramatic intensity.

Was the idea for the opera truly Auguste Mariette's? Did perhaps someone else deserve credit for it? If the accounts were more convincing, we might perhaps trace the concept that became *Aida* to the outline and notes that his brother, Edouard, claimed to have jotted down in 1866 for a proposed novel, *La Fiancée du Nil*. Edouard himself certainly seemed to take credit for originating the idea of the opera. "I would have been justified in this circumstance," he wrote some years after his brother's death, "to invoke a sort of owner's right."* What little we can know of the *Fiancée*, however, doesn't suggest a significant source for the plot of the opera, and Edouard himself admitted that his outline contained "not an identical story ... but certain similarities, certain analogies."† It's hard to read Edouard Mariette's comments, published in 1904 in his *Mariette Pasha: Letters and Memorials*, and not suspect that long after the fact and long after the astounding success of Verdi's opera, Edouard was straining hard to claim part of the credit for himself. Mary Jane Phillips-Matz, who had studied Mariette's correspondence, assures us that "given the content of Auguste's letters to him [Edouard]," his claim to have originated the plot of *Aida*, "seems impossible."‡

---

*Quoted in Busch, *Verdi's Aida*, p. 438.
†*Ibid.*, p. 439.
‡Phillips-Matz, *Verdi: A Biography*, p. 572.

Mariette Bey, provided we are willing to assign the credit to him, put his story together in an act-by-act, scene-by-scene synopsis of an opera and arranged for the printing of four copies of the twenty-three page booklet. Printing, it seems, was considerably less expensive in Egypt than paying a copyist would have been. More than twenty years later, Verdi recalled a four-page booklet, but his memory was not serving him well and probably he had confused the four copies with four pages. Mariette then sent his synopsis to Du Locle, who forwarded it on to Verdi attached to a letter dated May 14, 1870. Verdi hesitated, but he was clearly intrigued, and once the details of the contract had been settled upon, he agreed to move forward with the opera. The Khedive was more than willing to meet any demands that Verdi made for financial recompense and for the nature of the production of the opera. His only stipulation was that the opera be ready for performance by the end of January 1871.

Verdi found Mariette's summary of the plot "well done," and commented to Du Locle that it contained "a splendid *mise-en-scène*, and ... two or three situations which, if not very new, are certainly very beautiful. But," he added, "who did it? There is a very expert hand in it, one accustomed to writing and one who knows the theatre very well."* Du Locle responded a few days later that the synopsis was the work of Mariette and the Khedive, but the consensus of recent scholarship is that although Ismail Pasha may have made a few suggestions, he did not actually collaborate on the outline with Mariette. In any case, Verdi more than once expressed doubt concerning the role of the Khedive in the synopsis and probably had a few questions as to whether an outline so clearly designed for the operatic stage could have been the work of anyone without an intimate knowledge of the theatre.

Is it possible, Phillips-Matz suggests, that Temistocle Solera wrote the synopsis that came into Verdi's hands?† He was at the time employed by Ismail Pasha in Egypt, and he was assuredly knowledgeable when it came to the requirements for a successful plot for the opera stage. Could Solera have provided Mariette with the bait he needed to attract Verdi's interest? Almost anything, of course is possible, and given the strained relationship of the composer and his sometime librettist, Solera would probably not have wanted his name revealed to the composer. Along with a great many other hypotheses, however, this suggestion falls victim to the simple fact that the one name clearly and repeatedly identified as author of the twenty-three page summary of *Aida* is Mariette Bey. Perhaps the *coup de grâce* to all theories that deny Mariette credit for the original story of *Aida* was delivered by Du Locle, who surely knew the origin of the opera better than anyone other than the author himself, in an undated letter to his wife: "The true author of the libretto is

---

*Verdi du Camille Du Locle, May 26, 1870 (in Busch, *Verdi's Aida*, p. 17).
†Philips-Matz, pp. 572-573.

Mariette Bey, who invented an Egyptian story of a kind and gave the viceroy the idea of having it made into an opera."*

Were there perhaps other sources in the background of the *Aida* synopsis, not for the basic plot itself but for details in the action and the background? Over the years, scholars have sought to identify various earlier works that might have influenced the author, and there was, of course, one indisputable source—Mariette's own knowledge in depth of ancient Egypt. *Aida* is certainly not based on an actual historical event. Mariette was careful to avoid any attempt to pin down closely even the era of the action by placing his story only "during the reign of the Pharaohs,"† a period of something like three thousand years. Since the author includes the pyramids in the stage setting for the first scene, we can assume that the story takes place after their erection, roughly during the second half of the third millennium B.C. Conflicts between Egypt and the Ethiopians, or more accurately the Nubians, the people to the south of Egypt—a central feature of course of the opera—arose from time to time over an extended period, apparently with greater intensity toward the end of the second and into the first millennium B.C. Carol Andrews offers an informed guess that places the action during the twenty-fifth dynasty, that is from roughly the mid-seventh to the mid-sixth century B.C.‡ The precise period, nevertheless, remains a mystery, and the truth of the matter, as Andrews points out in her article, is that Mariette drew the details of his story from a broad spectrum of the history and culture of ancient Egypt. Whatever the precise period, however, Mariette certainly constructed a plot that makes historical sense for ancient Egypt. He was indeed not a stickler for details, and there are points in his synopsis that historians of ancient Egypt question. On the whole, however, out of his vast knowledge of the background, he was careful not to offend greatly against either historical possibility or the sense of dramatic credibility, and the questionable points are adequately justified in the stage worthy effectiveness of his synopsis.

Drawing on an idea from L. Pèrez de la Vega's *La Prosapia de Aida* brought to his attention by Joseph Kerman in *Opera as Drama,* Charles Osborne, in his book *The Complete Operas of Verdi,* claims that *Nitteti,* one of Pietro Metastasio's numerous librettos, is "clearly ... one of the sources of the plot of *Aida.*"§ Osborne summarizes a number of interesting parallels with *Aida*, including a triumphal scene, the rivalry

---

*Du Locle to his wife, undated (in Budden, The Operas of Verdi, III, 165).

†Mariette's *Aida* document is reprinted in Busch, *Verdi's Aida*, pp. 440–447. All quotations from the synopsis are taken from this version. Verdi and his wife translated Mariette's French into Italian. It is the Italian text that is translated in English in Busch's book.

‡See Carol Andrews, "The Ancient Egyptian Background," pp. 15–18. This article is included in the documentation for the 1962 recording of the opera as issued by Decca/London in 1987, No. 417 416-2.

§Charles Osborne, *The Complete Operas of Verdi* (New York: Alfred A. Knopf, 1970), p. 378. Osborne includes (pp. 378–380) a detailed synopsis of the plot of Metastasio's libretto.

of two princesses for the love of the same man, the refusal of a condemned man to accept the intervention of Princess Nitetti, and the threat of being buried alive. *Nitetti* was a popular libretto in the eighteenth and early nineteenth centuries, set by many different composers, but it is highly doubtful that Mariette would have known it. Osborne, however, suggests that Du Locle probably would have been familiar with Metastasio's text and drew on it to flesh out Mariette's "bald and unconvincing narrative."* He also mentions Racine's tragedy *Bejazet* as a possible source because it also includes a love triangle not unlike that of Aida, Amneris, and Radamès. Possible? Of course it is. We cannot know what influences may have touched Mariette's mind, and he might well have entertained some suggestions from conversations with Du Locle. The simple fact, however, is that Du Locle ascribed the synopsis that became *Aida* to Mariette and took no credit for a role in its creation even though later, as we shall see in the next chapter, he would claim to be the origin of the libretto itself.

Another possible source is a third-century A.D. novel, generally known by its short title *Aethiopica*, the work of the Greek writer Heliodorus. Mary Jane Phillips-Matz makes a convincing case for Heliodorus' romance as an important influence on Mariette's synopsis.† As a student of ancient culture, Mariette might well have been familiar the *Aethiopica*, which was one of the best known and most often read works of its genre, and there are, once again, some striking parallels with the opera in details of the plot. including an Ethiopian princess who turns out to be a slave in the service of an Egyptian princess, a heroine who is "almost buried alive," and a grand triumphal scene, albeit in Ethiopia rather than Egypt. One very telling detail is the name of a character in Heliodorus' book, Termuthis. The name is hardly a household word, and it turns up in Mariette's synopsis and in the early printings of the libretto of the opera. The influence, however, would only have been in the details and not in the actual outline of Mariette's plot. The *Aethiopica* is a work of remarkable complexity, with many characters and overlapping plots, but *Aida*, it turns out, is a story of wonderful and profound simplicity.

Mariette certainly did not develop his story in an intellectual vacuum. Many varied influences may have been at work in his mind as he created the plot of *Aida*. The best guess, however, is that the plot of the opera is essentially his work alone, and that is the position advanced in this book.

It isn't difficult to discover why Verdi was favorably impressed with Mariette's *Aida* synopsis when he read it. The outline follows the eventual structure of the opera almost scene by scene. The first scene of Act 1 is set, just as it is in the opera itself, in a hall in the palace at Memphis with the famous pyramids visible in the distance. Contemporary productions frequently omit the pyramids, but Verdi and

---

*Osborne, *The Complete Operas of Verdi*, p. 382.
†Phillips-Matz, *Verdi: A Biography*, pp. 571-572.

his eventual librettists kept them in their text. The action begins, not with the immediate encounter of Ramfis and Radamès, but with a chorus. We miss the familiar "Celeste Aida" aria of Radamès, although the content of the aria is at least suggested in Mariette's comment that Aida's remarkable beauty far exceeds that of the Egyptian Princess and that Radamès has now fallen completely in love with her. With the arrival of Amneris, the plot follows closely the action of the opera, and when Aida is added to the mix, Mariette has demonstrated his awareness of the importance of offering the composer situations that will lend themselves to operatic ensembles. As in the final opera, we have the messenger who brings the news of the Egyptians' defeat at the hands of the Ethiopians and the appointment of Radamès to lead the troops. Alone now, Aida agonizes over her divided loyalties between her own nation and her love for Radamès, the material that ultimately became her great aria, "Ritorna vincitor." Mariette's second scene in Act 1 is the consecration ceremony described very much as it finally appears in the opera, complete with the voices of the priestesses "in the distance," the massed chorus of priests, and even the sound of the harp, which Verdi employed in this scene, and a drum, which Verdi apparently rejected.

Mariette's second act is in a single setting, at the entrance to the city of Thebes. It is here that Amneris tricks Aida into revealing her love for Radamès, apparently but incongruently in the presence of the people of Thebes milling about as they wait for the appearance of the King and the triumphant return of Radamès from the battlefield. The wisdom of transferring this scene to Amneris' intimate apartments in the palace apparently originated with Du Locle and Verdi. The trumpets then sound the fanfare that eventually gave birth to the famous *Aida* march, and the action of the Triumphal scene continues, much as it is in the opera, with the entry of the conquering leader, the ballet performed by extravagantly dressed dancers, the appearance of the Ethiopian captives, and the events surrounding Aida's recognition of her father Amonasro and the release of the other prisoners. Once again, Mariette gave Verdi the opportunity for a wonderful ensemble and, of course, the important second act finale.

The Nile scene that constitutes Act 3, needed — and received — some important changes when first Du Locle and then Verdi and Antonio Ghislanzoni, his Italian librettist, began to shape the final text of the opera. In Mariette's version, Amneris first appears conveniently but without any apparent motivation only at the end of the scene, when she overhears the conversation of Amonasro, Radamès, and Aida, and there is none of the dramatically effective climax we have in the opera as Radamès protects Amneris from Amonasro's dagger and then surrenders to Ramfis. The most serious weakness in the scene as Mariette imagined it, however, is the ease with which Amonasro wins Aida's agreement to his scheme. The result would have been a heroine with no stamina or spunk, and worse still, no tragic, emotional conflict. To his credit, however, Mariette managed to give Verdi the raw material he needed for Aida's "O patria mia," the composer's last major addition to the score, and for Amonasro's eloquent final appeal to Aida, "Pensa, che un popolo..."

At the beginning of the final act, Mariette apparently realized the necessity for filling in the action that occurs between Acts 3 and 4: the defeat of the Ethiopians in their renewed war against Egypt, the death of Amonasro, the supposed escape of Aida, and the imprisonment and impending trial of Radamès. All of this would be done through the conversation of members of the royal court. Verdi had managed this kind of exposition effectively in the opening scene of *Il Trovatore* and might have done it again in *Aida*, but how much more effective to let the information emerge naturally in the dramatic duet of Amneris and Radamès. Verdi and his librettists shaped the Judgment scene somewhat differently, but the value that Verdi found in Mariette's scene was the opportunity to develop fully the tragic dimensions in the character of Amneris. When it came to the second scene of Act 4, Mariette painted vividly Radamès' discovery of Aida in the burial chamber and the emotions that led to the concluding ecstasy of her death. Although he described the stage setting on only one level in the burial vault itself, a hint of the divided, two-level setting that fascinated Verdi was already here in Mariette's comment that the worship of the Egyptian priests was taking place above the tomb in the same temple represented in the Act 1 Consecration scene above the tomb. The final dramatic touch, however, came from Verdi and Du Locle and not from Mariette — Amneris' prayer for peace.

In spite of the occasional changes and additions that Verdi, Du Locle, and Ghislanzoni made, however, they clearly found in Mariette's outline of *Aida* a sound, solid plot that made a far sight more sense than many another opera libretto, characters with strong personal feelings that invited lyrical expression, intense emotional conflicts as characters reacted and responded to each other, and ample opportunity for large-scale ensembles that would be both musically satisfying and dramatically apt. For Verdi personally it's easy to imagine how strong was the appeal of a story in which personal desires ran headlong into the call of duty and honor, a theme that he returned to over and over in his operas. Mariette had clearly done his work well.

It wasn't long before Verdi replied to Du Locle, "Now let's hear the financial conditions from Egypt, and then we shall decide."* No doubt it was primarily Mariette's tempting synopsis that led to Verdi's positive response, but the "financial conditions" were never far from Verdi's mind.

However, there was also a little note that Du Locle had included in the May 14 letter along with the plot outline. It was a brief letter, dated April 28, that he

---

*Verdi to Camille Du Locle, May 26, 1870 (in Busch, *Verdi's Aida*, p. 17).

had received from Mariette Bey. It appears that the Khedive Ismail Pasha was considering two other composers* if Verdi turned down the commission, Charles Gounod and Richard Wagner.† Since the death of Meyerbeer in 1864, Gounod was certainly the most prominent French operatic composer, and Wagner's was the name above all names among German musicians. One suspects that Verdi was not seriously challenged by the Frenchman. "Gounod is a very great musician," he wrote six years later, but then added, "he isn't an artist of dramatic fibre ... his treatment of situations is weak, and his characterization is bad."‡ Those are accusations that no critic could have made of Verdi himself.

Wagner, however, was another matter entirely. More and more, Italian artists were looking to the north, to Verdi's German contemporary, for inspiration, and Verdi often had to face those critics who branded him an imitator of Wagner. Such comments were a challenge not only to his own decidedly unique accomplishments but also to what he saw as the melodic essence of true Italian music. His attitude toward Wagner and his music was always ambiguous although he clearly respected his rival, a respect that was not returned by Wagner and his circle of admirers. To fail to claim this important opportunity to demonstrate his own gifts and those of Italian artistry in general would have been to confess defeat before the entire world. We can hardly doubt that Du Locle knew precisely what he was doing when he enclosed Mariette's note in his May 14 letter to Verdi.

Nothing demonstrates quite so fully the eagerness of Ismail Pasha to have his Verdi opera as the terms, financial and otherwise, to which he agreed in order to secure it. From June 19 to 25, 1870, Du Locle visited Verdi at St. Agata. Together they worked out a detailed scenario for the opera, and Verdi also trusted his friend to convey to the Egyptian authorities a statement of his contract demands. On the whole Verdi's expectations were met with only a few largely insignificant changes in the final contract.§ Verdi would compose the music in accordance with the plans already outlined for *Aida*. The opera would have its premiere at the Vice-Royal Theatre in Cairo in January 1871. The composer would choose his own author for the Italian libretto, would be permitted to send his own agent to direct the opera, and would select his own cast from among the singers engaged for the opera house in Cairo. He, however, would not be required to come to Cairo himself. Once the premiere was given, Verdi would be permitted to present the opera in European

---

*More than two, as a matter of fact. Apparently József Poniatowski's name had also been suggested and rejected, perhaps for political reasons. Poniatowski was a Polish nobleman, a singer, and composer, whose operas had achieved a measure of success in Italy and France. When Napoleon III was sent into exile, Poniatowski joined him in England.
†Mariette Bey to Camille Du Locle, April 28, 1870 (in Busch, *Verdi's Aida*, p. 12).
‡Quoted in Osborne, *Verdi: A Life in the Theatre*, p. 253.
§The document is printed in full in Busch, *Verdi's Aida*, pp. 473–474.

theatres (and presumably any other theatres outside Egypt). The libretto and score of the opera, which the composer would submit at the proper time to the Egyptian authorities, would belong to the Khedive insofar as Egypt was concerned, but Verdi would keep for himself the rights to the opera for the rest of the world, a significant financial consideration. Included among the provisions, of course, was the payment Verdi would receive for the opera, 150,000 francs, the amount he had stipulated. It was an uncommonly large amount, more than twice what he had been paid for *Don Carlos*, but apparently Ismail Pasha did not hesitate to guarantee it.

Verdi added to the contract two stipulations: that "the payments be made in gold," and that "if through any unforeseen circumstance whatever, independent of me (that is *through no fault of my own*), the opera should not be presented at the theatre in Cairo during the month of January, 1871, I shall have the option to have it performed elsewhere, six months later." After he received the contract, Verdi held onto it for almost a month before he signed and returned it on August 26, 1870. Verdi's added stipulations and his delay in returning the contract, as Hans Busch suggests, were no doubt a result of the formal opening of the Franco-Prussian War on July 18, 1870. Who could tell what might happen to the value of the franc as result of the conflict? The War might also necessitate a delay in the premiere of the opera. Verdi was covering his bases carefully — and quite wisely as it turned out.

For all of his practical caution and business acumen, however, *Aida* was a project that had clearly captured Verdi's mind and heart. He had chosen his story well, and he was far too eager to start to let the matter of a contract and the threat of a war stand in his way.

2

From Story to Stage

A number of personal problems and sorrows, as we have mentioned, weighed heavily on Verdi during the three years before he received Mariette Bey's synopsis — the death of his father on January 14, 1867, and of his patron, Antonio Barezzi, on July 21; the sudden and completely debilitating stroke suffered by Francesco Maria Piave five months later. Piave had not only written librettos for ten of Verdi's operas and completed the final act of *Attila* after Solera's defection, he was also a good and loyal friend, and it could not have been an easy friendship for him: Verdi was the most demanding of taskmasters when it came to his librettists and frequently gave Piave a difficult time. Piave's devotion, however, never wavered. It was returned in the financial support that Verdi and his wife provided for Piave and his family until his death in 1875.

Not the least of the problems Verdi faced in 1867 was the struggle to complete *Don Carlos* and see it through its initial performances at the Opéra in Paris. The Opéra was probably the most important, or at least the most famous, theatre in Europe, but it was bound in the straightjacket of cumbersome bureaucracy, encompassed by a multitude of inviolable performance traditions, hampered by inadequate professional discipline on the part of the artists, and subject to every imaginable delay and roadblock in the path of a successful and timely production. As Verdi wrote to his friend Count Opprandino Arrivabene, "We progress, but, as always at the Opéra, at a snail's pace."*
There were also artistic conflicts between Verdi's understanding of opera and that of the Paris establishment. He simply was not comfortable with the basic approach of the Opéra, where the conventions of the theatre insisted on lengthy, five-act works, burdened by heavy demand for scenic spectacle and the inevitable full-scale ballet, preferably early in the third act. The wonder is that given the restrictions placed on him and Verdi's admittedly negative attitude about the Paris Opéra *Don Carlos* turned out to be one of the greatest of Verdi's works. Unfortunately, when the opera had its premiere in Paris in March of 1867, the critics and the audience were on the whole not yet prepared to acknowledge its greatness. The opera, however, was a success three

---

*Verdi to Opprandino Arrivabene, September 28, 1866 (quoted in Budden, *The Operas of Verdi, III*, p. 22).

months later in London in a considerably cut Italian version and began to win an enthusiastic Italian public in its uncut form in Bologna in October of 1867.

The Paris reception had been disappointing and discouraging, and Verdi might well at this point have carried through on his occasional desire to retire from music and spend the remainder his life happily engaged in farming at St. Agata. Those close to him, however, knew that Verdi without an opera in the works was inclined not only to be unhappy but also to make those around him unhappy. Soon he was engaged in preparing a revised *La Forza del Destino* for performance at La Scala in Milan, and the overwhelming success of those performances in March 1869 apparently spurred him on to seek a new libretto for his next opera. He had plenty of encouragement from his French friend Du Locle, from Giulio Ricordi, his publisher; and we can well imagine from his wife, who no doubt found him easier to live with when he was busy putting notes to paper. This was the opportune situation when Mariette Bey's synopsis of *Aida* came into his hands in May of 1870.

Although Verdi waited until August 26 to sign and return the actual contract for *Aida*, it is clear that the idea for the opera fired his imagination and he was eager to start work almost immediately. Under pressure from Du Locle, early in June he dictated his basic terms very much as they would appear in the final contract, and on the same date, June 2, he wrote Giulio Ricordi, second in command at the Ricordi publishing company in Milan, to ask about the possibility of having the Italian libretto prepared by Antonio Ghislanzoni. Giulio replied to the composer immediately to guarantee Ghislanzoni's help and express his own delight in "that blessed letter of yours which reopened our heart to the dearest of hopes!"*

The House of Ricordi was Italy's most prominent publishing company in the nineteenth century. It had been founded by Giovanni Ricordi in 1808, and after his death it was directed by his son Tito with the help of his son Giulio, who eventually took over the reins. Ricordi accumulated the publishing and performing rights to an incredible number of operas, Italian and otherwise, during the nineteenth century. Their only rival — a fierce rivalry indeed — was the firm of Francesco Lucca, which had made the wise decision to secure the Italian rights to the operas of Richard Wagner, but in 1888 Ricordi acquired the Lucca company. Throughout most of the century, Ricordi represented the cream of Italian composers. Three of Verdi's operas in the 1840s — *Attila, I Masnadieri,* and *Il Corsaro* — had been published by Lucca. Otherwise the composer was faithful to the Ricordi company, which had formed that association early by publishing *Oberto*, the first of his operatic works, in 1839. That faithfulness reached in both directions. First Giovanni, then from 1853, Tito and Giulio became not only Verdi's business associates but

---

*Giulio Ricordi to Verdi, June 4, 1870 (Busch, *Verdi's Aida*, p. 20).

also his personal friends. They were cultured men, particularly Tito and Giulio, and were musicians themselves. Giulio composed vocal and instrumental music and eventually produced his own opera, *La Secchia Repita*. From time to time, there were business and artistic differences of opinion, but the relationships survived, and by 1870, when he was beginning to work on *Aida,* the composer could depend on Giulio particularly to handle countless details on his behalf. It was through his influence that later in his life Verdi would be brought together with Arrigo Boito to produce his two final masterpieces, *Otello* and *Falstaff.*

Before Verdi could begin work with Ghislanzoni on the Italian libretto, however, he needed to make any necessary modifications and changes in Mariette's original story. In this task, he sought and received the help of his friend Du Locle, who visited the composer at St. Agata, apparently June 19–25, to produce a detailed prose scenario for the opera.* The document itself reveals the haste with which it was prepared. Names are occasionally mistaken, there are many strike-outs and corrections, some scenes appear in more than one version as if Du Locle and Verdi couldn't quite make up their minds, and the final act is left incomplete with only a brief comment on the second scene. It is clear that there was a great deal left to be done, and at the end of that June week, Verdi wrote to Giulio Ricordi, "I have made and am still making new changes."† What had been accomplished, however, was apparently enough to assure Verdi that he had the basis for a successful opera.

Reading through Verdi and Du Locle's scenario, we notice right away some differences in light of the completed opera, and some of them are significant differences. There is still no "Celeste Aida" in the opening scene, and we miss the "Sul del Nilo" ensemble before Aida's "Ritorna vincitor" aria. The opening of Act 2, set now in Amneris' private rooms and not at the entrance of the city of Thebes, will eventually be lightened and brightened with the dance of the Moorish slaves, and the closing of the first scene of the act will certainly benefit from Aida's despairing prayer to her gods. The Triumphal scene itself will need to be both tightened dramatically and expanded musically. The largest changes are made in the third act, placed now on the banks of the Nile, and Verdi and Du Locle have worked hard to make the motivation of the primary characters clearer and on the whole more sympathetic. There are still problems to be solved, Aida's too easy acquiescence to her father's demand and the unsavory willingness of Radamès to betray the Egyptian plan of attack at Napata, among them. It was the third act that gave Verdi the greatest difficulty through the process of composition, and he was still toying with it almost up to the time of the eventual premiere of the opera. Almost nothing of the last act is included in the scenario, but the two-level setting of the final scene is included along with the final appearance of Amneris.

---

*See Busch, *Verdi's Aida,* pp. 448-471.
†Verdi to Giulio Ricordi, June 25, 1870 (in Busch, *Verdi's Aida,* p. 27).

Du Locle later claimed to have prepared a complete libretto in French: "I wrote the libretto, scene by scene, line by line, in French prose at Busetto, under the eyes of the Maestro who took part to a large extent in this work."* Perhaps he did, but Hans Busch's comment on this claim, which Du Locle also made in a letter to his wife, is that "no evidence is available in the correspondence or elsewhere to show that a complete play was ever written in French."† If this document ever existed, it seems strange that no reference to it turns up in Verdi's correspondence with Du Locle and especially later with Antonio Ghislanzoni, whom he had chosen to prepare the Italian libretto. There is simply no suggestion in the correspondence between the composer and his Italian librettist that Ghislanzoni was translating a French text into Italian verse, and every indication that he was composing a completely new text according to Verdi's ever-changing demands. The background for Du Locle's claim, along with much else in the story of the creation of this opera, remains a mystery, but Alessandro Luzio ascribes Du Locle's statements about the French libretto to his resentment following Verdi's insistent demands for the repayment of the loans.‡ It's possible that Du Locle has simply overstated what was actually included in the prose synopsis that he and Verdi had made.

Verdi had chosen his librettist well. Ghislanzoni, who was born in 1824, was a man of many gifts, literary and otherwise, and of a varied background and equally varied interests and abilities. As a young man, he studied for the priesthood, switched to a school of medicine, tried his hand at managing an opera company, and became a singer, one of whose roles was Carlo V in Verdi's *Ernani*, which he sang in Paris in 1851. Following a serious attack of bronchitis, he was forced to give up his career as a baritone and to focus his attention instead on the work of a writer. He wrote novels, critical essays on music and literature, and librettos and edited *La Gazzetta Musicale* and *Rivista Minima*, journals published by the Ricordi firm. Ghislanzoni is generally recognized as the best of the Italian librettists of the mid-nineteenth century, and he had written texts for a number of composers, including Erico Petrella, Carlos Gomes, and Amilcare Ponchielli. Unfortunately, his works for these composers are rarely performed today, and he is known primarily for his work with Verdi.

In 1869, Ghislanzoni came to Verdi's aid when the composer undertook the successful revision of *La Forza del Destino*. The opera had received a mixed reception ever since its premiere in St. Petersburg. The criticisms ranged from what many considered the excessive length of the work to the gloomy conclusion in which the three main protagonists all die within a very few musical minutes of one another.

---

*Du Locle to the editor of *L'Italie*, March 28, 1880 (in Busch, *Verdi's Aida*, p. 423).
†*Ibid.*, p. 425.
‡See Budden, *The Operas of Verdi*, III, p. 167, note.

Verdi's revision of *Forza* didn't do a great deal to reduce the length, but it did polish and tighten the score at several points, and the conclusion was completely rewritten both dramatically and musically so that there was one less death and a second protagonist was dispatched less offensively off stage. It was there that Ghislanzoni proved his worth to Verdi, and when the need for an Italian libretto for *Aida* arose, Verdi turned naturally to a writer who had already served him well and who also had a built-in association with his publisher. He would call on Ghislanzoni again when he worked on the 1872 revision of *Don Carlo*.

Writing a libretto for Verdi was not an easy job, a fact that Verdi himself apparently realized. "Poor Ghislanzoni!" he wrote to Giulio Ricordi, "I torment him so much, but I can't help it."* Part of the problem was the composer's keen sense of what worked and what did not work on the stage and his resulting insistence that the libretto follow his lead carefully and precisely. What Verdi wanted was a text that would provide at significant points a quality that he called *parole sceniche*, the scenic or perhaps theatrical word. It was a term, as he explained to Giulio Ricordi, that meant words "that carve out a situation or a character, words that always have a most powerful impact on the audience."† *Parole sceniche* pointed to a quality easier to demand than to define, "the word that clarifies and presents the situation neatly and plainly,"‡ but it was a quality that Verdi recognized when he encountered it. The *parole sceniche* somehow enabled the audience, as the poet Coleridge said, to suspend their disbelief and accept fully the reality of the emotions and conflicts being represented on the stage. Of course, it was never the words alone that produced the effect, but the words were somehow necessary in order to give the music the kind of dramatic specificity that would fully engage the audience. Verdi acknowledged that it was difficult to achieve these scenic words in the neat poetic forms traditionally employed in librettos, but Verdi suggested in the same letter—he branded his suggestion a "blasphemy"—that "both the poet and the composer must have the talent and the courage, when necessary, *not* to write poetry or music."§

It was also difficult to write a libretto for Verdi because his responses to the dramatic situations were often immediate and spontaneous and therefore, infinitely changeable. What had seemed to him almost right one day might well be less than acceptable the next day. His second thoughts were many and inevitably great improvements over the original, but the poor librettist would frequently find himself rewriting the lines that he thought he'd done well to begin with. It's easy to imagine that a creative writer like Ghislanzoni must have been a bit frustrated when a note from Verdi would suggest a whole new approach for a scene the two had

---

*Verdi to Giulio Ricordi, October 7, 1870 (in Busch, *Verdi's Aida*, p. 75).
†Verdi, to Giulio Ricordi, July 10, 1870 (in Busch, *Verdi's Aida*, p. 31).
‡Verdi, to Antonio Ghislanzoni, August 17, 1870 (in Busch, *Verdi's Aida*, p. 50).
§Verdi, to Giulio Ricordi, July 10, 1870 (in Busch, *Verdi's Aida*, p. 31).

worked on earlier, and more often than not, the note would include Verdi's own version of the dialogue to be set to music. He was almost invariably polite in his letters to Ghislanzoni, but reading between the lines, we can hear him saying, "Here's what the characters must say and do. Now, your job is just to put it into verse for me." As a matter of fact that's almost precisely what he did say to Ghislanzoni, for example, in a letter concerning the finale of Act 2. "I fumbled about with the words, which you will render into good verse for me."*

Verdi could be a demanding taskmaster. He composed quickly compared to those who labor for years over a single major work. He had certainly slowed down somewhat since his "galley years." After all, the days when a new opera was demanded from him every few months were well behind him, and his financial situation generally enabled him to resist that kind of pressure. *Aida*, however, was a special case. He simply had to move forward as quickly as he could. After all, his contract called for the score to be completed in time for a Cairo premiere in January 1871, and that was little more than seven months from his first encounter with Mariette's synopsis and hardly five from the date he received the contract for the opera. As it turned out, that pesky Franco-Prussian War actually provided a few extra months, but through the summer and fall of 1870, he was still facing the deadline imposed by the contract and the calendar. It's not surprising that he urged Ghislanzoni to write in a hurry and send him more material quickly so that he could move forward with his composing. On occasion, if the text he needed wasn't immediately available, he would write his own, set it to music, and then call on Ghislanzoni to put it in good libretto form.

We may be inclined to think, "Poor Antonio, wouldn't you rather write another novel and leave Verdi's opera for someone else to do?" If Ghislanzoni had complaints, however, he kept them to himself. When in October of 1870 he wrote to Eugenio Tornaghi, an assistant manager at the Ricordi company, "I am afraid to be recalled to St. Agata from one moment to the next,"† it was apparently the expense of the trip that concerned him rather than any frustration in working with the composer. In any case, Verdi reminded him more than once that what mattered was not the difficulty of the task they were undertaking but the ultimate success of the result.

The correspondence between Verdi and Ghislanzoni demonstrates how the details of the opera took shape under their hands, and often it truly was the "details" that concerned Verdi. We notice perhaps more than anything else that the creative initiative and the dramatic tone of the opera came first from Verdi himself. He wrote much of the text himself in great detail so that Ghislanzoni's task was essentially to polish it up for the final form.

---

*Verdi, to Antonio Ghislanzoni, September 12, 1870 (in Busch, *Verdi's Aida*, p. 66).
†Ghislanzoni to Antonio Tornaghi, October 1, 1870 (in Busch, *Verdi's Aida*, p. 74).

There were problems, of course, from scene to scene. Working out the Radamès and Amneris duet in the first scene of Act 4 raised a number of questions, and special difficulties arose in the Triumphal scene, particularly the passage in which Aida recognizes her father, Amonasro, among the Ethiopian captives. Typical of Verdi's technical concern and, of course, of his practical knowledge as well, is a suggestion for this passage that he sent to Ghislanzoni after the libretto as a whole had been completed: "It was easy for me to say ... *o padre mio* ... , but the accent, or the strong beat, fell on *mio*, and it is much better on *padre*; that also avoids the three notes of upbeat."*

Act 3, the Nile scene, however, was the greatest challenge for Verdi and Ghislanzoni. The composer returned to it over and again in order to tighten the action and to make the psychological motivation, especially for Aida herself, clearer and in the long run more sympathetic. How indeed would Aida respond when at the climax of their duet her father brands her as a slave of the Pharaohs? Not, Verdi suggests, with a typical operatic gesture, but "only ... in broken phrases." What about Radamès when Amonasro identifies himself as the King of Ethiopia? "Radamès must hold and control the scene, almost by himself, with strange, mad, highly agitated words."† A *romanza* for Aida was originally included early in the scene, but Verdi wanted it shortened so that the soprano would not expend all of her vocal and dramatic energy before the two large duets to follow. In August 1871, however, Verdi made one of last changes to the Nile scene. He added at this point in the opera the second of Aida's major arias, "O patria mia." "A little piece for Aida alone,"‡ Verdi called it. A "little piece" indeed! The soprano who survives its manifold difficulties still has the rest of this monumental third act to sing and act.

Throughout the process, Ghislanzoni clearly realized that the composer is in charge of the opera, and he did not challenge Verdi's authority to alter and modify — and to command. At almost the last moment, however, Verdi suggested to Giulio Ricordi that a few lines in the final scene might be changed. Radamès sings to Aida, "Morir! Si pure e bella.... No, non morrai! Troppo t'amai! Troppo sei bella!" ("To die! So pure and beautiful.... No, you shall not die! I have loved you too much! You are too beautiful!") The problem, Verdi said, was that the time might come when the singer cast as Aida wasn't beautiful at all. "The audience might joke about it, and that would displease me because that moment is too important."§ Two weeks later, Ghislanzoni asked Ricordi to persuade Verdi to leave the lines as they were on the grounds that "in the theatre all women are beautiful, or at least are made beautiful by musical idealism." He felt that Verdi's effective musical phrase would

---

*Verdi, to Antonio Ghislanzoni, January 13, 1871 (in Busch, *Verdi's Aida*, p. 132).
†Verdi, to Antonio Ghislanzoni, September 28, 1870 (in Busch, *Verdi's Aida*, p. 69).
‡Verdi, to Antonio Ghislanzoni, August 5, 1871 (in Busch, *Verdi's Aida*, p. 196).
§Verdi, to Antonio Ghislanzoni, September 7, 1871 (in Busch, *Verdi's Aida*, p. 219).

carry the day, and "even if we had a monster from Lapland onstage, the public would go into ecstasies."* For once, it was the librettist who called the shots, and the lines remained in the libretto. Of course, in a sense both men were correct: There have certainly been Aidas who were anything other than ravishing beauties, and Verdi's musical setting of the words has persuaded countless audiences not to notice.

Among the other issues that concerned Verdi as he and Ghislanzoni began work on the libretto was the historical background for the opera. He asked Giulio Ricordi to gather information on the culture and customs of ancient Egypt and, as a first response, Ricordi sent him a copy of François Joseph Fétis' *Historie Générale de la Musique*. Verdi did not find it helpful, but he was clearly concerned with the nature of musical instruments that would be appropriate for the Egyptian setting. Through Du Locle he received from Mariette information about the ritual dances of old Egypt and the music the accompanied them: "twenty-four stringed harps, double flutes, trumpets, timpani, and smaller drums, enormous castanets (rattles), and cymbals."† Audiences through the years should be grateful that Verdi followed his own inclinations rather than Mariette's suggestions for the orchestration of the sacred dance in the Consecration scene in Act 1. There were, of course, other concerns about instrumentation. Verdi, for example, responded to the proposal that he include the saxophone in his orchestration with disgust. It might be permissible in a modern setting, Verdi commented, but surely not among the Pharaohs! He experimented with a new type of flute and paid special attention to the famous long trumpets for the triumphal march in Act 2. Verdi insisted that they must not only sound right but also look right in an ancient Egyptian parade. As Julian Budden comments, it was "false antiquity; the trumpets are Roman."‡

Ricordi provided him with relatively detailed answers from a knowledgeable authority to his questions about ancient culture. Verdi wanted to know if women were included in the sacred rites. The answer was a qualified maybe, but Mariette, who could be a stickler on some points, told him to go ahead and use as many as he wanted. Verdi was informed in response to one of his questions that the appropriate historical setting was the reign of Ramses III, who had among his other accomplishments subdued Ethiopia, but in the final version of the opera the designation remained merely in the time of the Pharaohs. How far, Verdi wanted to know, is it from Thebes to Cairo, the setting of the ancient city of Memphis? The answer was 115 leagues. He asked also about the rites relating to the mysteries of Isis and about the Egyptian thoughts on death and immortality and was told that the mysteries of Isis involved a complicated series of actions (in some details similar

---

*Antonio Ghislanzoni to Giulio Ricordi, September 21, 1871 (in Busch, *Verdi's Aida*, p. 223).
†Camille Du Locle to Verdi, July 9, 1870 (in Busch, *Verdi's Aida*, p. 30).
‡Budden, *The Opera of Verdi*, III, p. 181.

to what we encounter in Mozart's *Die Zauberflöte*) and that these ancient people believed in immortality. In the long run, the research into ancient Egypt probably didn't affect the finished product a great deal. Even Mariette was remarkably flexible in what was permitted and what wasn't in terms of historical accuracy, but the mere gesture may have seemed important to Verdi as an indication of his sincere concern to please the nation where the opera would have its premiere and the ruler who was paying for it.

No doubt a more important concern for Verdi was assuring that the right conductor and singers would perform the opera, both in its Cairo premiere and in the first Italian performances to follow in Milan. The contract he had signed with the Egyptian authorities on August 21, 1870, gave him the right to "choose the artists who will perform his score from the company of the Italian Theatre in Cairo."* This clause may have seemed to make the composer's decisions absolute when it came to casting, but it actually contained an ambiguity that could have become a serious problem. Verdi could choose, but the choice was apparently limited to those artists engaged by "the company of the Italian Theatre in Cairo."

Selecting just the right conductor and cast for *Aida* brought Verdi into contact with Paul Draneht, the general manager of the Cairo Opera House. The design and execution of the *mise-en-scène*, both costumes and stage settings, were matters assigned to Mariette, who, it was assumed, would be best qualified to reproduce ancient Egypt on the stage, but the general management of the opera company and the theatre in which they performed was the responsibility of Draneht Bey, as he was generally known. He was not a man of the theatre. His education had centered on scientific, medical, and pharmaceutical subjects. His professor of pharmacy, Louis-Jacques Thénard, honored him by giving him his own name — spelled backwards, of course. His Greek family from Cyprus had fled to Egypt to escape Turkish persecution, and there young Paul had won the favor of the ruler of Egypt. In the service of the government, he had been influential in the creation of the Suez Canal, the beginning of Egypt's railway system, and the arrangements for foreign loans to the government. Now, in his fifty-fifth year he was managing the Cairo opera company, and that was a position that demanded every skill he had learned in the field of international diplomacy.

Had it been possible to present the premiere of *Aida* as originally intended, in February of 1871, there would have been no casting problems, but the intervention of the Franco-Prussian War trapped Mariette and his still unfinished scenery and costumes in Paris until the lifting of the siege. Verdi had apparently already given preliminary approval to a cast drawn from the Cairo company for the premiere performances, chosen no doubt on the advice of his friend Emmanuele Muzio,

---

*Quoted in Busch, *Verdi's Aida*, p. 473.

who had conducted the first season at the Cairo Opera House. They included Isabella Galletti Gianoli, probably as Amneris, and Ginevra Giovannoni Zacchi in the title role, although how the roles would have been distributed is not entirely certain. Emilio Naudin, a tenor, would surely have been Radamès, and Paolo Medini and Giovanni Maré would probably have sung Ramfis and the King respectively (both listed in the Cairo roster as basses). The leading baritone with the company was Luigi Colonnese, and it's a fair assumption that he would have been Amonasro. They were all respected artists, although only Naudin, who had been the first Vasco de Gama in Meyerbeer's *L'Africaine,* and Medini, whom Verdi later chose as bass soloist for tour performances of the *Messa de Requiem,* earned significant places in the annals of nineteenth-century Italian opera singers. By the time *Aida* actually reached the stage in December 1871, however, only Medini was left in the cast.

Draneht was rapidly learning the challenges that face any opera impresario. His leading soprano, Galletti Gianola: wrote to him in July 1870, "I *want* to be the interpreter of the afore-mentioned score,"* and for a time Draneht continued to recommend her to Verdi. Eventually, however, even after Draneht, fearing that her "capricious" nature would wreck the whole season,† refused to reengage her, she appealed to Giulio Ricordi to recommend her for Cairo. It was a fruitless appeal, one, as Ricordi commented, among "no less than twenty sopranos, ten tenors, ten baritones, and forty basses."‡ Draneht also discovered soon enough that a stage parent can be amazingly insistent when it comes to advancing a young singer's career opportunities, and Giuseppina Vitali's father was no exception. "It would be a mortification for my Giuseppina," he wrote Draneht, "if la Giovannoni were chosen in her place."§ Later, when indeed Giuseppina, who was probably still a teenager at the time, was not cast in *Aida,* her father wrote to accuse Muzio of blighting the young lady's chances with this "*most powerful blow* to my daughter's morale and one that will certainly cause considerable damage to her professional status."** What must have become increasingly clear to Draneht was that vocal artists in general coveted roles in the new Verdi opera as a way of advancing their own careers, but at the same time, they were not above making more or less unreasonable financial demands for their services. Impresarios then, as now, still had to balance their budgets.

When the Franco-Prussian War delayed the premiere for ten months, Verdi and Draneht had virtually to begin anew in choosing a cast. One name after another entered into their correspondence. Some were rejected as inappropriate. Other

---

*Isabella Galletti Gianoli to Paul Draneht, July 28, 1870 (in Busch, *Verdi's Aida,* p. 28).
†Paul Draneht to Verdi, April 3, 1871 (in Busch, *Verdi's Aida,* p. 149).
‡Giulio Ricordi to Verdi, June 14, 1871 (in Busch, *Verdi's Aida,* p. 173).
§Raffaella Vitali to Paul Draneht, August 6, 1870 (in Busch, *Verdi's Aida,* p. 42).
**Raffaella Vitali to Paul Draneht, August 21, 1870 (in Busch, *Verdi's Aida,* p. 53).

possibilities had either accepted contracts at other opera houses or made what Draneht considered unreasonable financial demands. Among those who might have sung the title role was Barbara Marchiso, whose mezzo-soprano sister, Carlotta, could well have essayed Amneris. They were noted for their *bel canto* accomplishments, but according to Giovanni Lampugnani, a Milanese agent, "the Marchiso sisters are quite ugly."* Gabrielle Kraus, the distinguished Austrian soprano just beginning the Italian phase of her career, and Marie Sass, who had been Elisabeth in the first performances of *Don Carlos,* were among those suggested for Aida, and in Sass' case, also for Amneris. Verdi's opinion of Sass was decidedly negative for either role. No doubt he remembered her less than supportive relationship with Pauline Gueymard-Lauters, the original Eboli in *Don Carlos*. "Doubtless," Julian Budden tells us, "this was one of the factors that led to the eventual dropping of their one duet."† Verdi's candid advice to Draneht was that Sass should be assigned operas "in which she is the only *soprano,* or at least an opera which has no other role equal or superior to hers."‡

Verdi's final choice for the title role, a choice with which Draneht concurred, was Antonietta Pozzoni. She was singing *La Traviata* in Florence during March 1871, and after hearing her there, Verdi gave his stamp of approval to her "figure," and found her a "good actress" with "much spirit and true artistic *material.*" "But," he added, "the wobble in the voice and the sagging intonation cause me to fear that her voice is on the decline."§ The vocal difficulties sound problematic, but they were apparently not serious enough for Verdi to withhold his approval. A few years later, however, she gave up soprano roles and began to specialize in the mezzo-soprano repertoire. When in 1875 Pozzoni was scheduled to sing Amneris in Rome, Verdi, who obviously thought of her as a soprano, doubted that her lower notes would be adequate, but she went on to have a rather extensive career primarily in mezzo-soprano roles.

The possibilities for Radamès were many and varied, among them Gaetano Fraschini, one of the leading tenors of the day and a favorite of Verdi. Verdi, however, advised Draneht that Fraschini would probably not agree to a Cairo engagement. In any case, he had already accepted a contract to sing in Lisbon. Another suggestion was Ernesto Nicolini, a tenor perhaps more remembered for the scandal of his relationship with Adelina Patti, whom he finally married in 1886, than for his vocal gifts, which were — and still are — the subject of critical debate.

Radamès eventually became one of Nicolini's major roles, but at the Cairo premiere it went to Pietro Mongini, dubbed by Julian Budden, a "swashbuckling,

---

*Giovanni Battista Lampugnani to Paul Draneht, March 12, 1871 (in Busch, *Verdi's Aida*, p. 143).
†Julian Budden, *The Operas of Verdi*, III, p. 22.
‡Verdi to Paul Draneht, June 8, 1871 (in Busch, *Verdi's Aida*, p. 170).
§Verdi to Giulio Ricordi, March 10, 1871 (in Busch, *Verdi's Aida*, pp. 141-142).

ex-dragoon."* As an artist, he may not have demonstrated a great deal of subtlety. One Milanese journalist, who apparently remembered Mongini from earlier performances, was surprised by his success as Radamès, so much so that he commented, "it did not seem to be him."† Contemporary reports grant him a large, ringing voice appropriate for the role of the victorious Egyptian general. His career came to a sudden end with his death in 1874, but his name lives on in Italy through the annual international "Pietro Mongini" vocal contest in Varese.

Apparently there was little discussion of who would sing Amonasro. Draneht suggested the young Victor Maurel, who had made his debut as recently as 1867 and was just beginning what would be one of the most outstanding careers of any nineteenth-century artist. In the years ahead, he would introduce Tonio in Leoncavallo's *I Pagliacci,* and be Verdi's choice to create the title role in the revised *Simon Boccanegra,* Iago in *Otello,* and Falstaff in the composer's final opera. In the long run, however, the role of Amonasro was assigned to Francesco Steller, a relatively obscure Italian baritone. At forty-five years of age, he was probably a more believable father for twenty-five year old Pozzoni than Maurel, at twenty-three, would have been. Singing Amonasro in the *Aida* premiere was certainly the high point in Steller's career.

What about Amneris? As it turned out, casting this important role was one of the greatest challenges in the process of bringing *Aida* to the stage, and it led to a serious conflict between Verdi and Draneht. Part of the problem seems to have been based on a misunderstanding about the voice type actually required for Amneris. Perhaps Verdi himself had confused the issue, as Budden suggests, so that "from being in Verdi's original conception a soprano with good low notes she had become a mezzo-soprano with good high ones."‡ A number of singers were considered and rejected. In spite of Draneht's ardent support, Verdi would not agree to Sass for either role, and nothing came of the suggestion of Marie Destinn-Löwe, whom Verdi approved with a few reservations about the bottom and top of her voice. She is remembered today primarily for a student who respected her enough to change her name from Ema Kittl to Emmy Destinn.

Draneht's problem was two-fold: on the one hand supply and demand and on the other shrinking financial resources. As the weeks and months sped by, the quest for an Amneris became increasingly urgent. Then, as now, singers made their plans well in advance of the opera seasons, and the better the artist the greater the chance that they would be engaged early. Wait too long, and the supply of the truly desirable singers for a difficult role would be decidedly limited. As the opening of

---

*Julian Budden, *The Operas of Verdi,* III, p. 186.
†Quoted in Giorgio Gualerzi, "The Singers," in *Aida in Cairo,* Maria Codignola and Riccardo de Sanctis, eds. (Cairo: Banca Nazionale dei Lavoro, 1982), p. 178.
‡Julian Budden, *The Operas of Verdi,* III, p. 185.

the season drew nearer, there was also the issue of dwindling finances. In other words, Draneht had committed fully the funds provided for his use, and adding another expensive artist to the roster of the season would require money that might well not be available to him. Why not, then, use an artist already engaged by the Cairo opera company, Eleonora Grossi?

The more strongly Draneht recommended her, the more adamantly Verdi refused. The debate began with a simple statement from Verdi: "I am afraid that the role of *Amneris*, which is for a mezzo-soprano, may be a little too high for Mlle. Grossi."* From then on, the correspondence became more heated, although it was always in the context of professional politeness. To his colleague Mariette, however, Draneht expressed himself more openly: "The Maestro wants to take over the selection of the artists from me, and I don't know how to deal with him regarding certain claims he raises that don't seem very logical to me."† Draneht wanted to see the original contract with Verdi, no doubt to determine just what rights were involved. Verdi, for his part, threatened to take the matter up with Mariette, who had, of course, originally signed the contract for the opera. Whatever the contract said, however, Verdi wanted a mezzo-soprano for Amneris and as far as he was concerned, Grossi was a contralto and thus did not fit the bill. He wrote to Du Locle and requested that he seek Mariette's help in the matter, that "Draneht Bey has not yet found, or rather has not wanted to find, the *mezzo-soprano* for the role of Amneris, and now he writes me repeatedly that he has no more funds!"‡

For Draneht the contract issue hinged primarily on the requirement that Verdi choose his cast from singers engaged by the Cairo opera company. Verdi apparently felt that it was the impresario's responsibility to provide a company that included the singers he chose to use. In a letter to Verdi dated July 21, 1871, Draneht finally agreed to engage a mezzo-soprano at Verdi's request, even though he would be "acting against the interests of the administration entrusted to me."§ However, that wasn't enough for Verdi. He countered that what he required was not merely a mezzo-soprano, but a mezzo-soprano of great artistic gifts. So tense did the issue become that Draneht feared Verdi would refuse to provide the libretto and score unless he bent to the composer's will, and he wrote to Mariette that "I am obliged to obey or go to court, which I would never want to do."**

It seems likely that by this time the issue had become for Verdi a struggle to assert his own authority over the will of the impresario of an opera company, and that was the kind of battle that Verdi had fought over and over again in the past.

---

*Verdi to Paul Draneht, April 14, 1871 (in Busch, *Verdi's Aida*, p. 152).
†Paul Draneht to Auguste Mariette, June 17, 1871 (in Busch, *Verdi's Aida*, p. 175).
‡Verdi to Camille Du Locle, July 20, 1871 (in Busch, *Verdi's Aida*, p. 177).
§Paul Draneht to Verdi, July 21, 1871 (in Busch, *Verdi's Aida*, p. 189).
**Paul Draneht to Mariette, July 24, 1871 (in Busch, *Verdi's Aida*, p. 190).

Draneht may have been to him little more than the symbol of operatic management standing against the realization of artistic values. Of course, he wanted the best possible performance of his new work in the premiere, but there's no indication that he had even given Eleonora Grossi a fair hearing and he didn't exactly exert himself to appreciate the situation that Draneht was facing.

As it turned out, a third party intervened, and thus a crisis that might have prevented the Cairo premiere was averted. That third party was Franco Faccio, the dynamic young conductor who would serve Verdi well in the first La Scala performances of *Aida*. Faccio had already won Verdi's respect, and after looking over the *Aida* score, he assured the composer that Grossi was capable of performing the role capably. Verdi gave his assent, but not without reminding Draneht that Grossi was somewhat less than the ideal. "Although a few passages in the role of *Amneris* may prove a little high for la Grossi, I confirm what Sig. Ricordi told you in person — namely, to entrust the role of *Amneris* to that artist, rather than taking a chance at this point with a new artist, since it would be quite difficult to find a talented one."*

Not a great deal is known about Eleonora Grossi or her subsequent career. She had sung extensively on the Continent and in Great Britain before she was entrusted with Amneris. Her early death at thirty-nine years of age cut short her career in 1879.

In the meantime, there were other problems that had to be faced as a result of the eleven-month delay in the premiere of *Aida*. It had been Verdi's intention that the Italian premiere of *Aida* would take place at La Scala during February of 1871, shortly after the anticipated first performances in Cairo. If anything, Verdi was more concerned with the preparations for the Milan performances than he was for those in Cairo, although his care with the casting for Egypt demonstrates that he sincerely wanted good performances of the opera in both venues. When it became clear that the siege of Paris would delay the Cairo performances for several months, Draneht was understandably concerned that as a result Egypt might be denied the premiere of the opera. He still had not seen a copy of Verdi's contract and thus, was not aware of the clause that gave Verdi permission to perform the opera elsewhere if the Egyptian premiere was delayed — but only after a six-month delay. Draneht shared his concern with the Khedive, who had an obvious personal interest in the honor that would come to Egypt as a result of Verdi's opera. If as a result of the delay Verdi should choose to go ahead with a performance in Milan, the Khedive, Draneht informed Verdi, "would be extremely grieved by your decision."† Verdi, however, had already anticipated the problem and made plans to delay the Milan performances. He responded to Draneht quickly to assure him "that I would

---

*Verdi to Paul Draneht, August 2, 1891 (in Busch, *Verdi's Aida*, p. 193).
†Paul Draneht to Verdi, December 21, 1870 (in Busch, *Verdi's Aida*, p. 117).

never have demanded my rights at this time (even if I had any) and that, although with great regret, I forgo my desire to give my opera this season in Cairo and at La Scala." Draneht's — and Khedive's — fears in this case were easily quieted.

The question of a conductor for the Cairo performances remained an open issue. Verdi had first asked his friend Muzio to supervise the premiere, a position that would have included conducting the performances, and Muzio, in spite of his reluctance to return to Egypt, had agreed. It was not a completely happy decision all the way around. Muzio and his family had not been completely happy in Egypt, and as Verdi sensed from Draneht's correspondence, Draneht had been no happier with Muzio. Nicola De Giosa had conducted in Cairo during the 1870 season, and he took Verdi's decision to send Muzio for *Aida* as a personal affront. Verdi's response to De Giosa in January 1871 was more a defense on the grounds of the composer's artistic rights than it was an apology. He and De Giosa had apparently had a disagreement in the past over the proper orchestral *diapason,* that is, the pitch to which an orchestra tunes its instruments. When Verdi asked Draneht if De Giosa had been reengaged for the next season, the question was certainly more than a matter of idle curiosity. He was probably relieved to learn that De Giosa would not be conducting again at Cairo. Later in the process of selecting a conductor, Verdi tried once more to persuade Draneht to engage Muzio, this time through Giovanni Lampugnani, the Milan artist's agent, but Muzio was not engaged.

Another possibility was Angelo Mariani, probably the most outstanding among the Italian conductors in the mid-nineteenth century. Beginning with Mariani's participation in the premiere performances of *Aroldo*, Verdi's revised version of the earlier *Stiffelio,* a close friendship developed between the conductor and the composer and his wife. Frank Walker, in his book *The Man Verdi*, devotes an entire chapter to that friendship and its ultimate sad dissolution,* and reading through the lengthy quotations from Mariani's letters, we are struck with the almost obsessive nature of Mariani's affection and respect for Verdi. He writes often, usually in long, rambling essays that demonstrate "his boundless devotion to Verdi and all his works," and Walker is surely justified in his evaluation of the situation: "Mariani *worshipped* Verdi, and would have allowed himself to be cut to pieces to give him pleasure."† Verdi, for his part, humored Mariani, instructed him as a father might a son, called him by not always complimentary nicknames, and perhaps did not take him completely seriously but always appreciated his gifts as a musical artist. By the time *Aida* was in the works, however, Verdi and particularly his wife, Giuseppina, had turned against Mariani abruptly, firmly and even cruelly.

What had produced the breach in this friendship? Scholars have suggested a num-

---

*Frank Walker, *The Man Verdi* (New York: Alfred A. Knopf, 1962), pp. 283-392.
†*Ibid.*, p. 301.

ber of reasons, and the real answer no doubt lies somewhere in the middle of them. First of all, there was the matter of the memorial requiem that Verdi had proposed to honor the first anniversary of Gioachino Rossini's death. Each section of the mass would be written by a different composer with Verdi himself contributing the *Libera Me,* and the work would then be performed in Bologna on November 13, 1869. The plans fell through, and Verdi blamed the failure on Mariani, who, he complained, had demonstrated neither enthusiasm nor initiative in the project. Greater responsibility probably rested with the committee that had been charged with responsibility for the mass with perhaps a little left over for Verdi himself and his publisher friend Giulio Ricordi.*

The friendship might have survived, even if not quite intact, had there been no further problems. From the beginning of the *Aida* project, Mariani had hoped that he might be called on to conduct and supervise the Cairo premiere and apparently had been given some encouragement, although not directly from Verdi, that he might be called on. Verdi sent him a curt answer to let him know that he had assigned the Cairo performances to someone else. When he was unable to arrange for Muzio to conduct the opera, however, Verdi turned to Mariani in spite of his personal animosity toward him and sought his help. This time, Mariani hesitated, delayed giving a definite answer one way or the other, and finally refused. Although he wanted nothing to do with Mariani personally and he and Giuseppina blamed him for his refusal to go to Cairo, Verdi acknowledged his superiority to other conductors and continued to encourage Draneht to engage him, but it was too late. By the end of April 1871, he had engaged another conductor.

There may have been other reasons why Verdi had turned so strongly against Mariani. The conductor had formed a romantic attachment to Teresa Stolz, the Bohemian soprano, and they were engaged to be married. From approximately 1870 on, however, Stolz began to play an ever-larger role in Verdi's life. She proved herself, both in *Don Carlo* and *Forza del Destino,* to be an outstanding interpreter of his roles, and Verdi took a special interest in her, both artistically and personally. If there truly was a romance between them, it surely happened later, after the first performances of *Aida,* but the attraction may have begun during the rehearsals for the revised *Forza* early in 1869. Some of Verdi's biographers have speculated that it was Verdi's interest in Stolz that led to the break with Mariani. There were rumors to that effect, and it is certainly true that by 1874, Giuseppina, Verdi's wife, seemed to be almost at the point of emotional collapse in her concern about the relationship and how it was affecting her marriage.

Then there was the matter of Wagner's *Lohengrin.* Mariani conducted the work at Bologna in November 1871, the performance that first introduced Wagner's operas

---

*The composers, however, were certainly not at fault. They completed their portions of the Rossini Mass. In recent years it has been reassembled, performed, and recorded. Verdi's *Libera me* was recycled in his Requiem Mass in memory of Manzoni.

to Italy. One of those in the audience was Giuseppe Verdi, hidden away in the back of a box. Verdi generally spoke of Wagner with measured respect, and his notes on this performance, jotted into the margins of a score of the opera, were not entirely negative. Of course, the friendship with Mariani had already ended, but is it possible that Mariani's advocacy of the German master deepened the break? Well, yes, possible, but I believe it highly unlikely that Verdi would have objected strongly to the introduction of Wagner's work to the Italian public, nor would he have blamed Mariani for conducting it.

The tragic figure in all of this unhappy story is Mariani himself. His own unstable personality and emotional insecurity were surely part of the problem. Even in an age when the emotions were expressed more openly, often in language of poetic hyperbole, the intensity of Mariani's attachment to Verdi as seen in his letters goes beyond the ordinary boundaries of friendship and artistic respect. Mariani wrote too often and at too great length and said far too much, and to Verdi, it must have seemed almost overbearing. It's easy to imagine that there was some relief to the composer when the relationship came to an end. On the other hand, once the break had taken place, Verdi and his wife were often thoughtless and cruel in the way they treated Mariani, and even before that time they had often taken his concerns lightly and disparaged his illnesses, which were indeed quite serious and ultimately proved to be fatal in 1873. Unfortunately, Verdi's attitude toward his one-time friend is perhaps the ugliest episode in a life that was otherwise marked with generosity and kindness.

The man Draneht finally chose to conduct the premiere of *Aida* was Giovanni Bottesini. Verdi did not approve. "Great musician that he is," Verdi wrote, "[Bottesini] is not a good conductor for me or for my operas."* Bottesini was, according to Phillips-Matz, "an apostle of the Music of the Future and founder of an avant-grade circle in Tuscany,"† not precisely the best qualifications to appeal to Verdi. He was, however, not only a respected conductor, he was also a composer of some note and a renowned virtuoso on the double bass, a world-wide performer who triumphed not only in Italy, but also in France, Spain, Great Britain, Russia, Austria, Mexico, the United States — and Havana, Cuba, where his first opera *Cristoforo Colombo,* had its premiere in 1848. Verdi respected his abilities even though he would have preferred another conductor, and sent him suggestions to help in the first performances of *Aida*. Years later, he recommended Bottesini for the position of director of the Parma Conservatory.

The performing roster for the *Aida* premiere was not, then, exactly what Verdi would have preferred, but on the whole, it was a thoroughly competent group, if not quite top drawer.

---

*Verdi to Giovanni Battista Lampugnani, May 4, 1871 (in Busch, *Verdi's Aida*, p. 156).
†Mary Jane Phillips-Matz, *Verdi: A Biography*, (Oxford and New York: Oxford University Press, 1993), p. 583.

Conductor	Giovanni Bottesini
Aida	Antonietta Anastasi-Pozzoni
Amneris	Eleonora Grossi
Radamès	Pietro Mongini
Amonasro	Francesco Steller
Ramfis	Paolo Medini
Il Re	Tommasso Costa
Messenger	Luigi Stecchi-Bottardi
Priestess	Marietta Allievi

The visual production had been largely in the hands of Mariette, who was very keen on reproducing more or less authentic architectural details in the settings and costume designs that would at least not offend against history. In fact, he proved to be a skillful designer, and his costume sketches, many of which have been preserved, are both attractive and beautifully executed in water colors.*

Aside from the *mise-en-scène*, Mariette was not closely involved in the actual production of the opera, but a handful of issues arose to give him some slight concern. He certainly wanted his beautiful costume designs to make a strong impression on stage, and he had to deal with the delay of some of the artists in submitting their measurements. There was also the matter of beards. "I consider it absolutely necessary that there be neither beards nor moustaches.... Can you see the King of Egypt with a turned-up moustache and a goatee?"† A few days later, Draneht replied that he had ample authority to insist on the removal of facial hair if necessary. Illustrations from later nineteenth and early twentieth century performances, however, suggest that impresarios since Draneht have either been unable to remove the beards or haven't bothered even to try.

Then there was the sleepless night that troubled Mariette, probably in October of 1871. It was the final scene of the opera, the unusual setting of the underground chamber with a temple above it, that kept him awake. What about the sight lines in the opera house? "The matter is worth examining," he wrote Draneht "otherwise we expose ourselves to the disapproval of people of taste, if there [are] any such in Egypt."‡ What about the Khedive, who would be able to see everything easily from his elevated royal box, but who would see nothing if he chose instead to view the opera from his lower box? Mariette need not have worried. Stage designers have managed to meet that challenge successfully through the years.

By December 24, 1871, when the premiere performance took place, Cairo was astir with activity. The Khedive and his staff had been eager to focus the attention

---

*For five examples, see William Weaver, *Verdi: A Documentary Study* (New York: Thames and Hudson, 1977), Illustrations 202-206.
†Auguste Mariette to Paul Draneht, August 30, 1871 (in Busch, *Verdi's Aida*, p. 208).
‡Auguste Mariette to Paul Draneht, October 6, 1871[?] (in Busch, *Verdi's Aida*, p. 233).

of the artistic world on Egypt. The theatre was filled with the important, influential, and presumably wealthy people, and of course the Khedive himself was there along with his harem, who occupied three boxes. Apparently, the audience consisted mainly of invited guests, a fact that did not please Verdi, and at least one observer noted that they were primarily European in background, Noted musical journalists were summoned to Cairo for the occasion to ensure full press coverage in Europe. Verdi, by the way, was not particularly happy about the publicity surrounding the premiere. He did not plan to be there himself, and he truly preferred for his operas to earn their success not from an invited audiences of celebrities but from the regular opera-going public.

The critics and the audience, however, approved of *Aida,* and Ismail Pasha, who must have been delighted, received a lengthy, resounding ovation for having provided this opera for his theatre. He honored Verdi by naming him a Commendatore of the Ottoman Order. Among the music critics present on that Christmas Eve night were Ernest Reyer, the distinguished French composer and music journalist, and Filippo Filippi, the most prominent of the Milanese critics. Both men were thought to have "Wagnerian" sympathies, and both of them pointed to what they heard as Wagnerian influences in *Aida.* Reyer particularly, although he praised the composer "toward whom, as is well known, I have never shown either great admiration or much fondness," pointed out affinities with "Germanism" and assured his readers that "the works of Richard Wagner are familiar to [Verdi]."*
From the viewpoint of Reyer and Filippi, any influence that Verdi absorbed from the German master was worthy of praise. That was a viewpoint that Verdi did not share and it was an influence that he assuredly would never admit.

Aida, however, had clearly enjoyed an auspicious beginning in Cairo, but for Verdi, the real test was yet to come. How would the opera be received in Italy, first at La Scala in Milan, and then in the other theatres? How would it fare as it made its way around the world?

---

*Quoted in Weaver, *Verdi: A Documentary Study,* p. 229.

3

Aida for the World — and for the Ages

Christmas Eve 1871 marked the premiere of *Aida* in Cairo, Egypt; and February 8, 1872, its introduction to the rest of the world in Milan, Italy.

Verdi took few, if any, chances with the initial and early performances of his operas. He wanted the best casts, under the best conductors, with the best choruses and orchestras, in the best possible productions that could conceivably be achieved, and above all, he wanted it done his way. For Verdi, it was a case of the composer rules. He could sometimes, of course, make compromises. After all, he was a practical man of the theatre. However, the compromises were never easy and were always accompanied with protests and complaints. We have seen that attitude at work in the preparations for the first performances in Egypt. As Draneht discovered, when it came to the choice of cast and conductor, Verdi was not an easy man to please. He would be just as demanding or perhaps even more so for La Scala. After all, La Scala was home territory, and it was also the great symbol of Italian opera for the entire artistic world, a position that the new company in Egypt certainly did not hold. In the long run, Milan simply made more difference for the future of *Aida* than Cairo did.

La Scala prided itself on being the leading opera house in Italy, and in the eyes of much of the artistic world it was the true symbol of the musical life of the nation. It earned its original full name, Regio Ducal Teatro alla Scala, by virtue of the former church that stood on the site, S. Maria della Scala, which in turn had included in its title the name of an eminent lady of Milan, Beatrice della Scala. It had opened with a gala evening of opera and ballet on August 3, 1778, when Salieri's opera *L'Europa Riconosciuta* was performed along with two ballets — one by Salieri himself and the other by Luigi de Baillou. During the first few decades of the nineteenth century the fame of La Scala grew as Italy's most important composers premiered operas there. Gioachino Rossini honored the house with *Il Turco in Italia* in 1814 and occasional other works, although he generally preferred to introduce his operas in Naples or Rome. Vincenzo Bellini's handful of operas included three La Scala premieres, one of which was the famous *Norma* in 1831, and Gaetano Donizetti, who was not inevitably happy with the artistic quality of La Scala performances, was none the less represented by premieres of five of his sixty-five operas. There were, of course, other composers, more famous in their own time than in ours, who saw their works first on the stage of La Scala, among them Simone Mayer, Saverio Mercadante, and Giacomo Meyerbeer, during his Italian years.

At the same time, there were productions in other Italian cities that sometimes outdid La Scala in artistic terms, and many of them could claim outstanding premieres of their own. When Verdi's first opera, *Oberto,* was mounted at La Scala in 1839, however, he was surely in good compositional company. Bartolomeo Merelli, the impresario of the opera house in Milan, encouraged Verdi, and his next three operas — *Un Giorno di Regno* (1840), *Nabucco* (1842), and *I Lombardi* (1843) — were given La Scala premieres. When Verdi returned to La Scala for the 1844–45 season to supervise a revival of *I Lombardi* and to present the first performances there of *Giovanna D'Arco,* however, he found the situation far from his liking. Artistic standards were low, casts inadequate, and the orchestra underpowered. His friend Muzio commented that during the rehearsals for the revival of *I Lombardi* Verdi "shouted like a madman and stamped his feet so much he looked as though he were playing the organ."* According to biographer George Martin, it was at this time that Verdi acquired one of his less admirable nicknames, "the bear of Busetto."† He refused to appear for the opening performance of *Lombardi*, which was nonetheless a success. With the premiere of *Giovanna D'Arco,* the audience was happy, the critics somewhat less so, and Verdi himself decidedly unhappy. He refused permission for a revival of *Ernani* and declared that he was finished with La Scala. "He will not write any more for La Scala," Muzio reported, "or stage or conduct any opera of his there; and he says he will never set foot on that stage again."‡ The next season Merelli mounted performances of *I Due Foscari* in which the third and fourth acts were reversed, one more offense against a composer who intended for his works to be performed his way. Verdi was as good as his word, and it took twenty-four years, a new management at the opera house, and a whole new attitude toward fidelity to a composer's wishes to bring him back to La Scala.

Verdi's publishers, the Ricordi firm of Milan, were eager for a rapprochement with La Scala, where artistic standards were now greatly improved, and were equally eager for the composer to complete the revision of *La Forza del Destino.* Verdi agreed and in the fall of 1868 began work on a revision of the opera. Since the original librettist, Francesco Piave, was now completely incapacitated, revisions to the text were turned over to Antonio Ghislanzoni, and soon a number of smaller changes

---

*Quoted in George Martin, *Verdi: His Music, Life and Times* (New York: Limelight Editions, 1992), pp. 121–122
†Martin, *Verdi: His Music*, p. 121.
‡Muzio to Antonio Baarezzi, February 27, 1845 (in William Weaver, *Verdi: A Documentary Study*, New York: Thames and Hudson, 1977, p. 162).

had been made and the unremitting gloom of the final scene had been somewhat alleviated by reducing the number of deaths from three to two. An excellent cast was assembled, including Teresa Stolz as Leonora, and under the inspired leadership of Angelo Mariani, the problematic *Forza* received a triumphant welcome. Within a few months, Verdi's friendship with Mariani would come to its unhappy end, but the success of the revised *Forza* effectively healed the breach between Verdi and La Scala.

From very early in the process, it had been Giulio Ricordi's hope that the Italian premiere of *Aida* would take place at La Scala. He wrote Verdi in July 1870, "I continue to hope for the realization of my ideal — that is ... Verdi ... *Aida* ... La Scala."* Verdi expressed some hesitation still, but by November 1870, the performance was assured. Apparently, the powers at La Scala were as eager as Ricordi to see the Italian premiere of *Aida* on their own stage. Even the mere announcement that a new Verdi opera would be performed at their theatre could have enormous financial benefits to the company. As Ricordi informed Verdi, for La Scala it "would mean that, at the very least, 300 more subscribers could be gotten. Calculating these at an average of 100 lire each, this would amount to 30,000 lire that the management would have immediately in cash."† Then, as now, opera companies operated under severe budget restraints, and La Scala was obviously no exception.

As we have seen, the Franco-Prussian War pushed the La Scala performance back a year, from February 1871 to February 1872, and the delay necessitated some important changes in the originally planned casting. Verdi's first choice for the title role was Antonietta Fricci, an Austrian soprano whose real name, Frietsche, had been "Italianized" for international consumption. She had proved her worth as a dramatic soprano in Great Britain and Italy in some of the most demanding roles of the repertoire, and she was Verdi's enthusiastic choice to sing Aida. For Radamès, the choice was Mario Tiberini, who had sung Alvaro in the revised *Forza*. As it turned out, Fricci was already under contract in Lisbon for the 1871–72 season, and neither she nor Tiberini would be part of the La Scala company. Verdi, Ricordi, and the management were forced to turn their eyes and ears elsewhere.

Other singers were considered, among them Antonietta Pozzoni, who would sing the title role in Cairo, and Giuseppina De Giuli, but Verdi had clearly been impressed with Teresa Stolz as the *Forza* Leonora. He first considered her as a possible Amneris. Stolz's extensive vocal range, however, made it feasible for her to sing either of the leading female roles, and when Fricci was no longer available, Stolz became the preferred choice for Aida. Of course, there were problems to be overcome. Would Mariani, her fiancé, agree, particularly with his growing estrangement

---

*Giulio Ricordi to Verdi, July 14, 1870 (in Busch, *Verdi's Aida*, p. 31).
†Giulio Ricordi to Verdi, November 13, 1870 (in Busch, *Verdi's Aida*, p. 105).

from Verdi? Verdi feared that *"Mariani will ruin* everything, if he can think of a way."* Mariani, however, apparently offered no objections. The problem with Stolz's engagement arose primarily because of the exorbitant demands, financial and otherwise, that the soprano made. When he responded to the letter detailing her expectations, Ricordi informed the "esteemed Lady, that never in my life have I experienced such a lively displeasure and such a strong disillusionment as that which your letter of the 6th brought to me."† It took patience and perseverance, but in time an agreement was reached and Stolz agreed to be La Scala's first Aida.

Stolz centered her career on the major soprano roles in Verdi's operas and continued to sing them until her relatively early retirement after the 1876–77 season. Photographs show a woman with a strong facial profile, more strikingly noble than conventionally beautiful, and contemporary reports suggest a singer of vocal refinement and dramatic involvement — precisely the kind of artist Verdi would prefer. To what extent the composer's interest in Stolz went beyond close friendship and sincere appreciation of her artistic gifts is a matter of continuing debate among Verdi scholars. There was ample contemporary gossip, some of it in the public press, and Giuseppina, Verdi's wife, was concerned and at least for a time deeply hurt by the attention her husband showered on Stolz. It is to Stolz's credit and perhaps to Giuseppina's as well that she remained one of the closest of friends of both husband and wife throughout their lives. About her artistic accomplishments there was no question. She was, as Andrew Porter called her, "the Verdian dramatic soprano par excellence."‡

For Amneris in the La Scala performances, the choice fell on Maria Waldmann. Verdi was initially reluctant. She was a young singer, still in her twenties, either eight or ten years younger than Stolz, depending on which of the ambiguously reported birth dates one accepts. There were questions about the quality and size of her voice, and at one point Verdi complained that "she has defects in pronunciation,"§ by which he apparently meant the little dramatic accents that he alone could teach the singer — if there were time. On the whole, the reports Verdi received of her performances were positive, but he clearly believed that the success of the opera as a whole depended a great deal on a strong Amneris. As he wrote to Giulio Ricordi, "A mediocre *Amneris* means a ruined opera."** For this role "one needs an artist with highly developed dramatic sensibility who is a mistress of the stage."†† As it turned out, Waldmann proved her worth and won Verdi's approval, and with

---

*Verdi to Giulio Ricordi, December 30, 1870 (in Busch, *Verdi's Aida*, p. 121).
†Giulio Ricordi to Teresa Stolz, January 7, 1871 (in Busch, *Verdi's Aida*, p. 129).
‡Andrew Porter, in *The New Grove Dictionary of Opera*, ed. Stanley Sadie (New York: Grove's Dictionaries of Music, 1992, 1998), IV, p. 549.
§Verdi to Giulio Ricordi, December 13, 1871 (in Busch, *Verdi's Aida*, p. 265).
**Verdi to Giulio Ricordi, May 24, 1871 (in Busch, *Verdi's Aida*, p. 163).
††Verdi to Giulio Ricordi, July 10, 1871 (in Busch, *Verdi's Aida*, p. 182).

it a friendship that continued throughout his life. He regretted the early termination of her career when in 1877 she left the stage to marry Count, later Duke, Galleazzo Massari.

For Radamès, Giuseppi Capponi was the choice. Illness, however, forced his withdrawal a month before the La Scala premiere, and much to Verdi's regret, he was replaced by Giuseppe Fancelli, who according to contemporary reports must have been the prototype for every cartoon description of vocally gifted and intellectually deprived opera singers. Verdi's candid comment? "Beautiful voice, but a blockhead."* Jules Massenet named Fancelli "cinq-et-cinq-font-dix"† — Mr. Five Plus Five Equals Ten — a reference to his stock gesture with arms stretched out before him and fingers widely separated. Fortunately, Capponi recovered to sing Radamès in other Italian theatres and joined Stolz, Waldmann, and Armando Maini for the initial performances of Verdi's *Requiem* in 1874.

Francesco Pandolfini, who sang Amanasro, was the most distinguished Italian baritone of the period, a position he had established through outstanding performances in the 1860s. Verdi's only question about Pandolfini was whether this famous artist would accept a role that was not only brief but also offered no aria in which he could shine. Artist that he clearly was, however, Pandolfini appreciated the possibilities of Amonasro and wrote to Giulio Ricordi that "even if the role had been a hundred times smaller, I would have been equally content."‡

Others in the cast of the Milan performances were Orlando Maini as Ramfis and Paride Povoleri as the King. Both of these basses had outstanding careers, and Povoleri, like Maini, took part in some of the performances of the *Requiem* as it made its way around Europe in the later 1870s. All in all, it was a remarkably strong cast, and that in spite of Fancelli. Few performances either on stage or in sound recordings in the years since 1872 have offered more — or, we might add, have been better conducted.

The choice of a conductor was, as always, a sensitive issue with Verdi. With his earlier operas, he had usually led the initial performances himself, but by the 1870s composers were more and more inclined to trust their works to specialists in the field of conducting. Leading a new Verdi opera under the scrutiny of the composer, however, was no easy task. He insisted on someone with musical sensitivity aligned with the ability to communicate with the musicians under his charge and command them, when the need arose, with authority. What he did not want, however, was a conductor — or a singer either for that matter — who attempted to become a co-creator with the composer. It was a position he defended adamantly.

---

*Verdi to Opprandino Arrivabene, January 13, 1872 (in Busch, *Verdi's Aida*, p. 276).
†Budden, *The Operas of Verdi: From* Don Carlos *to* Falstaff (New York: Oxford University Press, 1981), p. 189
‡Quoted in Giulio Ricordi to Verdi, November 12, 1871 (in Busch, *Verdi's Aida*, p. 250).

"I want only one creator.... I don't concede the right to '*create*' to singers and conductors."*

Angelo Mariani was not available and, given Verdi's estrangement from his former friend, would hardly have been a comfortable choice for the La Scala premiere of *Aida*. The possible La Scala engagement of Hans von Bülow, the great German maestro, as music director was opposed by Giulio Ricordi, probably on the grounds that Bülow would bring his Wagnerian baggage with him to Milan with resulting profit to the rival Lucca music publishing firm, the company that represented Wagner's operas in Italy. It was even suggested that if Bülow became the music director of the Milan opera house, Ricordi would refuse permission for Verdi's operas to be performed at La Scala. In any case, the German pianist/conductor was not engaged, and with Ricordi's encouragement the appointment went to Franco Faccio.

Faccio was a young friend of Arrigo Boito, who would become Verdi's last librettist, and the two had served together briefly in Garibaldi's forces. Music, however, was his destiny, and Faccio soon devoted his attention to composition and conducting. As a composer his success was limited, and the failure of his opera *Amleto* at La Scala led to his decision to write no more music dramas. As a conductor, however, he became the best that Italy had to offer, the logical successor in artistic achievement to Mariani, who died in 1874. Faccio's own career was cut short by debilitating illness and he died in 1891, but not before bringing to the stage the first performances of Ponchielli's *La Gioconda*, Puccini's earliest works, and Verdi's *Otello*.

Excitement ran high in Milan in the days immediately before the Italian premiere of *Aida,* and on the evening of February 8 La Scala was crowded with every seat taken, large numbers standing, and the boxes jammed full of eager opera-goers. They were not disappointed. *Aida* was a triumph, and Verdi was feted like a conquering hero. He received thirty-two curtain calls and was presented with a gold, gem-encrusted scepter. Some of the critics were a bit more cautious than the general public, and Verdi, who like many artists sometimes claimed to be unaffected by criticism, was actually very sensitive to what the musical press had to say about his works. Three years later, some of the comments made after the initial performances of *Aida* still rankled. "Endless chatter," he commented to Giulio Ricordi, "that I didn't *know how to write* for the singers; that the second and fourth acts had some tolerable moments (nothing in the third); and finally that I was an imitator of Wagner!!! What a fine result after a career of thirty-five years — to end up as an *imitator*!!!"† The actual critical notices following the Milan premiere were hardly as severe as Verdi remembered them, and his personal evaluation the morning after the La

---

*Verdi to Giulio Ricordi, April 11, 1871 (in Busch, *Verdi's Aida*, p. 150).
†Verdi to Giulio Ricordi, April 4, 1875 (in Busch, *Verdi's Aida*, p. 382).

Scala premiere was typically low key but completely indicative of the opera's future: "...this opera is certainly not one of my worst. Time will afterward give it the place it deserves."*

And that is precisely what "time" has done. After Milan, *Aida* made its way first to Parma, then to other Italian cities, Buenos Aires, New York, Berlin, and Vienna. By its tenth birthday in 1881, the opera had been performed in at least twenty-three different nations, and it continues as one of the most popular operas in theatres all around the globe.

Audiences and even the critics, sometimes rather begrudgingly, praise *Aida* as one of the greatest of all operas, Italian or otherwise. One early auditor, however, had a decidedly different view. It's an oft-repeated account. Prospero Bertani had traveled from Reggio to Parma to hear *Aida*. He was not happy with the opera, but given its favorable reception by other people, he decided to return two days later to give the opera another chance to win his approval. His second exposure satisfied him no more than the first, and he wrote Verdi to ask for a refund of 31.80 lire for his expenses — the train fare, his dinner, and his theatre tickets. Verdi instructed Giulio Ricordi to send the man a check for 27.80 lire for train fare and theatre tickets, but he would not pay for the dinner. After all, Prospero could have eaten at home. Verdi's only demands were that Bertani was to provide a receipt and promise never to attend another new Verdi opera.†

The first performance of *Aida* in the United States took place on November 25, 1873, in New York's Academy of Music. Aida was Ostavia Toriani, a soprano of German origin in spite of her Italianized name. Others in the cast were Annie Louise Carey as Amneris, Italo Campanini as Radamès, and Victor Maurel, who was making his American debut, as Amonasro. The conductor was Verdi's friend and protégé, Emanuele Muzio. Within three months, the same company with largely the same cast had introduced *Aida* to Philadelphia, Chicago, Milwaukee, and Boston.

The opera entered the repertoire of the three-year-old Metropolitan Opera on November 12, 1886, sandwiched between two presentations of Wagner's *Die Walküre*. From 1884 to 1891, all Metropolitan performances were sung in German. This one, along with the nine presentations of the opera to follow, was no exception. The cast included Carl Zobel, whose only appearances with the company were four outings as Radamès; Marianne Brandt, the distinguished mezzo-soprano, as Amneris; Adolf Robinson as Amonasro; and Emil Fischer as Ramfis. As Aida, the audience heard Theresa Herbert-Föster, who had come to American with her husband Victor Herbert, a cellist in the Metropolitan orchestra. His career as America's top-

---

*Verdi to Opprandino Arrivabene, February 9, 1872 (in Busch, *Verdi's Aida*, p. 281).
†This incident is included in most accounts of the performance history of *Aida*. The correspondence that confirms it is to be found in Busch, *Verdi's Aida*, pp. 303–305.

ranking operetta composer was still in the future. W.J. Henderson, the dean of New York music critics, found little to admire in the performance and nothing to praise in the conducting of Anton Seidl, whom he found guilty of "unconscionable dragging of the tempos."* It was clearly the wrong cast singing the wrong opera in the wrong language, and obviously something beyond German routine would be necessary if *Aida* was to succeed at the Met.

What that something was emerged when the Metropolitan abandoned the "all–German" policy and presented *Aida* in Italian, first while touring in Chicago on December 10, 1891, and then on December 28 at home base. The cast was headed by Lily Lehmann, an outstanding artist in any language (she had earlier sung the title role in German), and Jan De Reszke, the prince of tenors, as her lover Radamès. De Reszke was known on occasion to omit "Celeste Aida," the tenor aria in the first scene, apparently because he found it too strenuous at such an early point in the opera. He managed to get away with it, but one can only imagine the unhappy fate of a tenor nowadays who disappointed the audience so early in the evening. *Aida* went on to become one of the most often performed works in the entire Metropolitan repertoire. For many years it was number one, and only recently has Puccini's *La Bohème* moved ahead. As of the 2001–2002 season, *Aida* had graced the Metropolitan stage 1,051 times,; *La Bohème*, 1,123. Add to that the countless performances of *Aida* in opera houses all over the world and it is obvious that, as Verdi anticipated, "time" has indeed given "it the place it deserves."

So why has *Aida* achieved the kind of international popularity that most other operas never manage to gain? The reasons, no doubt, are many. It is, first of all, a work of musical beauty and dramatic power, subjects that will be addressed in the next chapter. It's also a work that offers a strong visual appeal. With *Aida* there is almost always something interesting to look at even for newcomers to opera or the people who've been turned off by previous encounters with musical drama. At the most conspicuous level, it is a big, splashy, spectacular feast for the eyes, and that effect can work, by the way, even in some of the small-scale productions if they are effectively designed and directed.

Consider, for example, the scenic possibilities: a triumphant victory parade set amid the archeological wonders of ancient Egypt, a moonlit night outside a temple of Isis with the waters of the Nile rippling in the distance, the interior of a mysterious sanctuary with an underground vault for the burial alive of enemies of the state. Then there is the cast, sometimes an incredibly large cast, elaborately and often colorfully costumed — not just the six principal singers but also the chorus, the stage extras, and the dancers. Some operas have *no* ballets, some have one, but *Aida* has *three*— sacred

---

*W.J. Henderson, quoted in *Metropolitan Opera Annals: A Chronicle of Artists and Performances*, William H. Seltsam, ed. (New York: H.W. Wilson Company, 1947), p. 22.

temple dances, Moorish slaves cavorting for the amusement of an unhappy princess, and an eye-filling victory ballet. There are animals, too — occasional horses and camels, and there have even been performances in which an African or Indian elephant or two appeared, (it wouldn't matter since the Egyptians trained both kinds of pachyderms). Even a confirmed opponent of opera could hardly be bored.

It should come as no surprise that *Aida* has been the subject of spectacular stage productions. One suspects that Verdi would be pleased provided the spectacle was subservient to high artistic standards. Show merely for the sake of show was one of the vices the he condemned at the Paris Opèra, but he was always concerned that his operas come to the public not only in superior musical and dramatic performances but also with effective, impressive staging values. The Milan critic Filippo Filippi, who was present at the first performance in Cairo, confirmed that the sets and costumes for the premiere were "magnificent,"[*] which must have pleased both Verdi and Auguste Mariette, who had supervised the designs. The composer himself commented that the *mise-en-scène* at La Scala was "very good"[†] and was equally impressed with the visual aspects of the next production, which opened in Parma on April 20, 1872.[‡] Verdi was clearly the complete man of the theatre and concerned himself with the total performance of his opera in all its aspects. In the broadest sense he wanted "good elements for the performance," and by that, he wrote, "I don't mean to speak of the singers alone, but of the orchestral and choral masses, the costumes, the scenery, the props, the *stage movement*, and the *subtlety of coloration*."[§]

Aida is also an opera that has flourished in the most varied surroundings — under the roof of an opera house, under the stars, and occasionally even under the sun. The vast amphitheatre at Verona, Italy, is a case in point. Through the years, *Aida* has been the most popular of the productions there.

Verona's great outdoor arena has actually offered a widely varied repertoire over the years, as have some of the other outdoor theatres. It's certainly true, however, that some works thrive best enclosed within the walls of an opera house, and the issue is apparently not so much whether the setting of the plot is essentially "outdoors" or "indoors." It has more to do with the scope of the action and the size of the work musically and dramatically. Contrast, for example, Verdi's *Forza del Destino*, in which large, romantic human emotions are played out against a background of international conflict, and his *Traviata*, in which the tragedy is equally profound but the milieu is decidedly intimate. There's always a danger that Violetta and Alfredo, the lovers in *Traviata*, will be lost amid the overpowering ruins of the

---

[*]See Busch, *Verdi's Aida*, n. 2, p. 269.
[†]Verdi to Opprandino Arrivabene, February 9, 1872 (in Busch, *Verdi's Aida*, p. 281).
[‡]Verdi to Cesare De Sanctis, April 21, 1872 (in Busch, *Verdi's Aida*, p. 297).
[§]Verdi to Vincenzo Torelli, August 22, 1872 (in Busch, *Verdi's Aida*, p. 317).

Verona amphitheatre. The differences can sometimes be subtle, but they are nonetheless real. For an example, take a look at Harvey Phillips' parallel reviews of the videos of Verona productions of Puccini's *Tosca*, a more intimate story, and his *Turandot,* set as it is among the storied wonders of imperial Peking. It goes without saying that *Turandot* has thrived in the Verona arena.* When it comes to *Aida*, there's no question: It is entirely at home in the wide open spaces.

Among the outdoor opera performances, Verona's Roman amphitheater claims pride of place not only for size and quality of performance but also for perseverance. Since the origin of the festival in 1913, there have been inevitable breaks in continuity during the troubled, war-torn years of the twentieth century, but the eightieth season of opera at the amphitheater was celebrated in 2004. The possibilities of the huge arena inspired the tenor Giovanni Zenatello, who was a native of Verona, and impresario Ottone Rovato to produce the first Verona festival. The opening opera was the most obvious choice of all — Verdi's *Aida*— and it has continued to grace the enormous outdoor stage in the years since. During that first season, Zenatello sang Radamès, and his Aida was Ester Mazzoleni. From the viewpoint of ninety or more years later, Zenatello was certainly the better artist of the two with a strong, vibrant voice also capable of considerable refinement, as many of his recordings demonstrate. Mazzoleni was very much typical of her *verismo* period, a large voice roughly used and a dramatic temperament to match. Amonasro was Giuseppe Danise and Amneris, Maria Gay, Zenatello's wife. From 1947 to 1948, Zenatello, having retired as an opera singer, served as general manager for the Verona performances, and in this capacity he introduced Maria Callas to Italy — and to the world — as Gioconda in Amilcare Ponchielli's opera.

In 1937, the ruins of the notorious Emperor Caracalla's public baths from the early third century became the home for outdoor performances of opera in Rome. It was a project much loved by Mussolini, who on performance evenings would enter the theatre through the underground passageways of the ancient baths and appear suddenly at his box. Although *Aida* became the most famous of the productions at Caracalla, the first opera performed there in 1937 was Gaetano Donizetti's *Lucia di Lammermoor* with Toti Dal Monte as the hapless heroine and Beniamino Gigli as her beloved Edgardo. Early performances of *Aida* at both the Verona Amphitheater and the Roman Baths frequently included elephants in the Triumphal scene of Act 2. The pachyderms, however, were not, as sometimes suggested, responsible for the structural threats that led to the temporary end of the opera performances at Caracalla in 1993. Time, too much use by too many people, and the destructive city smog were the prime culprits. In 2003, however, opera returned to the Baths with performances of Georges Bizet's *Carmen*.

*In *The Metropolitan Opera Guide to Opera on Video,* ed. Paul Gruber (New York and London: W.W. Norton, 1997), pp. 236–237 and 255–256.

Spectacular alfresco *Aida* performances have in no way been limited to Italy, and outdoor sports arenas have sometimes hosted performances of Verdi's Egyptian opera. At Ebbet's Field in Brooklyn, N.Y., baseball yielded to opera for 1925 performances of *Aida*. Football also made room for opera on occasion. In 1941 Marjorie Lawrence, the Australian soprano, had been stricken with crippling polio, but she was a brave and determined artist who continued to sing, both in opera and concert. After her retirement from performing, she taught voice and headed the Opera Department of the University of Southern Illinois at Carbondale, where she directed a performance of *Aida* at what, during the fall and winter season, would double as a football field. The setting might well have inspired special enthusiasm from the Pharoah's singing subjects as they cheered for the home team returning victorious from their struggle with Ethiopia.

In Mexico, a bullring became an open air opera house in the fall of 1919 at the behest of impresario Josè del Rivera, who discovered that an ordinary theatre would not hold the thousands of fans who clamored to hear Enrico Caruso in person. A few performances of *Samson et Dalila, Ballo in Maschera, Aida,* and other operas were given on a temporary stage erected inside the enormous arena, and audiences of more than twenty thousand crowded in to hear "the world's greatest tenor." No doubt the crowds helped Rivera balance the financial books. He probably needed the help since he was paying Caruso one of the highest fees of the tenor's entire career. Unfortunately the only other artist of stature who appeared in these performances was Gabriella Besanzoni, the famous Italian mezzo-soprano who sang Dalila and Amneris. Otherwise, according to Caruso's biographer Michael Scott, the singers were "deplorable."* One wonders in any case just how much of the performances the audience was able to hear in that setting without the benefit of modern amplification, but if nothing else they could return to their homes happy that they had at least "seen" Caruso.

It didn't take long for some clever promoters to realize the appealing possibility of *Aida* with the archeological wonders of ancient Egypt as the actual stage setting. The sixth edition of *The Victrola Book of the Opera* includes a photograph of a 1912 performance at the foot of what appears to be the Great Pyramid of Khufu.†
It is obviously broad daylight and the men in the audience are decked out in straw

---

*Michael Scott, *The Great Caruso* (New York: Alfred A. Knopf, 1988), p. 177.

†*The Victrola Book of the Opera,* sixth edition (Camden, New Jersey: The Victor Talking Machine Company, 1921), p. 8. My copy includes a newspaper clipping and handwritten notes of unknown provenance about a radio broadcast of a portion of *Aida* from the new Chicago Civic Opera House on November 4, 1929. The notes tell us that the broadcast lasted from 11:45 p.m. to 1:00 a.m., that it "took 10 hundred and 80 'kilo-cycles'" and that the listener heard the "thud of priests walking beneath stage." In the cast that evening were Rosa Raïsa, Cyrena Van Gordon, Charles Marshall, Cesare Formichi, and Virgilio Lazzari, with Giorgio Polacco conducting.

hats, necessary protection no doubt from the Egyptian sun. As with Caruso in Mexico in 1919, the question, of course, is how much they could hear. With a little electronic assistance, more recent performances have no doubt gone far to solve the audio problem. There have been spectacular productions of the opera in recent years, first at Luxor, and then in 1998, after the deaths of fifty-eight tourists at Luxor, in the shadow of the pyramids at Giza. Spectacular indeed, these productions employed up to one thousand artists to fill the vast stage areas.

Even the largest indoor stages can't quite accommodate that crowd, but the most colorful of nineteenth-century impresarios, Colonel J.H. Mapleson, assured the readers of his autobiography that on a memorable evening in 1885, he entertained the audience at the Chicago Opera Festival with a memorable *Aida*.* For the occasion, a large theatre seating six thousand had been constructed inside the festival hall. The architects were two of the most distinguished, not only in Chicago but in the entire nation — Dankmar Adler and Louis Sullivan. According to Mapleson's report, "An increased chorus had been organized of 500 voices, whilst the orchestra had been augmented by a hundred extra musicians." The audience of twelve thousand overflowed into the wings of the stage and added to the confusion of "some 500 supernumeraries with blackened faces, in oriental garb, chasing round to try to find their places, others with banners arranging their dresses." For the Triumphal Scene, there were six hundred members of the Illinois State Militia and three hundred fifty extra choristers. It took the Chicago police to clear a way for Adelina Patti, the Aida of the evening, to make her way from her dressing room to the stage. Mapleson's comment on the occasion? "Well might the audience cheer as it did on the fall of the curtain."

A considerably smaller entourage of a mere one hundred eighty sufficed for performances before an audience of fifteen hundred in the Roman stadium at Tyre in Lebanon in the summer of 2003, but according to Ramsay Short, in spite of the heat, the busy mosquitoes, and a two-hour delay on opening night, "the performance well and truly made up for the long wait."† There's no readily available information about how many Egyptians and Ethiopians crowded the stage for the Triumphal scene at the Stade de France, Paris on Friday, September 21, 2001, but the audience of seventy thousand may well be a record for *Aida*.

It doesn't take a vast outdoor theatre to make a success of *Aida,* a fact that New York's Amato Opera Theater has demonstrated. The Amato, located now on the Bowery in New York City, has been performing operas for more than fifty years. Their venue is a twenty-foot stage in a shoe-box theatre with a seating capacity of

---

*Harold Rosenthal, ed., *The Mapleson Memoirs: The Career of an Operatic Impresario 1858–1888* (New York: Appleton-Century, 1966), pp. 230–232.
†Ramsay Short, "Verdi's Aida, on a grand scale, shines in Tyre despite delay before curtain rises," Lebanonwire Web site, July 5, 2003, from *The Daily Star*.

slightly more than one hundred. *Aida* would not appear to be a likely prospect here, but Anthony "Tony" Amato has innate musicality and an active imagination working for him. There are obvious limitations when it comes to the massed choruses, the full orchestrations, and the splendid processions of the Triumphal scene, but apparently artistic sensitivity and sincerity and a cast of gifted young singers are adequate compensation. Edward Rothstein reported on their production of *Aida:* "...everything is proportioned for the space ... everything was worked on with such taste an[d] care that Verdi seemed not only to survive, but also even now and then to thrive."*

What Verdi himself would have thought about either the outdoor spectaculars or the indoor miniature is a matter of pure speculation since he composed with neither setting in mind. His milieu was the opera house, and he certainly created his operas for the sonic resonance of the theatre without artificial amplification and the visual perspective of the framed and enclosed stage. Given those limitations, he was greatly concerned that his operas sound good in the auditorium and look good on the stage.

What we can recapture from stage photographs of early opera house productions of *Aida* often seems to our enlightened twenty-first century cluttered and crowded. The scenery is obviously constructed of flimsy canvas flats and back cloths, and there usually appears to be too much of it, too many sphinxes and columns and palm trees. In crowd scenes, there are frequently lines of people, row on row, like a massed concert choir, in awkward, bulky costumes. The mind's eye, however, needs to adjust for the bright, glaring lighting necessary for an interior group photograph in those long-ago days. Stage lighting in the second half of the nineteenth century and the early years of the twentieth was capable of far more subtle effects than the contemporary technology of the photographer could reproduce.

Styles in staging, however, have certainly changed over the years, generally but not inevitably in favor of simpler lines with larger scenic elements that at least appear to be solidly constructed. Costume design has entered the era of high fashion with particular attention to coordination of the overall picture and appropriateness for the emotional tone of the scene and the psychology of the characters. In a sense, the original production of *Aida* was ahead of its time with Mariette's skillful reproduction of Egyptian architectural details and beautifully detailed costuming. In too many other opera houses, the principal singers brought their own costumes to any production, the chorus was clothed in whatever could be devised with the greatest economy, and the stage settings might be badly worn or put together from odds and ends from the storage rooms of the opera house. Production styles have certainly changed over the years. At the Metropolitan Opera House

---

*Edward Rothstein in the *New York Times* (quoted on the Amato Opera Theater Web site, amato.org).

there were six fully new productions of *Aida* during the twentieth century. They varied from the cluttered, crowded settings in 1908, typical of their era and much praised at the time, to the moderately stylized designs of 1976. The current production, introduced in 1988, is solid, architectural, realistic, and impressive. Through all six, the Met has kept *Aida* always within the framework of a basically conservative approach to stage design with due respect for the historical setting of the opera.

On the whole, *Aida* has been spared the excesses of the revisionist designers and directors intent on up-to-date "concept" productions. The opera appears to be firmly enough grounded in ancient Egypt to resist in most cases being reset in fascist Italy, political Washington, or the Star-Wars future. Overall designs may be attractively simplified and streamlined to avoid the effect of a cluttered stage, although a few successful productions of *Aida* have set out consciously to reproduce the styles of an earlier age. La Scala, for example, in the 1960s offered an historical reproduction of a nineteenth-century performance, and in 1997, the Verona Amphitheatre duplicated the settings of their initial 1913 version with the singers clothed in costumes designed from Mariette's original drawings. Even with historical reproductions, however, directors today are more concerned than in the past with dramatic meaning, clear motivation, psychological penetration, and honest emotional conviction, and the styles of operatic acting have gratefully advanced beyond the stock arm waving gestures and the advance-to-the-footlights-and-deliver stance of the singers.

Directorial restraint, however, has occasionally given way to the misguided desire to make *Aida* "relevant" to contemporary audiences, who are assumed to be unable to appreciate the import of the opera without the help of a guiding hand. A 2002 performance by the Helikon Opera in Moscow apparently raced across two or three thousand years of history to combine ancient Egyptian autocracy and twentieth-century fascism.* The women of the chorus were clad in military camouflage reminiscent of Latin American rebels. Amneris wore leather boots, lashed out at Radamès with a bullwhip, and kept the slave Aida controlled with an animal leash. Ramfis delivered his entire role while standing in a sarcophagus, and a defenseless female soldier was tossed mercilessly about the stage on elastic cords for the amusement of her fellow warriors. According to the review, the music was performed effectively, but did the director truly believe that this foolishness would enhance the tragic beauty of Mariette's story, Ghislanzoni's libretto, and most of all Verdi's masterful musical score?

Olga Maynard, in her book *Enjoying Opera*, describes a production in which the Egyptians were portrayed as Spanish conquistadors and Ethiopians as native

---

*Details of the performance are taken from Neil McGowan's entirely favorable review, "Mukeria triumphant in the Valley of the Kings," from the S and H International Opera Review, included on music web.uk.net for April, 2002.

Mexicans. The plot required some twisting to exonerate the Spaniards from the cruelty of burying the hero and heroine alive. To Maynard, "the new idea for *Aida* in this Aztec scene appeared perfectly valid."* She also describes a production in which Radamès turned out to be an American Marine sergeant at the Guantanamo Base in Cuba and Aida was a Cuban guerilla fighter. This performance required serious changes in the music of the final scene. Another set in Viet Nam had Aida as a Saigon night club singer and spy for the Viet Cong, and the "frug" was introduced into one of the ballets. Unfortunately, Maynard expressed her approval of these absurdities. "The experiments here described," she commented, "do not abuse *Aida*, because Verdi saw to it that the intrinsic values of *Aida* were incorruptible."†

It might just be possible to place the music and the plot of *Aida* successfully in an historical setting other than ancient Egypt — although one could legitimately wonder why a director would bother when the original works quite well as it is. One attempt that almost succeeded opened on Broadway on October 10, 1952, and lasted eleven weeks before the lack of public response brought its closing, not exactly a bomb but hardly long enough to repay the enormous investment of bringing the show to Broadway. The title was *My Darlin' Aida*, the music was essentially Verdi's original, and the cast was drawn largely from the ranks of American opera singers. The setting, as the mock-southern "*Darlin'*" would suggest, was the American southland during the years of the Civil War, a not unlikely parallel with the original setting of the opera itself. Aida, the slave girl, was played by Elaine Malbin, with Eileen Schauler as her alternate. Dorothy Sarnoff sang Amneris' music in the role of Jessica, the plantation owner's daughter (Betty Dubrow was alternate); William Olvis, seconded by Howard Jarratt, was Raymond, or Radamès, as we know him in the opera; and William Dillard was Adam, a character based on the original Amanasro. A future Aida in European and American opera houses, Gloria Davy sang the small role of Susie. The title of the show became the opening words of "Celeste Aida," and "Ritorna vincitor" was transformed into "March on for Tennessee." What *My Darlin' Aida* apparently lacked was the kind of dramatic and verbal imagination that had made a notable success of *Carmen Jones*, a similar adaptation of Bizet's opera that came to the Broadway stage in 1943.

Aida can be — and has been — used and misused in some amazing ways. The comedian band leader Spike Jones at least had the good judgment not to use Verdi's music when he performed "FBAida" in one of his on-the-air programs, although he did manage a little bit of *Samson et Dalila* to liven up his highly eclectic musical score. He also avoided the original plot when he told the story of "Aidalot," who for all the evidence otherwise did not actually stab her husband but who did live up to the pun suggested by her name.

---

*Olga Maynard, *Enjoying Opera* (New York: Charles Scribner's Sons, [1966]), p. 295.
†Maynard, *Enjoying Opera*, p. 298.

The highly successful contemporary Broadway musical *Aida,* a much more serious affair than Spike Jones' parody, was, as the performance playbill announces, "suggested by the opera" although the suggestions had nothing to do with Verdi's music.* The major changes in the plot include a prequel taking the action back to the original capture of Aida and other Nubians; the replacement of the High Priest Ramfis with Zoser, Radamès' father and an influential but traitorous figure at the court of the Pharaoh; a considerable emphasis on the internal politics of ancient Egypt; and Amneris, initially introduced for comic relief, at last as the beneficent influence who enables the lovers to die together. The music is roughly pop-rock, nothing too raucous, all of it, as is often the case on Broadway, overamplified in performance. Song after song works up to a grating vocal climax. For this listener the only memorable musical moment was the finale of the first act, when Aida and the other slaves sing an exciting anthem in gospel style, "The Gods Love Nubia," but Elton John's music in general is clearly no substitute for the real thing. To their credit, however, the various authors of the book, composer Elton John and lyricist Tim Rice, had the artistic judgment to avoid clothing in music the dramatic and emotional climaxes of Verdi's opera — namely, the intense encounter of Aida and Amonasro in the Nile scene and Amneris' climactic Judgment scene in Act 4. The audience loved the show and rewarded the performers with a noisy standing ovation. Perhaps they weren't aware of what they were missing.

Since its premiere in 1871, Verdi's *Aida* has had a far longer run than the Broadway musical, and it's still going strong. It is a major staple for opera houses all over the globe, and that in spite of the fact that it's not an easy opera to produce. Even the small-scale productions require careful musical and dramatic preparation, a cast of gifted singing actors (or acting singers), and the effective coordination of all of the elements in the opera company. Bringing it all together can be a daunting task, and it's no wonder that through the years performances have been subject to almost every possible kind of on-stage mishap.

For starters, *Aida* is a difficult opera to cast. There are five major (and I do mean "major") roles — Aida, Radamès, Amneris, Amonasro, and Ramfis — and Il Re, the Pharaoh or the King, had darn well better be able to hold his own in the big ensembles. To find (and afford to pay) six major singers who possess the voices their roles demand stretches the resources of many, if not most, opera companies, and the six voices must constitute a balanced vocal group. If the King carries less vocal weight than the High Priest the dramatic credibility begins to suffer, and woe be to the Aida who can't hold her own against a powerful Amneris. It might be possible to portray Aida dramatically as a shrinking violet, but vocally she absolutely must offer a real challenge to the Egyptian princess.

---

*These comments are based on my experience of the performance of *Aida* at the Palace Theater in New York City on July 13, 2004.

There were no questions about the quality or the balance of the cast on the evening of November 16, 1908. The Metropolitan Opera was entering a new era under general manager Giulio Gatti-Casazza, and strung across the front of the stage in the Triumphal scene of Act 2 were six artists fully equal to the task—Antonio Scotti as Amonasro, Emmy Destinn as Aida, Enrico Caruso as Radamès, Louise Homer as Amneris, Adamo Didur as Ramfis, and Giulio Rossi, in his debut, as Il Re, a role that he went on to sing ninety times at the Metropolitan. It didn't hurt that the conductor in the pit that night was Arturo Toscanini. The performance on that November evening was the kind of event on which operatic legends are built.

Toscanini had conducted his first *Aida* twenty-two years earlier on June 30, 1886. He was nineteen years old at the time, and he had come with a touring company to Rio de Janeiro. His regular positions were assistant chorus master and cellist in the opera orchestra, but the incompetent Brazilian conductor resigned, the Italian conductor who replaced him couldn't even make it through the Prelude, and Toscanini, who had impressed the company with his musical knowledge, was sent to the podium to try to save the scheduled performance of *Aida*. Perhaps he could at least hold it together. He could and he did—and it was his first conducting assignment. He conducted the score from memory and did it so well that he won an ovation from the audience and rave reviews in the local newspapers. "This boy, barely nineteen years old but already an excellent musician, succeeded admirably, revealing directorial qualities of a superior level." "This beardless maestro is a prodigy who communicated the sacred artistic fire to his baton and the energy and passion of a genuine artist to the orchestra."* Toscanini later confessed that he had committed two errors that night, "one wrong downbeat and one short memory lapse."†

Toscanini was just one in a long line of star conductors who have taken up the baton for performances of *Aida*, and they have been joined by an army of opera singers eager to vie for one of the six leading roles in the opera. Self-respecting tenors who can muster anything beyond a *tenorino* whisper are almost bound to attempt Radamès, and baritones regularly covet Amonasro even though he has no large-scale aria to sing.

Not that the tenor and baritone roles are fool proof—the many anecdotes from the stage are adequate proof. Radamès, for example, with its demands for both lyrical sensitivity and stentorian dramatics, is a difficult role for any tenor, and some of the wisest among the tribe have refused to risk it. Jan Peerce said "No" to the role, even at the behest of Arturo Toscanini. "I'd have to push and it could hurt my voice ... at any stage of my career, I'd have looked ridiculous wearing a leopard

---

*Quoted in Harvey Sachs, *Toscanini* (New York: Harper and Row, 1978), p. 18.
†*Ibid.*, p. 17.

skin."* Many other tenors might have advisedly followed Peerce's example for either or both of his reasons. Peerce's brother-in-law, Richard Tucker, was equally cautious about the role. He recorded it twice, including the 1949 broadcast concert with Toscanini, before he brought it to the stage in 1965. In the recording studio and in the concert hall, where the performance was spread over two days, he knew he could sing Radamès safely, but performing it in one evening before four thousand people in a mammoth opera house was something else.

Giacomo Lauri-Volpi was surely one of the superstar tenors in the first half of the twentieth century, and no doubt he sang many admirable performances of *Aida* in his long career. On at least one occasion, however, he overreached his limitations and sang a falsetto high B-flat at the end of his first-act aria. He was rewarded for his effort with a barrage of hisses from his Barcelona audience, a reaction, as the Aida of the evening, Iva Pacetti, reported, that "put the fear of God in all of us, as it meant it was one of those bloodthirsty audiences."† When Lauri-Volpi sang the role in London in 1936 one critic praised him for "singing with all his old ease and lovely quality but with a notable refinement of style," but another wondered why the tenor found it necessary to "take his breath so often in the wrong places and so seldom in the right ones."‡ So much for the critics! It's easy to understand why some opera singers treat their opinions scornfully.

Peerce's concern about his appearance in the leopard skin might well be echoed by the slender, young baritone who, according to Robert Merrill's account, was called on to substitute for a portly Amonasro. The costume had not been properly altered, and when the young man took a deep breath and began to sing, his costume descended to his knees. Merrill's comment? "It had not occurred to the new singer to wear an athletic supporter."§ Merrill himself sang his first Amonasro in Newark, New Jersey. Part of his makeup included a large moustache stuck to his upper lip with spirit gum. In the Triumphal scene of Act 2, when Amonasro embraced his daughter, Aida, the moustache left Merrill and stuck instead to the soprano's neck. Aida was not amused. The audience was.

What happens on that rare occasion when the members of the cast know the opera well but not in the same language? The result is a multilingual performance. Astrid Varnay recalls a London *Aida* in which Edith Coates sang Amneris in English, Hans Hopf sang Radamès in German, and Varnay sang Aida in Italian. Jess Walters,

---

*Alan Levy, *The Bluebird of Happiness: The Memoirs of Jan Peerce* (New York: Harper and Row, 1976), p. 127.
†Quoted in Lanfranco Rasponi, *The Last Prima Donnas* (New York: Alfred A. Knopf, 1982), p. 204.
‡Quoted in J.B. Steane, *Singers of the Century* (Portland, Oregon: Amadeus Press, 1996), p. 89.
§Robert Merrill, *Between Acts: An Irreverent Look at Opera and Other Madness* (New York: McGraw-Hill, 1976), p. 143. Merrill's book is filled with delightful anecdotes for both friends and enemies of opera.

Amonasro, demonstrated his versatility by switching from one of the three languages to another.* Trying to follow the libretto must have been a frustrating experience for the audience.

So the stories go, and their number is legion. No doubt every opera singer who has ever trod the boards in *Aida* more than once has a repertoire of similar anecdotes. Some of them might even be true.

For all of the wonderful music of Radamès, Amonasro, Ramfis, and the Pharaoh, when it comes to this opera Aida and Amneris are surely the plum roles for which sopranos and mezzo-sopranos stand in line to beg the impresarios. As a matter of fact, in a handful of cases the same artist has been known to reach up or down, as the case may be, for *both* of the roles. Since Aida must have not only the soprano's high notes but also a considerable lower range and Amneris requires a mezzo-soprano who can handle comfortably more than one high A-flat, A-natural, and a couple of B-flats, many an Amneris has sung Aida and a few Aidas have given up the title role to sing the Egyptian princess instead. After all, Verdi's La Scala Aida, Teresa Stolz, had first been considered for Amneris. In recent years, Ghena Dimitrova, an erstwhile Aida, has also sung and recorded Amneris, and somewhat earlier, Marjorie Lawrence, the Australian soprano who was stricken tragically with crippling polio, discovered that she could sing Amneris reclining on a convenient Egyptian couch and moved about the stage on a litter borne by the princess' slaves. To the extent that there is a problem in switching from one role to another it has more to do with tessitura (the prevailing range of the role), vocal color, and contrast than with the actual high and low notes in a part. Verdi surely intended the darker tone of the true mezzo-soprano to contrast with the brighter and somewhat gentler sound of the lyric-*spinto* soprano voice.

One singer who went from Amneris to Aida and then back again, albeit briefly, to Amneris was the American soprano Rose Bampton. She began her Metropolitan Opera career in 1932 with success as a mezzo-soprano and one of her roles was Amneris. Later, she retrained her voice as a soprano and appeared in 1937 as the soprano Leonora in Verdi's *Trovatore*. The afternoon of January 19, 1940, she was Aida to Bruna Castagna's Amneris, but eight days later she became Amneris, this time with Zinka Milanov as her Ethiopian servant. Too much careening from high to low or from bright to dark and too much forcing upwards of the chest tones too often can damage a voice seriously. Bampton, however, survived to continue her career into the 1950s.

There is a rather lengthy record of mezzo-sopranos who aspire to the roles of their soprano colleagues. Among those who made that transition with some measure of success are Grace Bumbry and Shirley Verrett, who have sung both Amneris

---

*Astrid Varnay with Donald Arthur, *55 Years in Five Acts: My Life in Opera* (Boston: Northeastern University Press, 2000), p. 158.

and Aida. Although Verrett dropped Amneris from her repertoire before her first stage appearance as Aida, she refuses to characterize herself as either soprano or mezzo soprano: "I didn't set out to put a tag on my voice," she wrote in her autobiography. "I refused to be boxed in."* To Grace Bumbry, however, belongs the distinction of singing both roles simultaneously, at least in a recording. The duet for Amneris and Aida in Act 2, Scene 1, pits Bumbry against herself through the miracle of modern recording technique, a feat that she would be hard put to duplicate on stage. (You can hear the performance on compact disc, Gala GL 100.539.) She sings both roles quite well, including a glowing high C for Aida, although without a knowledge of the score and the text we'd be hard put to tell which character is singing which lines. We can imagine Maria Callas, with her infinite palette of vocal colors, bringing off this two-headed duet and maintaining an adequate contrast between the two voices, but Bumbry isn't quite Callas.

For all of her multifaceted talents, however, Callas never attempted Amneris on either stage or disc, but the title role was in her active repertoire during the early years of her career. Her 1950 and 1951 performances of Aida in Mexico City quickly entered the annals of great operatic legends primarily because of the spectacular, unwritten high E-flat that she interpolated at the end of the Triumphal scene. In this case, the legend can be documented historically because her 1950 and 1951 Aidas were broadcast and have been made available on compact disc. When the idea was suggested to Callas by the manager, Antonio Cazara-Campos, she demurred on the perfectly legitimate ground that Verdi had not written the note. Campos, however, showed her a score in which Angela Paralta, a nineteenth-century diva, had written in the note, and apparently the idea remained in her mind. The tenor scheduled to sing Radamès, Kurt Baum, had been something of a problem to Callas and other members of the cast, and just before the second act of the opera began, she agreed to sing the note as a challenge and no doubt a corrective to him. The response of the audience was spontaneous and overwhelming, and needless to say the note stayed in her Mexico City performances and was repeated the next year, when her Radamès was Mario del Monaco, who required neither a challenge nor a corrective. Would Verdi have approved? The answer is surely "No." He didn't like singers or conductors altering his scores, and it is out of keeping with Aida's character or her situation at this point in the opera. It, however, does make for a great deal of opera house excitement as the recordings prove. To her credit, Callas apparently did not repeat the feat in other performances of *Aida*.

In many ways Aida is a difficult role to pin down vocally. Perhaps the ideal is a strong *spinto* soprano with the power to ride over the large ensembles in Act 2 and still produce the *dolce* piano tones called for in the Nile scene and in the final

---

*Shirley Verrett, with Christopher Brooks, *I Never Walked Alone: The Autobiography of an American Singer* (Hoboken, New Jersey: John Wiley and Sons, 2002), p. 236.

duet with Radamès. Emmy Destinn, in that famous Metropolitan performance of 1908, fit the description precisely, as did Elisabeth Rethberg a few years later and, more recently, Zinka Milanov, Renata Tebaldi, and Leontyne Price, to mention just a few of those who sang the role to great acclaim in the United States. Sopranos of all vocal weights, however, have sung the role with varying degrees of success. The huge dramatic voices of the Wagnerian soprano might seem overwhelming as Aida, but Kirsten Flagstad sang the role twenty-seven times in her pre-Wagner days, and Birgit Nilsson kept it in her repertoire, both on stage and in recording, right beside her Isoldes and Brünnhildes. By the way, Radamès was also a role that the greatest of all heldentenors, Lauritz Melchior, performed a number of times in Germany from 1928 to 1930.

By way of contrast, in the past a number of the light-voiced lyric sopranos found Aida to be a congenial role. Nellie Melba's lack of success in *Aida* may have had more to do with the failure to communicate dramatically than with any vocal shortcoming. We wonder, however, about Adelina Patti, whose voice and artistry were more closely identified with the so-called coloratura roles, but Patti had great success in *Aida*. Her vocal means were more than adequate, as one London critic commented, "Her voice, so equal in its *timbre* throughout her register, came out with electric force at times, towering above the *fortissimo* of her colleagues, band, and chorus."* What's more, Patti was a gifted actress, often praised as much for her dramatic projection as for her remarkable vocal prowess. The distinguished British critic Herman Klein heard her in the role and noted the "new note of tragic feeling in the voice" and the "shades of poignant expression ... that seemed to embrace the whole gamut of human misery and passion."† Even Beverly Sills risked her essentially lyric/coloratura voice in *Aida* on a couple of occasions on the stage — once in 1954 in Salt Lake City for outdoor performances, but, as she tells us, with "lots of microphones, which meant I would not have to strain my voice"‡ and again in the jewel box opera house at Central City, Colorado, where she had gone to sing *Lucia* and found herself instead in *Aida*.

It was inevitable that singers and impresarios alike would realize early in the game the logic of an African-American soprano in the role of the Ethiopian princess. But breaking the color barrier on stage, particularly in the United States, was easier dreamed than accomplished. Florence Cole Talbert from Detroit had sung Aida at the Teatro Comunale in Cosenza, Italy, in 1927, but in too many situations at home the only true operatic opportunities were in such all-black companies as the National Negro Opera Company, established after black artists were denied roles

---

*Quoted in John Frederick Cone, *Adelina Patti: Queen of Hearts* (Portland, Oregon: Amadeus Press, 1993), p. 109.
†*Ibid.*
‡Beverly Sills, *Bubbles: A Self-Portrait* (New York and Indianapolis: Bobbs-Merrill, 1970), p. 55.

in an *Aida* at the Boston Opera House. The first performance by the National Negro Opera Company was inevitably. *Aida,* and the star was the Louisville, Kentucky, soprano La Julia Rhea.*

To perform in a major American opera company, to perform at the Metropolitan, for many years must have seemed almost impossible to the African-American artists. It took Rudolf Bing, who became the general manager at the Metropolitan in 1950, to make the impossible happen. The 1951–1952 opera season at the Metropolitan opened with a new production of *Aida*, and the stage was graced with its first African-American solo performer, Janet Collins, who took the leading role in the ballet. Bing was blissfully free of any lingering American racial prejudice. "I never had the slightest question about engaging Miss Collins," he wrote later, "and I told the board about it after the contract was signed."† Four years later, Marian Anderson was the first black singer to perform a major role at the Metropolitan when she sang Ulrica in Verdi's *Un Ballo in Maschera*, and in 1958, Gloria Davy, who had been hidden away in a small role in the 1952 *My Darlin' Aida*, became the Metropolitan Opera's first African-American Aida. Soon she was followed by artists of the quality of Leontyne Price, who sang her first Met Aida in 1961, and Martina Arroyo, who on February 6, 1965, substituted in *Aida* for an ailing Birgit Nilsson and in the process scored her breakthrough at the New York opera house.

The list of great artists who have appeared in *Aida* is virtually endless, and it continues to grow every year because *Aida* remains one of the most popular operas ever composed. Among the artists, however, we shouldn't forget the animals who have made their way onto the stage with the singers and, as one great conductor noticed, have occasionally expressed pointed and strong critical opinions about the performances of which they were part. One that deserves a special place on the honor role of *Aida* casts is Anna, the beautiful white mare who brought on Radamès' chariots in scores of Triumphal scenes and in so doing taxied such distinguished tenors as Enrico Caruso and Beniamino Gigli. Anna, who died in 1940 at thirty-nine years of age, also had a Hollywood career that included serving as Rudolph Valentino's mount in the old silent film *The Sheik*. Nicolas Slonimsky, in his volume of operatic anecdotes, reports the legend "that Anna had a high standard of musical appreciation, and that once when the tenor got off pitch, she emitted a couple of critical neighs."‡ Verdi, who loved his horses as much as he loved singers who sang on pitch, would probably have given Anna a pat on the back and an extra serving of oats.

---

*Rosalyn M. Story, *And So I Sing: African-American Divas of Opera and Concert* (New York: Warner Books, 1990), pp. 91–92.
†Rudolf Bing, *5000 Nights at the Opera* (Garden City, New York: Doubleday and Company, 1972), p. 184.
‡Nicolas Slonimsky, *Slonimsky's Book of Musical Anecdotes,* reprint edition (New York and London, Routledge, 2002), p. 291.

4

Words and Music

Before there can be an opera on the stage, there must be an opera on paper. The libretto and the musical score come first.

In the case of *Aida,* the words and the music took shape almost simultaneously. Once Verdi had accepted the detailed outline from Auguste Mariette, he went to work first with Camille Du Locle to flesh out and adjust the plot and then with Antonio Ghislanzoni to prepare the libretto. At point after point, the correspondence that has been preserved shows both how carefully Verdi oversaw Ghislanzoni's work on the libretto and how much of the musical composition was actually accomplished while Verdi corrected and amended and occasionally wrote himself the words that would be sung in the opera. In spite of the debt that he owed to Mariette, Du Locle, and Ghislanzoni, the end result was truly *Verdi*'s opera and every part of *Aida* bears his personal stamp.

There is a tendency to think of Verdi as an essentially instinctive composer who had little concern with theories and philosophies of musical art. Wagner was the great intellectual. Words poured from his pen as freely as musical notes, and he delighted in writing essays and entire books about art and music and politics and religion and philosophy and just about anything else. Verdi was a composer, not an author, and it's impossible to imagine him churning out volumes on *The Art-Work of the Future, Music and Drama, Judaism in Music, On the State and Religion*—all of these titles that appear in the sixteen volumes of the most nearly complete edition of Wagner's writings. We should not assume, however, that Verdi did not think and think quite profoundly not only about the art of dramatic music but also about literature and about politics. He was certainly instinctive in his music, and he could afford to be: He had very good instincts. He was also an intellectual, although he probably would have denied it if you'd asked him. He read widely, he was interested in the prose works of Richard Wagner, and he thought consciously about his art and wrote about it intelligently to his correspondents.

He understood, for example, and sought to express in each of his operas the individual *tinta* or *colorito,* the basic musical and dramatic "coloring" appropriate to the work at hand. George Martin makes a convincing case that by these terms,

Verdi actually meant not only the sound of the music, but the "settings, costumes, and stage movements as well as types of melody, rhythm, and orchestration."* This is the quality that separates *Il Trovatore* from *Rigoletto* and *Rigoletto* from *Traviata*. Herein is the reason that *Aida* doesn't sound like *Otello* and the tone of *Otello* is radically different from that of *Falstaff*. It was a skill that he honed to razor sharpness as his early operas merged into the masterpieces of his middle and late periods.

He was also a very practical man, as down to earth in the way he composed as he was in managing—and managing quite efficiently—his farm at St. Agata. "Art for the Sake of Art" would hardly have been his motto. He was far too much aware of those who would see and hear his operas for any type of ivory-tower artiness to invade his work. "Art for the Sake of the Audience" comes closer to the Verdian ideal because he appreciated the great classical purpose of drama to move the audience and to deepen their experience of life. When he defined for Giulio Ricordi the evasive *parole sceniche* that he wanted in his operas as those words "that carve out a situation or a character, words that always have a most powerful impact on the audience,"† it was the effect on the people who attended his operas that concerned him particularly. That he also appreciated a *paying* audience was simply one more symptom of his practicality, but it did not interfere with his keen and serious concern for his art and how it would affect his audience. One of the secrets of his great success both artistically and financially was his ability to combine these practical aims without denigrating his art.

Verdi certainly grew and developed primarily within the traditions of Italian opera as they had been handed down through Rossini, Bellini, and Donizetti, but he was not satisfied merely to repeat those traditions or, for that matter, to repeat himself. He was hardly the kind of revolutionary that Wagner claimed to be, but the possibility of change, even somewhat radical change, was not absent from his fertile imagination. He was surely enough of a revolutionary to write, as he did in the letter referred to above, "But ... (pardon the blasphemy) both the poet and the composer must have the talent and the courage, when necessary, *not* to write poetry or music.... Horror! horror!"‡ Verdi could and did use the musical forms and the formal structures that had defined Italian operatic music in the past. They can be found in *Aida*, perhaps, as Philip Gossett suggests in his discussion of the four great duets in the opera, because Verdi had yet to find a librettist/collaborator ready and able to change.§ In Verdi's hands, however, the forms took on new dramatic life,

---

*George Martin, *Aspects of Verdi* (New York: Dodd, Mead and Company, 1987), p. 181; also Notes 1 and 2, pp. 281–282.
†Verdi to Giulio Ricordi, July 10, 1870, in Busch, *Verdi's Aida*, p. 31.
‡*Ibid.*
§Philip Gossett, "Verdi, Ghislanzoni, and *Aida*: The Uses of Convention," in *Critical Inquiry*, Vol. I, No. 2 (December, 1974), pp. 291–334.

and he employed them so adroitly that only a close, technical analysis of the text and music fully reveals their presence.

One result of Verdi's attitude toward the traditional structure of Italian operas was the softening of the lines between recitative and the arias, duets, and structured ensembles traditional in opera. Earlier composers had discovered the musical and dramatic value of recitative. Verdi took what Rossini, Donizetti, Bellini, and the others had accomplished and built on it, and for some traditionalists he apparently went too far. As early as *Rigoletto* in 1851, conservative critics had been disturbed by the musical continuity of the opera. There were still identifiable "numbers," but the music between the numbers was taking on a new significance so that it would become part of the overall musical fabric and considerably more than the mere connecting passages to move from one aria or ensemble to the next.

Verdi, for his part, was apparently moving, and moving quite consciously, toward one of Wagner's aims — unending or infinite melody (*unendliche Melodie*). In 1851 he wrote to Salvatore Cammarano, the librettist who was preparing the text for *Il Trovatore*, "If in operas there were no Cavatinas, or Duets, or Trios, or Choruses, or Finales, etc. etc., and the whole opera were only (I would almost say) a single number, I would find this more reasonable and right."* That was further than Verdi was ready to go, and certainly up to *Aida* and even beyond in the final two operas, the formal numbers although increasingly less obvious are still discernible. The extent to which he moved toward unending melody, however, is at once remarkable and also unfortunately often lost on us in performances in the opera house because audiences ordinarily interrupt the flow of the music with applause after the individual numbers. Listening to an uninterrupted recording of any Verdi opera from the middle period on, however, we can hear that continuous flow of melody, heightened, of course, in the arias and ensembles but never completely absent.

As we consider the plot, the words, the characters, and the music of *Aida,* we encounter all of these characteristics at work — the distinctive *tinta* of the score, the musical means used to move the audience and bring them into the emotional experience of the characters, the willingness and even eagerness on occasion to experiment with more open musical structures and forms, and the desire to create a continuous fabric of music. Instinctive, yes, but at the same time Verdi was profoundly aware of his artistic aims and the means necessary to achieve them.

Precisely what kind of opera is *Aida*? In many ways it is an Italian version of the classic nineteenth-century French *grand opéra* as defined in such works as Auber's *La Muette de Portici,* Halevy's *La Juive,* and Meyerbeer's *Robert le Diable, Les Huguenots, Le Prophète,* and *L'Africaine.* We often use the English term "grand

---

*Verdi to Salvatore Cammarano, April 4, 1851, in William Weaver, *Verdi: A Documentary Study* (London: Thames and Hudson, 1977), p. 183.

opera" to refer to any musical-dramatic work that is sung throughout, but in the 1830s and the years following there developed in France a special kind of opera with more or less clearly understood boundaries. These *grand opéras* were serious, intensely dramatic, and usually tragic works in four or five acts, more often than not based on historical events filtered through a fictionalizing imagination. They utilized a large cast of important soloists, a chorus frequently capable of being divided into two or more groups, and the full contingent of the ballet company. The musical scores were often highly complex with elaborate ensemble effects and the employment of the full resources of the orchestra. The productions were spectacular in their staging with ample opportunity for impressive crowd scenes and eye-catching scenic effects. In Auber's *La Muette de Portici,* for example, Mount Vesuvius erupts, and in the original production of *L'Africaine* there was a shipwreck realistic enough to induce seasickness.*

In many of its details *Aida* fits the description of *grand opéra*. It includes strong dramatic conflicts and contrasts in the unfolding of its tragic story. It is set in a roughly identifiable historic setting of conflict between ancient Egypt and Ethiopia. There are six major roles, a large chorus divided in the Triumphal scene of Act 2 into three identifiable groups, and a major role for the ballet. There are certainly opportunities for large scale scenic and musical effects, particularly again in Act 2, Scene 2, with massed choruses, complex ensembles, and elaborate stage settings. Verdi knew the form well: He had transformed *I Lombardi* into a *grand opéra* titled *Jèrusalem* in 1847 and had composed two new works of the genre, *Les Vêpres Siciliennes* in 1855 and *Don Carlos* in 1867. It was also the right type of opera for an important, almost ceremonial occasion at the Cairo Opera House, an opera that would at once hymn the glories of Egypt and demonstrate the full capabilities of Ishmael Pasha's new theatre.

Verdi, however, was also a better composer and a greater artist than Auber or Meyerbeer or Halevy. It isn't that the other composers of *grand opéra* were rank amateurs. They certainly weren't, and their works continue to appear successfully from time to time, and it isn't that they failed to communicate musically character and personality beyond the mere effect of the spectacle. It's only that Verdi did it better.

One feature that comes through particularly in a good performance of *Aida* is the extent to which Verdi focuses attention on the personal relationships among the characters. The large-scale, grandiose elements are found only in Acts 1 and 2. In Acts 3 and 4, the spectacular stage effects and the massed choral ensembles of *grand opéra* are replaced by intense concentration on the intimate and personal lives

---

*See Arthur Jacobs, "Machinery," in *The New Grove Dictionary of Opera*, ed. Stanley Sadie (New York: Grove's Dictionaries of Music, 1992; 1997), Vol. III, p. 131, for an illustration of the setting of this scene in *L'Africaine* and the elaborate stage machinery necessary to achieve it.

of the characters. Even earlier in the opera, however, Verdi reminds us repeatedly that the heart of the opera is in the dramatic and emotional encounters of Radamès, Amneris, and Aida. There is a massed chorus and ensemble section toward the end of Act 1, Scene 1, but it is sandwiched between an extended trio, that reveals the complex relationships among the three characters and the final, despairing soliloquy in which the heroine expresses her personal and private dilemma. Before the triumphal parade in Act 2, we encounter the remarkable duet of Amneris and Aida, once again an intensely personal and private moment. Then in the Nile scene in Act 3, we have only the developing and dissolving relationships of the major characters in the drama, and Act 4 takes us straight into the heart and soul of the suffering Princess Amneris and concludes with the most personal and private moment of all, when we join Aida and Radamès in the underground vault.

Verdi's artistic sensibility enabled him to weave these intimate moments effectively into the larger tapestry of a *grand opéra* during the first two acts, but the focus narrows radically in the concluding acts. So great is the difference when we arrive at Act 3, that one scholar has declared that "in the contrasts between ecstatic sounds of Verdi's greatest duet, Amneris' lament, and the stilled bodies of the temple dancers, we can hear the death knell of grand opera."* We may doubt that *Aida* actually drove the nails into the coffin of *grand opéra*, but it is certainly Verdi's musical clothing of the concerns of the individual characters that enables *Aida* to work effectively even in small-scale, decidedly "anti-grand" productions without the elephants and the pyramids and the masses of people who sometimes crowd the stage in the Triumphal scene.

Aida is clearly then a special kind of *grand opéra*, not only because it effectively incorporates the intimate, personal drama into the broad sweep of spectacular settings and a plot set against the military conflicts of two ancient nations but also because, unlike many works of this genre, it is what we may well refer to as a well-made play. The most obvious contrast is with *Don Carlos*, the Verdi opera that immediately precedes *Aida*. Both are *grand opéras*. *Don Carlos* was indeed composed for and received its initial performances at the Paris Opéra, the native habitat for works of this type, and eventually in 1880 *Aida*, with minimum changes beyond a French libretto, made its way into the sacred confines of France's major opera house.

Don Carlos, however, is a big, sprawling, occasionally confusing combination of plots and subplots, of romantic and political intrigues, and of ecclesiastical and personal conflicts. It could hardly have been otherwise given its major source in Friedrich von Schiller's equally big and sprawling and sometimes confusing poetic drama. It is also a long opera. In anything approaching a complete performance of

---

*Simon Williams, "The Spectacle of the Past in Grand Opera," in *The Cambridge Companion to Grand Opera*, David Charlton, ed. (Cambridge: Cambridge University Press, 2003), p. 75.

the five-act version,* it runs an hour or more longer than *Aida,* the length dictated no doubt by the excessive complexity of the plot. Verdi himself had a difficult time deciding just what to do with *Don Carlos* during and after its composition, and it exists in at least five different, more-or-less official versions and many more put together by different conductors and producers. It is certainly one of Verdi's major works, and it has very much come into its own in recent years. For many contemporary critics, the intellectual complexity and challenges of *Don Carlos* mark it out as a greater work than *Aida,* more penetrating in its psychology and more profound in its philosophical assumptions. It doesn't hurt that it also contains some of Verdi's finest, most thoughtful, and mature music.

Aida, on the other hand, is neat, relatively concise, clear in action and motivation, and not at all confusing. *Don Carlos,* as Julian Budden has pointed out, "is an adventurous 'questing' work (to use Schiller's term)," and *Aida* is "a moment of the purest classicism in Verdi's output."† It is, again in Budden's words, "the stuff of classical tragedy."‡ In that sense, *Aida* is a much neater opera than *Don Carlos,* as we commented earlier, "a well-made play."

The key term here may well be "classical tragedy." If we consider the tragic drama of ancient Greece as defined by Aristotle in his *Poetics* and as actually exemplified in the plays of the old Athenian dramatists, we find that *Aida* fits the model closely, if not always precisely. The plot as it progresses in the action through the four acts follows the structure of Attic tragedy.§ The first act constitutes the formal introduction and the initial segment of the drama, the *protasis,* which "stretches out" or puts before the audience the issues that will be presented in the drama. We are plunged immediately into the action and shown the basic conflicts that work together to govern all that follows — Radamès' call to honor and heroic service on behalf of Egypt, the romantic triangle created by his love for Aida and the love of both Amneris and Aida for Radamès, and Aida's torn loyalties between her love and her loyalty to her father and the nation of which he is king. The next segment of the traditional classical drama, the *epitasis,* occurs in Act 2. The action now becomes more intensely complicated as we move into the dual "turning points" of the drama, Amneris' jealousy, duplicity, and her open antagonism toward Aida along with the appearance during the Triumphal scene of Amonasro and his identification as Aida's father. We don't know at this point precisely what the results will be, but we know

---

*What constitutes a "complete" *Don Carlos* is a matter of infinite controversy. No two stage productions or recordings include precisely the same material.
†Julian Budden, *The Operas of Verdi: From Don Carlos to Falstaff* (New York: Oxford University Press, 1981), p. 197.
‡Budden, *The Operas of Verdi,* Vol. III, p. 198.
§The material on classical tragedy is taken largely from "Dramatic Structure" in C. Hugh Holman and William Harmon, *A Handbook to Literature,* sixth edition (New York: MacMillan, 1992), pp. 153–154.

that the result of Amneris' jealousy and Aida's reunion with her father are decisive actions that will shape the future of the characters in the opera. We know, as the old saying goes, that "the die has been cast."

The stage is set now for the *catastasis,* the final series of actions leading to the tragic conclusion in the classic Greek dramas. Frequently at this point in the plot there will be the possibility of escape from the impending tragedy, as here in Act 3 of *Aida.* Perhaps Amonasro's grand plan will work and the hero and heroine will make their way to a long and happy life in Ethiopia, or perhaps, as we move to the first scene of the final act, Amneris will persuade Radamès to plead his case and her intervention with the authorities will lead to his release. But the conflicts that have been set into motion move with conclusive inevitability to the final segment of the drama, the *catastrophe.* Aida and Radamès are buried beneath the Egyptian temple and Amneris is left with only a tragic appeal to the gods for peace.

What we have described here and what we will see in more detail in the analysis of the opera to follow is a clear linear plot development in which action leads logically to action with no distracting subplots to divert the audience's attention from those intertwined issues presented in the *protasis*—Radamès' commitment to both personal honor and his love for Aida, Aida's similar divided loyalty, and the destructive romantic triangle. They work together to create a single plot and to produce the dramatic unity that Aristotle insisted upon in the structure of a tragedy.

Aida, of course, does not observe the traditional unities of time and place. The action of the opera moves from Memphis to Thebes and clearly exceeds twenty-four hours. It's worth noting, however, that absolute insistence on the unities of time and place was not a binding principle for Aristotle. That insistence was, rather, primarily a development not of the ancient Greeks but of the authors and critics of the Renaissance.

Whether *Aida* fulfils the other characteristics of a classical tragedy—namely the fall of characters who are significant enough to engage our attention and the presentation of a total experience adequate to produce an emotional and intellectual catharsis—is a question best addressed as we look at the opera scene by scene and character by character.

The Characters

The King or Pharaoh of Egypt (Bass)—father of Amneris
Amneris (Mezzo-Soprano)—his daughter
Radamès (Tenor)—Captain of the Egyptian army
Ramfis (Bass)—Chief Priest of the Egyptians
Amonasro (Baritone)—King of Ethiopia
Aida (Soprano)—slave of the Egyptians, daughter of Amonasro

Messenger (Tenor)

Priestess (Soprano) — In the earliest lists of characters she was named Termouthis, but the proper name disappears from later lists.

Prelude

The brief Prelude that Verdi composed for *Aida* sets in motion the conflict that in one way or another will dominate the action throughout the opera. There are two contrasting themes. The first, introduced softly by the first violins, is associated with Aida herself. Keep this melody in mind. It will return in Act 1, Scene 1, when she first appears on stage and will reappear in the first scene of Act 2 and again in Act 3, once again to mark Aida's entrance.

Example 1

The cellos then play the second musical theme, softly at first but soon growing in volume. Aida's theme has a gentle curve to it, rising, then falling slightly on the closing notes of the first two phrases. The new theme is solid, almost military, and rather grimly insistent.

Example 2

The chorus of priests will sing this melody in the Triumphal scene of Act 2 of the opera and it will accompany their entry into and exit from the judgment hall, where Radamès is condemned to death, in Act 4. Verdi, who had learned the lessons of counterpoint during his student days in Milan, combines the two melodies and works them together into a *fortissimo* climax before the Prelude ends as a reminder of Aida's theme high in the strings fades away into silence.

When he begins the Prelude with a theme related solely to Aida, Verdi lets us know that he intends her as the central character and the focus of the audience's sympathy and concern, but her tragedy reaches out also to touch tragically the lives of Radamès and Amneris. Radamès is condemned to death, Amneris is left in despair, and Aida dies in her beloved's arms. In one way or another, all of them have fallen victim to the inexorable power of a hard, relentless, but doubtless necessary system that will not, indeed cannot, move in response to the individual's needs and desires. The public order must be maintained. That is the force that is represented and defined so well in their musical theme by the priests, Ramfis, and his fellows. In fifty-four measures and two themes, Verdi has managed to summarize the central conflict of the plot—the yearning of the individual human heart in conflict with the inflexible power of a hard, organized, closed society.

Some conductors linger over the Prelude and stretch it out to almost five minutes, but it makes its effect in three and a half or four minutes. Verdi's tempo marking is *andante mosso,* which is adequately ambiguous but surely indicates something beyond the *adagio* that a handful of conductors make of it.

Had Verdi wanted a longer musical introduction for *Aida,* he might perhaps have approved the use of the Overture or Sinfonia that he composed in the closing days of 1871. The Overture is a longer work, running ten or more minutes in performance. It begins with the same themes as the familiar Prelude and then branches out into a potpourri of various melodies from the opera, including the conclusion of Aida's "Ritorna vincitor" from Act 1 and various passages related to Amneris' jealousy, before it ends with a large and loud orchestral flourish. As a concert piece it works quite well. The themes are intertwined with admirable contrapuntal skill, and it offers ample demonstration of Verdi's skill in orchestration and symphonic development. As an introduction to the opera, however, it is far too grand and complex. The classic simplicity of *Aida* calls for something at once simpler and more direct, something, that is, that will point straight into the action and essential conflicts of the opera.

That is precisely what Verdi realized when the La Scala Orchestra gave this full-scale Overture a trial run. He withdrew it and it was never used to precede *Aida.* Three years later, he wrote the conductor Emilio Usiglio, "...the piece might have turned out well if the construction had been solid. But the excellence of the orchestra [La Scala] merely served better to illustrate the silliness of the supposed overture."* In spite of Verdi's low opinion of the work, he did not destroy the manuscript, and Toscanini played it with the NBC Symphony on March 30, 1940. On June 4, 1940, it was performed in Rome under the baton of Bernadino Molinari with Benito Mussolini in the audience.† A modern recording of the Overture with Claudio Abbado and the La Scala Orchestra has been issued on compact disc (CBS Records MK 37228).

Act 1, Scene 1

The first scene is set in a hall in the King's palace in Memphis with the buildings of the city and the pyramids in the distance. Ramfis and Radamès are alone on the stage. The scene opens with what appears to be a conversation already in motion as Ramfis tells Radamès that the Ethiopians are threatening Thebes and the Nile valley. A messenger with news from the front will arrive soon. In the meantime,

---
*Verdi to Emilio Usiglio, January 26, 1875 (in Busch, *Verdi's Aida,* p. 376).
†See Busch, *Verdi's Aida,* pp. 250–251.

Radamès is eager to know which fortunate military leader the goddess Isis has chosen to lead the Egyptian forces into battle. The choice, Ramfis tells him, has been made — a young, brave leader — and he will go now to report the name to the King. The subdued accompaniment over which this brief conversation takes place is set to relatively simple counterpoint scored for the lower strings. The musical dialogue is quite straightforward, and one thing we learn about Ramfis is that although he may on occasion be inflexible and even cruel, there is no duplicity about him. He has a clear understanding of his responsibility as High Priest, and he intends to carry it out.

As soon as Ramfis leaves on his mission, Radamès lets us know that he would like to be the triumphant leader of the Egyptian troops in the fight against the Ethiopians. The music suddenly becomes strongly militaristic with noisy brass fanfares interrupted by the strings only when Radamès thinks of his beloved Aida and dreams of returning to tell her that he fought and won solely for her. One more flurry of the brass and then Radamès begins his *romanza*, "Celeste Aida," one of the most famous of all tenor arias.

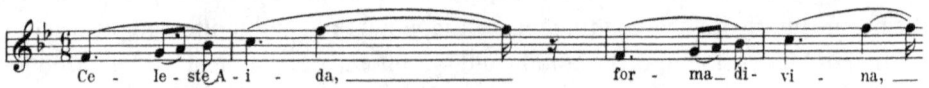

Example 3

We may legitimately wonder why defeating the Ethiopians and returning as a conquering hero will in any way benefit Aida. As he praises her beauty and sings of his love for her, however, Radamès gives us a hint. He hopes to be able to return her to her native land and see her installed on the royal throne of Ethiopia. Let's hazard a guess: As the military deliverer of his nation, he may be in a position to ask for and receive the kingship of Ethiopia for himself, and then Aida could reign beside him as both queen and wife. It's all a rather boyish dream, a hero receiving the ultimate reward of his true love, and the music in which he expresses his dream is more conventionally lyrical than most of the opera. It is, however, entirely appropriate for a heroic young lover as he daydreams. Before the end of the opera, however, his dream will fade into harsh reality and our boyish hero will be forced to grow up.

Listen particularly for the conclusion of Radamès' *romanza*. Verdi asks of the singer something that most tenors are either unable or unwilling to deliver — that the concluding high B-flat be sung softly and then fade away (the Italian term is *morendo*).

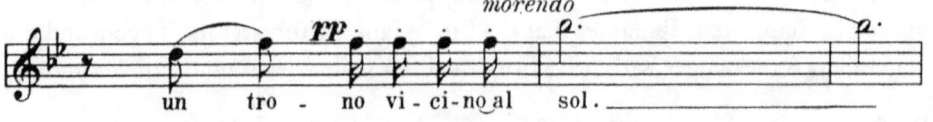

Example 4

4 — Words and Music

More often than not what the tenor produces is a stentorian high note trumpeted forth as loudly as possible. Then the orchestra plays the concluding bars softly and they fade away prior to the entrance of Amneris. Martial Singher, the distinguished French baritone and teacher of singers, admits that "not many dramatic tenors can achieve such a feat [the *morendo* high B-flat]," and he adds, "besides, the temptation to deliver a heroic high note is all but irresistible."* Verdi, however, knew the effect he wanted. Radamès' dream of Aida reigning in her native land as she now reigned in his heart must be precisely that — a beautiful daydream that ultimately in every sense would fall victim to Amneris. Her entrance at this point to a rapid *allegro* truly does break the spell, provided the spell has been created the way Verdi intended. Since the task of producing a genuine *morendo* on the B-flat, as Singher indicated, is extremely difficult for tenors of adequate vocal amplitude to sing Radamès, Verdi provided an alternative — a loud high note followed by the repetition of the final phrase, "vicino al sol," one octave below and softly. According to Julian Budden, he probably suggested it first for Giuseppe Capponi, and later he recommended it for Ernesto Niccolini, who had asked for — and been denied by the composer — permission to transpose the aria downward by a half-tone.† A few tenors, including Richard Tucker in Toscanini's broadcast/recording of the opera, have followed this suggestion. It is hardly the ideal solution, but to this listener it is surely better than the blaring high B-flat.‡ So pervasive in performance is the loud note at this point, however, that some audiences have come to expect and to value it. Rodolfo Celletti reports an incident in which tenor Carlo Bergonzi "was booed in an Italian theater for having taken the note *piano*, as Verdi wrote it."§

The theme that accompanies Amneris' entrance recurs at other times in the opera, probably to underline musically her love for Radamès. We'll hear it again in the final act when, at the beginning of the Judgment scene, she considers the possibility of saving Radamès' life. Notice the use of the triplets in the rhythm. That, too, is a characteristic of much of Amneris' music.

We learn a great deal about Amneris in this brief duet with Radamès and the trio that follows.

Example 5

---

*Martial Singher, *An Interpretive Guide to Operatic Arias: A Handbook for Singers, Coaches, Teachers, and Students* (University Park: Pennsylvania State University Press, 1983), p. 245.
†Budden, *The Operas of Verdi*, III, p. 193.
‡For a contrasting view, see Budden, *The Operas of Verdi*, III, p. 193.
§Rodolfo Celletti, "On Verdi's Vocal Writing," in *The Verdi Companion*, William Weaver and Martin Chusid, eds. (New York and London: W. W. Norton, 1979), p. 235, n. 6.

That she loves Radamès is never subject to question, nor is the fact that her love pushes her to extremes of jealousy. She is also a desirable woman, beautiful and appealing. From the beginning we need to be aware that were it not for Aida, Radamès might well have chosen Amneris. Surely there had been some degree of romantic attachment in the past strong enough to encourage her hopes for a union with Radamès. However, she has now begun to suspect that whatever his current interests are, she is not high on the list. As a result, she is unsure of herself and of her ability to gain and hold Radamès' affection. She turns on her feminine wiles at the beginning of this scene, and it's important that the artist portraying her let us know that Amneris is here all sweetness and light. "A great joy shines in your face," she tells Radamès. "How happy would be the woman who could inspire such joy in you." His response is that he is dreaming of the possibility of being chosen as the leader of Egypt's armies in the battle against the Ethiopians. "But perhaps it's something more," Amneris says, "something sweet and appealing here in Memphis that you're hoping for."

The pre-history of the relationship of Amneris and Radamès is a matter for speculation, but this is clearly not the first time that she has asked for reassurance of Radamès' affection and not the first time that the possibility of a romantic rival has entered her mind. She shares that information with us in a brief aside, accompanied by new theme, apparently relating to her jealousy, in the orchestra. This theme also will recur in the duet of Aida and Radamès in the Nile scene of Act 3 and the at the beginning of the first scene of the final act.

Radamès, too, knows something of Amneris' jealousy, and in his own brief aside he fears that she has discovered the love for Aida, her slave, buried in his heart. It is, dramatically speaking, the opportune time for Aida to appear. Amneris, ever attentive, notices the special look on his face as Radamès sees her.

Example 6

"Could Aida be my rival?" she wonders, and for the first time we encounter another aspect of Amneris' personality — her willingness to employ duplicity and prevarication in order to achieve her ends. The theme that accompanies her pretended sympathy and concern for Aida has about it a kind of serpentine quality as Amneris attempts to twist her way into her slave's secret heart.

"To me," she sings, "you're not a slave. You're a sister. Why are you weeping?"

"It is," Aida tells her, "fear about the war — fear for my fatherland, fear for all of us."

Vie - ni,o di - let-ta, appress-sa - ti

Example 7

What follows is a trio in which Aida, Amneris, and Radamès express their personal reactions to the situation in a series of asides. The sisterly concern that Amneris has expressed for her slave turns in her private meditation to hatred. "Tremble, wicked slave! I'm about to discover your secret!" Radamès has seen the anger in Amneris' face and fears what will happen if she discovers the love he and Aida bear for one another. Aida, for her part, confesses that in her hidden thoughts it is not only for her fatherland that she grieves but also for her love, a love that brings her such great unhappiness.

A fanfare in the brass heralds the entrance of the King with his full contingent of ministers, officers, and members of his court including Ramfis and the other priests. A messenger has just returned from Ethiopia, and he reports on the advance of the Ethiopian army into Egyptian territory toward the great city of Thebes. They are led, the messenger tells us, by a strong, charismatic leader — Amonasro. Aida, in an aside, recognizes the name of her father. The Messenger's brief part in this scene can be turned into a small personal triumph for a tenor who bothers to sing it with a sense of excitement and impending danger, and more than one Messenger, including Nicola Martinucci and James McCracken, has risen in rank to sing Radamès.

His message is, of course, a call to war, and the King reveals now the name of the leader chosen by Isis for the Egyptian army. It is Radamès. The King orders him to go to the Temple of Vulcan, where he will be equipped with the arms that he will take into battle. The call now is for "War! Guerra!," and led by the King, the gathered ensemble cries out for warfare and the defeat of the enemy. Ramfis and the priests remind them that it is the power of the gods that determines the outcome of battle. Radamès rejoices in the opportunity before him, and Amneris places in his hand the military standard while Aida expresses her despair that her love for Radamès binds her to the enemy of her fatherland and the ensemble calls for the gods to protect their sacred Nile River.

The great cry of "Return victorious! Ritorna vincitor!" is raised first by Amneris, then by the entire ensemble before all except Aida leave the stage.

Example 8

Alone now, Aida repeats the cry, "Ritorna vincitor!" and realizes that she has called for the defeat of her father and her nation. It is the introduction to her first major aria, generally

Example 9

known by those introductory words, "Ritorna vincitor." She imagines Radamès returning as the victor over her own brothers and her father paraded in chains behind his chariot. She prays that the gods will erase her words and bring defeat to the Egyptians, but those words, too, torment her. She loves Radamès, and she has, in effect, prayed for his death in battle. It is the heart of her dilemma — the love of her father and her homeland and the love of Radamès — and she can see no way to resolve the conflict. She prays to the gods to have pity on her and let her die.

Example 10

Aida is haunted by the realization that her dilemma can only find its resolution in death. From the beginning of the opera, she seems to realize that death is the only possible avenue of escape for her, and as it turns out, the only possible avenue of fulfillment. In Act 2, when Amneris, having tricked Aida into revealing her love for Radamès, threatens her, she begs for pity because, as she says, her love will end soon in the tomb. In Act 3, as she waits beside the Nile for Radamès, she fears that he will reject her for Amneris, and then she will end her life and her misery beneath the waters of the river. Even when her father offers her the possibility of a blissful life in Ethiopia with Radamès at her side, her response is that one day, one hour of that joy, "e poi morir — and then death." Finally, in the last scene of the opera, when Radamès discovers her in the tomb to which he has been condemned, she confesses that she has hidden herself there in order to die with him. In many ways, she is the unhappiest of opera heroines, and until the final moments there is no sense of real peace or fulfillment for her. As she dies in Radamès' arms, however, she finds the resolution that she had sought all along, and finds it precisely where she all along sensed it would be — in death.

Act 1, Scene 2

Verdi's "Great Consecration Scene and First Finale," which the composer wanted to follow immediately upon the end of the first scene of the act, is set in the Temple of Vulcan in Memphis. According to informed historians, the Egyptians did not worship Vulcan and, in any case, he was certainly not a god of war. The confusion grew from the mistaken assumption fostered by the Greeks that the Egyptian god Phtha was the equivalent of the Roman Vulcan and his Greek counterpart, Hephaestus. "Fortunately," as Julian Budden observes, "such solecisms are for the Egyptologist rather than the music-lover to worry about."*

*Budden, *The Operas of Verdi*, III, p. 172.

Verdi was at great pains to define this scene clearly and describe the setting and the actions of the participants in detail. Apparently he felt that its effectiveness was crucial to the opera. There is, however, a tendency to see it only as an added attraction, an opportunity for a little splendor and ceremony with no particular importance to the characters or the plot of *Aida*, and I have seen amateur productions that unfortunately simply omit the Consecration scene completely and proceed to the first scene of Act 2. The result is a significant loss to the opera as a whole.

First of all, the Consecration scene establishes clearly Radamès' commitment to both the gods and the battles of his nation. The impressive ceremony in which he is consecrated to the service of Egypt while prayers are raised to Phtha underlines the profound responsibility that he takes upon himself and thus the seriousness of his offense when in Act 3 he reveals the military plans and arranges to flee with Aida to Ethiopia. In an interesting way, this scene also vindicates the character of Ramfis and the priesthood, who are sometimes portrayed as the villains of the opera. Cold, inflexible, and invincible they surely were, but the sincerity and the zeal of their prayers here in the Temple of Vulcan should persuade us that they are fully persuaded of the efficacy of their gods and the rightness of their cause. When the fury of Amneris is unleashed against them in the Judgment scene of the final act, we need to understand that they are not the bad guys in *Aida*. They are the voice of justice, albeit justice completely untempered by mercy.

The Consecration scene is also of great interest musically. Whether the effect is "local color" or not is debatable. Neither Verdi nor anyone else for that matter knew a great deal about the actual sound of ancient Egyptian music, but he managed here to produce the effect of solemn worship of the gods in a highly flavored Oriental vein. The off-stage harp arpeggios that accompany the High Priestess* and the other priestesses as they invoke Phtha, the creator deity particularly associated with Memphis, lend a tone of mystery, and the fact that the voices themselves emerge from no visible source adds to the effect of strange practices in distant places. The song of the Priestess is prime pseudo orientalism, a sinuous minor melody, within a limited range from A-flat up to F-flat.

The priests offer their prayer in solemn E-flat major harmony, and the contrast of minor

Example 11

---

*After the first performances, she lost her proper name, Termouthis. It may have seemed pointless to attach a name to a character who never appears on stage. In some early performances and perhaps in some more recent recordings, apparently with Verdi's agreement, the role was sung by the same artist who appeared as Aida, feasible, of course, because the High Priestess does not appear on the stage.

and major has a slightly unsettling, ambiguous effect that contributes to the mystery.

The dance of the priestesses that follows continues to suggest the Orient with another close, winding melody carried primarily by the flutes. The priestesses created something of a problem for Verdi since he had already read that there were no priestesses in the worship of ancient Egypt. His historical conscience, however, was satisfied when Mariette informed Verdi through Du Locle that "you can use as many priestesses of Isis or Vulcan as you please."* Occasional modern productions substitute males for females in this ballet, but if the priestesses didn't trouble the archaeologist Mariette, why should they trouble contemporary stage directors? During the ballet, Radamès enters, approaches the altar, a silver veil is held over his head, and at the end of the ballet, Radamès is given the sacred, divinely forged sword that will bring death and defeat to the enemy.

Ramfis introduces the final movement of the Consecration scene with a noble theme in which he prays that the god will protect Egypt.

Nu - me, cu-sto-de e vin - di-ce di questa sa-cra ter - ra,

Example 12

Radamès and the priests join in this hymn to Phtha, which rises to two magnificent climaxes, both underlined in the orchestra with powerful alternating descending and ascending scale passages. The invisible priestesses join them in invoking the god, once more to the theme of Example 11, before the ensemble fades to a hushed, *pianissimo* prayer. A lengthy silence, accompanied only by quiet rolls on the timpani, is broken as Radamès and Ramfis and then the entire ensemble call out to their all-powerful god, "Immenso Fthá!"

Thus ends a wonderfully effective scene, ritual in nature but entirely germane to the opera as a whole. It may well be the finest ceremonial music that Verdi ever composed for the operatic stage.

Act 2, Scene 1

The war with Ethiopia is over, Radamès and the Egyptian forces have triumphed, and the day has come for his triumphant entry into Thebes. Amneris will, of course, be present for the victory parade, and now, in her private rooms, her

---

*Camille Du Locle to Verdi, July 26, 1870 (Busch, *Verdi's Aida*, p. 38).

slaves are dressing and adorning her for the celebration. They sing of the returning hero and the power of love, with comments from Amneris as she yearns to be again with Radamès in a typical, languorous closely-woven melody with a hint of that haunting uncertainty about her ability to win Radamès' love.

Example 13

Young Moorish slaves perform for her entertainment a light-hearted dance — "very lively and rather grotesque, without many complicated steps which could not be executed considering the speed of the music."*

This is the only point in the score where we might well question whether the music has any easily recognizable application to the dramatic context. Ritual dance in the Consecration scene and the celebratory ballet to come in the Triumphal scene are logical parts of the action — but a dance by young Moorish slaves while Amneris is being adorned for the victory parade? In many operas we could justify it as a nongermane interlude purely for the pleasure of the audience, but *Aida* otherwise presents a tightly knit plot with little room for extraneous matter. Is it too much of a stretch to accept it as a sympathetic attempt of Amneris' servants to lighten her mood and lift her troubled spirits? It's interesting how different productions have dealt with this brief ballet movement. In some cases, children are the performers, usually to the delight of the audience. Frequently the dance is played for laughs. In one version that I have seen the Moorish slaves were well-trained female athletes performing gymnastic feats. In another, there were two hunters pursuing and eventually killing a stag — a little story ballet, so to speak.

A brief repeat of the slaves' chorus and Amneris' yearning response (a reminder perhaps that the Moorish interlude hasn't done a great deal to relieve her anxiety) leads to her duet with Aida and the dramatic climax of Act 2, Scene 1. Philip Gossett has demonstrated that this duet includes the traditional elements, including the concluding *cabaletta,* that would have been expected in a nineteenth-century Italian opera albeit with the crucial connecting recitative that would ordinarily introduce the *cabaletta* moved forward between the first two, more lyrical sections of the duet.† Verdi's artistry, however, enabled him to adopt — and adapt — the convention so that it fully served his dramatic purpose.

---

*Quoted from *The Production Book* by Giulio Ricordi (in Busch, *Verdi's Aida*, p. 574).
†Gossett, "Verdi, Ghislanzoni, and Aida," pp. 321–324.

Amneris dismisses the other slaves, and we hear Aida's theme in the orchestra (Example 1) as she enters. Amneris' doubts are fully awakened now and she determines to discover once and for all whether her suspicions about Aida and Radamès are true. She approaches Aida first with feigned sympathy for the defeat of her people in battle and with the promise that she will do all in her power to restore her happiness. "But how can I be happy," Aida confesses, "away from my homeland and uncertain of the fate of my father, my brothers."

"Time will bring healing," Amneris suggests, "and greater than time — the power of love." In an aside, we learn that for Aida, the thought of her love for Radamès brings both joy and anguish, a reaction that Amneris notices carefully. "Perhaps," she tells Aida, "one of those who fought against your country has found a place in your heart. Some have survived the battle even thought their leader, Radamès, has been slain." Aida's reaction is immediate and strong. The pace increases and the accompaniment becomes more agitated as Amneris leaves her false sympathy and breaks out in anger. One final stroke, and she will be fully convinced. "I was lying," she says, "Radamès is alive." Aida's passionate thanksgiving to the gods is all the proof Amneris needs. Her jealousy and anger break forth in a wide-ranging phrase completely different from the closely bound musical phrases illustrative of her duplicity.

Example 14

For a moment Aida accepts the role of rival to Princess Amneris, for "Anch'io son tal — ... I also am." She was about to reveal that she too is a princess, but she catches herself and pleads instead for pity.

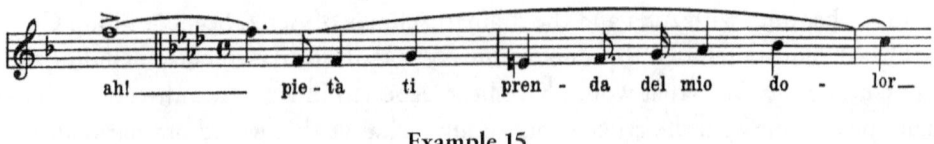

Example 15

Far from pity, however, Amneris' response is nothing but hatred and the desire for vengeance as she commands Aida, her slave, to tremble in fear — "Trema, vil schiava!"

Off stage, the chorus repeats the mighty prayer for the protection of Egypt first heard in Act 1, Scene 1 (Example 8), which becomes now the basis for the concluding *cabaletta* section of the duet. Amneris orders her slave to accompany her and kneel beside her in the dirt during the victory celebration, and Aida laments that her love will soon be buried with her in the tomb. The scene ends with Aida alone as she repeats the prayer that ended the first scene of the opera (Example 10).

Act 2, Scene 2

Act 2 ends with the grandest of grand finales requiring a full contingent of soloists, three choruses, the ballet company, the full orchestra, a stage band, and six very special trumpets. After the subdued conclusion of Aida's prayer in the first scene, the orchestra fades away into silence so that the forte rhythmic fanfare of the trumpets introducing the Triumphal scene comes as an aural shock. At least it should come that way provided the producers have planned for an instantaneous change of the stage setting so that there is not an extended pause at this point. In most stagings, at least part of the crowd of eager Egyptians will already be on stage and others will join them quickly since there are only twenty-four bars of rapid music before the massed chorus must break into jubilant song. They sing the praises of Isis, who has protected the nation, and the Pharaoh, who enters with his retinue and takes his throne to be followed by Amneris and her slave Aida. The theme of their anthem is big, bold, and rather pompous, but it is entirely appropriate for the occasion.

Example 16

The women in the crowd, in a gentler, contrasting melody, offer wreaths and flowers for the returning army and call on the Egyptian maidens to dance in celebration. In a somber, rather threatening theme, the priests thank the gods for the Egyptian victory, and then the conquering troops march in to the music of the most famous tune in the opera.

It was Verdi's intention that the six trumpeters march in before the Egyptian soldiers, but many recent productions tend to station them more or less permanently on either side of the stage.

Example 17

The six long trumpets that Verdi required for the triumphal march had been a source of considerable concern to him before the first performances of the opera. He wanted to be certain that they not only sounded right but also that they looked right, that is, that they looked authentically ancient Egyptian. Ancient, they may have appeared, of course, but there was nothing "Egyptian" about them. Three of them were to be A-flat trumpets, the other three B. They would play the theme of the march alternately and then the A-flat trumpets would carry the theme while the B instruments sounded a D-sharp, a clever device that looks strange on paper but that works since the D-sharp echoes the E-flat of the A-flat trumpets. It was the simplest of musical devices. The melody of the march required only five different notes, and it is wonderfully memorable, the kind of tune that audiences whistle on the way home from the opera house. Its familiarity may make it sound hackneyed and trite outside the opera house, but in the context of the Triumphal scene it is absolutely right — the Verdian equivalent of a rousing Sousa march.

The ballet follows immediately, a series of episodes in which Verdi draws on the full arsenal of Oriental effect in harmony, melody, and orchestration. The original ballet was relatively brief, but at the request of the officials at the Paris Opéra in 1880, he expanded it and instructed his publisher to include the additional music in future editions of the opera. In the original productions, the stage extras would carry on Ethiopian idols and other trophies of the war and the ballerinas would dance around them. The Moorish slaves, presumably the same ones who danced for Amneris while she was preparing for the celebration, were expected to join them.

In all candor, through the years the ballet has proved something of an embarrassment to producers and opera companies. Attempts to reconstruct ancient Egyptian dance are doomed to failure simply on the grounds that no one knows how the Egyptians danced. Angular movements modeled after the figures in the old tomb paintings inevitably look more awkward than graceful, but the forms of classical ballet seem completely incongruous in this warlike victory setting. In some productions, a program of sorts has been imposed on the ballet. At the Metropolitan Opera in 1976, male dancers representing Egyptian warriors and one of their Ethiopian counterparts engaged in conflict to the death. Some opera performances omit the ballet altogether, but for anyone who knows the score the result is a glaring gap in the middle of the scene. Perhaps the best solution is a simple ritual dance or procession in which the war trophies are presented to the King.

After the ballet, the victory choruses continue as the people praise the conquering heroes and the priests intone their gratitude to the gods. Additional soldiers parade and bring with them their banners and implements of war. (These soldiers are, of course, stage extras employed temporarily to fill the stage, not to sing. Don't be surprised if they look suspiciously like the same troops that entered *before* the ballet, and more often than not rather than battle-scarred veterans, they resemble teen-aged supers from a local high school.) At the climax of the victory chorus, Radamès himself enters, frequently in a horse-drawn chariot.

He is clearly the hero of the day, and the King descends from his throne to greet him as the savior of his fatherland. Amneris, accompanied by the same theme that announced her entry in the first scene of the opera (Musical Example 5), places a crown of victory on his head. When the King offers to give Radamès any gift he desires, he asks first that the Ethiopian captives be brought in. As they enter, the priests once more thank the gods in a doleful melody that seems to bode ill for the unfortunate prisoners. Aida suddenly recognizes the last of them as her father, Amonasro, and rushes to him. "Her father!" all of those assembled sing, and Amneris adds her threatening comment, "In our power!" Amonasro whispers a warning to his daughter not to reveal his royal position to the Egyptians, and then at the command of the King, steps forward and begins his appeal for the captured Ethiopians.

It is our introduction to Amonasro, who appears in the opera only in this scene and the one to follow. Obviously it's not a long role, but it is just as clearly a very important one, and the action of the Triumphal scene, which has been largely ceremonial up to this point, now becomes not only highly dramatic but also absolutely essential to the ongoing plot of the opera. Just as the full development of Amneris' jealousy in the first scene of this act is decisive in the ongoing action, the events in the remainder of Act 2, the revelation of Aida's relationship with Amonasro and the announcement to follow of Radamès' impending marriage to the Princess, set the stage for the dramatic complexities of the third act of *Aida*.

Amonasro's character comes through clearly in the words he sings and the music to which he sings them. There is something rather stiff and self-conscious about his opening address to the Pharaoh. After all, he is lying and he is no doubt reciting a speech that he has rehearsed over and again since his capture. Obviously, the King of Ethiopia did not, as he claims now, die on the battlefield. As he moves from the lie to the emotion that at the moment is no doubt completely sincere, the tone of the music changes. "If fighting for our fatherland brings guilt," he sings, "then we who fought are ready to die." His music rises to a *forte* climax on the word "die — morir," and then he stops abruptly in his tracks. Verdi's instruction is "*tronca* — cut off" at this point, and the composer followed it with a pause. Can it be that in his regal pride Amonasro senses that he has come dangerously close to revealing himself? After the *fermata*, he offers a moving appeal for the life

Example 18

of the Ethiopian prisoners that will become the basis for a fully developed ensemble.

The theme is taken up by Aida and the other prisoners, and soon Ramfis and the other priests are countering this appeal for mercy to call for the death of all the Ethiopian captives. The people who have been an audience to these events beg the priests to spare the prisoners and ask their king to be merciful. Radamès, for his part, is profoundly moved by Aida's grief on behalf of the Ethiopians, and Amneris notices his concern for Aida and it adds fuel to her burning jealousy and desire for vengeance. Aida's musical line, rising eventually to a high C, soars above the ensemble. It is in moments like this that lighter-voiced lyric sopranos often fail to deliver the goods.

This is the kind of ensemble that challenges all but the largest opera companies with unlimited resources of performing personnel. Verdi insisted on a large chorus divided here into three distinct groups — the Egyptian people, the priests, and the prisoners. For the 1872 premiere at La Scala, he had a mighty choir of one hundred seven members, most of whom would represent the people with proportionately smaller numbers for the prisoners and the priests. Smaller opera companies, however, would be unable to provide so large a chorus, as Verdi knew, but he insisted that the same proportions among the groups should be observed.* Gianandrea Gavazzeni, the noted Italian conductor, admitted that in many Italian opera houses, the controlling authorities refused the employment, even on a temporary basis, of a large enough chorus to fill all three groups. "Hence ... the chorus director must make use of tricks and artifacts which cancel the three parts ... the director knows it and feels it very much; and this is sufficient to disturb his conscience and his ear."[†]

Radamès now makes his request of the King. He asks that the Ethiopian captives be released. The not-unexpected response of Ramfis and his fellow priests is to insist that as enemies of Egypt they be condemned to death. His rationale is simple: Granted their freedom these Ethiopians will seek vengeance and renew the war. "Not," Radamès assures his king, "with their warrior king, Amonasro, dead." A compromise is reached: Amonasro, Aida's father and clearly the spokesman for the group, will be held, but the other Ethiopian prisoners will be released. Now, as a further honor to Egypt's young hero, he will be granted the hand of the Princess Amneris in marriage, and eventually with her at his side, he will reign over the entire nation. It is Amneris' moment of triumph. No mere slave maiden will be able to rob her of her love.

---

*Budden, *The Operas of Verdi*, III, p. 233.
[†]Gianandrea Gavazzeni, "Conducting Aida," *Aida in Cairo*, Mario Codignola and Riccardo de Sanctis, eds. (Cairo: Banca Nazionale del Lavoro, 1982), p. 46.

The powerful opening chorus of the Triumphal scene returns with priests and the people praising their nation and the prisoners expressing their gratitude to the King and the nation that have granted them their freedom. Aida and Radamès sing of their despair and Amneris of her victory. In a brief interlude, Amonasro assures Aida that all is not lost for Ethiopia, and then all of the voices join in expressing their own varied reactions to the events. In the vocal line, Verdi challenges Amneris twice to ascend with Aida to a high C-flat. We may well wonder how many mezzo-sopranos actually accept the challenge.

A reprise of the theme of the Grand March brings to a close this supreme example of Verdi's artistry in blending all the forces into the mightiest of finales.

Act 3

At the opening of Act 3, Verdi takes us to the banks of the river Nile beside a temple of Isis. He truly does "take" us there with his music. With occasional exceptions — the storm in the final act of *Rigoletto*, for example — Verdi preferred to get on with the action and leave the depiction of nature to the scene painters. In this case, however, the first bars of the Nile scene make the atmosphere of the vast river and the moonlit tropical night almost palpable. The combination of the octaves in the first violins, the gentle accompaniment from the other strings, and the soft melody of the flute is magical and highly evocative, and the effect is not destroyed when the off-stage chorus of priests from within the temple pray for the help of Isis as the "mother of overwhelming love." Verdi had first planned a small chorus "in the style of Palestrina"* to begin Act 3, but four months before the Cairo premiere he changed his mind. Audiences, particularly American audiences, will too often break into applause when the curtain rises on a particularly beautiful stage setting. They should be charged with disturbing the artistic peace if their applause drowns out the evocative opening notes of Act 3.

While Verdi paints the Egyptian night with his music, Amneris and Ramfis appear as passengers on a small boat and disembark to enter the temple. Arrival by boat probably suggests that the setting of Act 3 is an island in the Nile and thus a relatively isolated place. It is, as we learn, the day before Amneris' anticipated wedding to Radamès. Ramfis has brought her there and will remain with her while she prays for Isis' favor. Amneris responds (in a musical phrase, Example 19, that in its simplicity and sincerity leaves no doubt about her love) that she will pray that Radamès will give her his heart as completely as hers has always been committed to him.

Aida enters now to the accompaniment of her by-now familiar theme (Example 1). Radamès has asked her to meet him in this isolated location, where they can

---

*Verdi to Giulio Ricordi, August 12, 1871 (in Busch, *Verdi's Aida*, p. 202).

Example 19

be alone and not observed. We must assume, then, that Aida, although a slave, enjoyed a measure of freedom of movement. She is deeply troubled as she considers what Radamès may have to tell her. In her recitative, Verdi has asked for long pauses (*lunga silenzio*) between her first unaccompanied phrases. The music becomes increasingly troubled as she confesses to herself that if he comes to bid her a final farewell, she will seek peace and oblivion in the rushing waters of the Nile. As she contemplates death, she remembers the beauty of her native land ("O patria mia") and laments that she will not see it again.

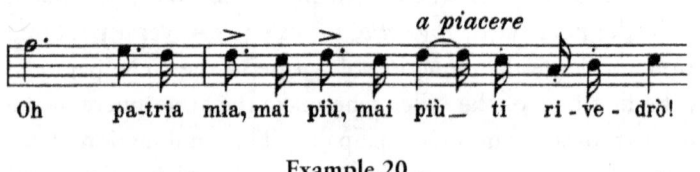

Example 20

It is the introduction to her aria, "O cieli azzurri," the *romanza* that was one of Verdi's last additions to the score. The aria may have been composed with Teresa Stolz's voice in mind, but there is no reason to believe that it was not sent to Cairo as part of the final score and first sung there by Antonietta Pozzoni. Aida's farewell to the beautiful land of her birth is repeated throughout the aria with several reminders that she will see Ethiopia *mai più*, which means simply "never more." The *romanza* and the recitative preceding it require the full range of the soprano voice, from high C to the B natural two octaves below. It demands the ultimate in *legato* phrasing and control throughout the entire dynamic range. The penultimate phrase has defeated many a soprano who otherwise had all of the gifts for the role.

Example 21

The Aida who can rise to a *dolce* high C and complete the phrase fully without increasing the tempo is rare indeed. The aria ends on a *piano* high A that should fade away into silence.

In live performances, wise conductors delay the orchestral postlude for the applause and cheers that are bound to follow if the soprano has accomplished even a part of what Verdi requested. On a recording of the complete opera, however, the orchestral music should continue without a long pause for the simple reason that Act 3 of *Aida* holds together as if it were a single musical composition. It is, in fact, made up of a series of more or less formal musical units welded together with passages of recitative. In other words, Verdi has not turned his back on the traditional structures of Italian opera. After the introductory material, we have a major aria, followed by a duet for Aida and Amonasro, followed by another duet for Aida and Radamès, and a brief concluding passage in which Aida and Radamès are joined first by Amonasro and then by Amneris and Ramfis. At the same time that we notice the formal musical structures, however, we should be aware that introductory, connective, and concluding material is so carefully interwoven with the aria and the two duets that the act as a whole can and should also be heard as a continuous single work of music.

Amonasro's sudden appearance at the conclusion of her aria comes as a shock to Aida ("Heavens! My father!" she cries, "Ciel, mio padre!"). It may well come as a shock also to any member of the audience who has not encountered the opera previously. In Auguste Mariette's original synopsis of the action, Act 3 took place in a garden of the Pharaoh's palace and Amonasro enters from a door in a pavilion. The change of venue from a royal garden to an isolated spot along the banks of the Nile raises a few questions. As a prisoner of the Pharaoh, Amonasro might well have been confined to the palace and the surrounding grounds but would hardly have been free to travel at will to a sequestered temple site along the banks of the river. Aida would perhaps not have been surprised to see her father in the royal gardens, even though he wasn't the person she was expecting. What we must assume now, given the new setting and the information we learn later in the scene, is that he has escaped and that his Ethiopian troops have now regrouped and have already begun a new offensive against Egypt. Aida's surprise, then, is not only to find him at the isolated temple of Isis but also no doubt to see him at all here in Egypt. In case we wonder how he knew where to find Aida, we can fall back on his assurance to his daughter that nothing escapes his attention. Let's make one more assumption and decide that he must have informants in the palace who manage to keep him well informed.

None the less, the revised setting for Act 3 truly does stretch credibility a bit. On the other hand, it's a great deal more convincing than Mariette's original version, in which Amneris has been concealed among the trees and, after Aida, Radamès, and Amonasro leave, emerges from her hiding place and declares that her vengeance will be complete — Aida and Radamès will both face judgment and execution. The Princess of Egypt hiding in the foliage!

For most listeners, the duet of Aida and her father is the musical and emotional highlight of Act 3. This is dramatic music at its best with the changing emotions fully revealed in the vocal and orchestral lines. Amonasro's task is to persuade Aida to presume on Radamès' love for her in order to learn from him the route the Egyptian army will take in pursuit of the Ethiopians. In order to achieve that end, he plays mind games with Aida. First, he assures her that she can choose not to be a slave in the power of Amneris and that she can again see her homeland and be united there with her true love, Radamès.

Example 22

"One hour of that joy," Aida responds, "and then I can die." Amonasro reminds her that Egypt has ravaged Ethiopia, profaned their places of worship, enslaved the people, and killed the defenseless elderly and the innocent children. Aida prays for the gods to grant peace to her nation.

Against an agitated accompaniment, Amonasro tells his daughter that the Ethiopian troops are ready to strike the decisive blow as soon as they know where to attack the enemy. "Who can provide that information?" Aida asks.

"You will," Amonasro answers. A simple figure punctuates his explanation to his daughter.

Example 23

"Radamès will soon be here.... He loves you.... He commands the Egyptian army.... Do you understand me?" She does, and she is horrified. She has no intention of betraying her beloved Radamès.

The allegro that follows is the perfectly motivated *cabaletta* to the duet. Amonasro vents his anger against Aida in music of great violence. She begs him to stop, but his curses become ever fiercer. "Then Ethiopia will go down in flames before the Egyptians. And you call yourself my daughter! See the spirits of the slaughtered Ethiopians accusing you. Your own mother's blessed hand will reach out to condemn you." He then rejects his daughter in the cruelest way possible. "You are not my daughter! You are a slave of the Pharaohs!"

4—Words and Music

It is more than Aida can take. She crawls to his feet and tells him that she is still his daughter and will not desert her homeland. The melody, introduced first in the accompaniment, is a beautiful example of the typical rising and falling phrase that Verdi often introduces in moments of profound emotional response.

Example 24

Just when we think that there is nothing else that the composer can offer to cap what we have already experienced, Amonasro assures Aida, in what many listeners consider the most eloquent passage in the entire opera, that she will be the true savior of her people. Once again, as so often in Verdi, it is the rising and falling of the melody that points to the deepest level of emotional involvement.

Example 25

Aida's response? "Oh patria! Quanto mi costi!— Oh my fatherland, how much you cost me!"

There is perhaps a tendency to condemn Amonasro for the way he tampers with Aida's emotions and browbeats her into acquiescence. He, however, is not only a father; he is also the King of Ethiopia. We may hate him for the way he has tortured Aida psychologically, but in the long run he is just as profoundly aware of his responsibilities to his nation as the high priest, Ramfis, is to his—and as ultimately Radamès will prove to be.

When he sees Radamès approaching, Amonasro hides himself among the trees so that he can overhear the lovers' conversation. The rapturous melody with which Radamès greets Aida expresses both his joy at seeing her again (he is instructed to sing *con transporto*) and what Julian Budden refers to as "his easy heroic optimism."*

Example 26

---

*Budden, *The Operas of Verdi*, III, p. 240.

The joyful enthusiasm of his greeting contrasts strikingly with the downfall he will face by the end of the scene. He is at this point a self-assured young man certain of his military prowess and equally certain that he can translate his victory into a happy marriage with Aida.

What could easily have become an ecstatic love duet, however, is tempered by Aida's abrupt reminder that he is to be married to Princess Amneris. Radamès, however, has devised a plan that he believes will enable them to live a happy married life in Egypt. The Ethiopians have arisen again and crossed the border into Egypt. Radamès will once more command the Egyptian troops, and when he returns for a second time victorious from the battle field, he will be in a position to confess his love for Aida and claim the right to share his life with her as his wife.

His scheme might have been enough to satisfy Aida had she not already accepted her responsibility as a loyal Ethiopian and the daughter of King Amonasro. She soon proves herself to be a cleverer person than Radamès and at the same time somewhat more of a realist. The accompaniment recalls a theme related to Amneris' jealousy (Example 6) as Aida reminds him that if he asked to marry Aida, Amneris' anger would flash out against her, her father, and her nation and that there would be nothing Radamès could do to defend them effectively. "But," Aida tells Radamès, "there is a way for us if you love me — that way is to flee Egypt." She offers him a blissful future of love and peace in her native land, there where fragrant virgin forests will shield them from the outside world. The theme she sings is seductive, alluring, and it shows us Aida in an entirely new light.

Example 27

Try to find a soprano who can let us know that here Aida is the temptress, using her persuasive charms to lure Radamès to desert his military duties and flee his native land.

He resists. He has defended Egypt on the battlefield, and after all, it was there that he first saw Aida and came to love her. He does not want to leave Egypt, but Aida turns on him immediately. "Go!" she sings, "You don't love me. Amneris is waiting for you, and only death is left for me and my father." His love for Aida, however, is too great, and in an exciting allegro *caballeta* to their duet, he agrees to flee with her to the earthly paradise she has described to him.

Example 28

Toward the end of the *caballeta* we encounter what seems to me to be one of Verdi's amazingly few miscalculations in this score. (You may not agree.) Aida has just reminded Radamès that they will find bliss together beneath the starry skies and the lush forests of her homeland when abruptly they join voices to an almost martial melody and sing "Vieni meco, insiem fuggiamo ... Come now, we'll flee together". For a scene in which the musical continuity is maintained with such great consistency, the lack of transition is abrupt and vaguely unsettling. Of course, Verdi may have had something to say at this point that I have not yet grasped.

Verdi does not provide an opportunity for applause at the end of the *cabaletta* just as Aida and Radamès should begin their flight from Egypt — although audiences frequently interrupt the flow of the music and the action at this point. Three measures of octaves played loudly by the full orchestra lead to the most crucial moment of the third act, and Aida, as if she suddenly remembers her mission, asks him by what road they should travel to avoid the Egyptian forces. It is, Radamès tells her, the path where tomorrow the Egyptians will attack the Ethiopian army. "Le gole di Nápata — the gorges of Napata." This is the moment Amonasro has been eagerly awaiting. He emerges now from his hiding place and identifies himself as Aida's father and the King of Ethiopia. His soldiers will be there at Napata to meet the Egyptian forces.

Radamès is overwhelmed. He can't believe what has happened. Although Aida and Amonasro try to reassure him that he has done nothing wrong and that a wonderful life awaits him in Ethiopia, he is devastated with the realization that he has revealed Egypt's military secrets and become a traitor to his homeland. They try to drag him away, but suddenly Amneris appears from the temple of Isis and grasps what has happened. "*Traditor*—Traitor!" she cries. This can be an awkward moment on stage if Amneris has not had an opportunity to observe and hear at least a little bit of what's happening. In some productions, the director has her come out of the temple early enough at least to grasp the situation.

Amonasro draws his dagger to kill Amneris, but Radamès stops him and urges Aida and Amonasro to flee. Radamès, however, surrenders to Ramfis, and thus ends one of the most remarkable scenes in all of Italian opera.

The action moves rapidly in these closing moments of Act 3 and it's easy to miss the skill and artistry with which Verdi has made his dramatic points. Many composers might have paused long enough for an extended ensemble since we have on stage five of the principal members of the cast, but Verdi knows precisely what he's about. The climax has been reached, and anything beyond that would be too much.

Within this Nile scene as a whole, however, Verdi has accomplished far more than the advancement of the plot. We come to a deeper understanding of the love Amneris bears for Radamès, and we learn more about the compulsion to fulfill his royal duties that governs Amonasro's actions even in the cruelty and harshness of his treatment of his daughter. Some commentators tend to view Aida herself as essentially a simple, faceless young woman totally subject only to her love for Radamès and her loyalty to her nation. She is, of course, much more than that. Her first-act aria has revealed the depth of her anxiety over her divided loyalties, and that conflict comes vividly to life in the third act. The weight of the decision she is forced to make becomes tragically real in the duet with her father, and her potential duplicity and seduction bring to light an otherwise hidden aspect of her character. Aida, it turns out, is a far more complex character than she appears on the surface. Then there is Radamès, who often receives the worst press of all when the characters in *Aida* are subjected to analysis. The cocksure young military kid who had it all added up for his life in his first appearance in this act changes into a man — and a rather admirable one, at that — by its end.

Act 4, Scene 1

The first scene of the last act is largely centered on Amneris, and the vocal and emotional range required of the artist who portrays her is ample justification for Verdi's insistence on finding just the right singer both for the Cairo premiere and for the initial performance at La Scala. A true contralto might not have the high notes, a soprano might not have the low notes, and whoever the singer happened to be he wanted an artist "with highly developed dramatic sensibility who is a mistress of the stage."* Verdi wanted it all for what we have called the Judgment scene.

To consider the opening scene of Act 4 as only a show piece for the mezzo-soprano, however, misses the point. Just as Act 3 had developed the dramatic stature of Aida, Radamès, and Amonasro, Act 4 reveals fully the frustrated heart and volatile emotional responses of Amneris. She is exposed to us in Verdi's wonderfully conceived and developed music, and we should feel at the end of this scene that there is nothing about Amneris that we do not know.

George Bernard Shaw, as astute a critic as he was a dramatist, attributed "the elaboration of the last three operas" to "the inevitable natural drying up of Verdi's spontaneity and fertility ... when in process of time the well begins to dry up, ... then it is time to be clever, to be nice, to be distinguished, to be impressive, to study instrumental confectionary, to bring thought and knowledge and seriousness to the rescue of failing vitality."† All of Shaw's brilliant descriptive terms are applicable to the Judgment scene, but far from demonstrating that Verdi's well of imagination

---

*Verdi to Giulio Ricordi, July 10, 1871 (in Busch, *Verdi's Aida*, p. 182).
†George Bernard Shaw, *London Music in 1888–89 as Heard by Corno di Bassetto (Later Known as Bernard Shaw) with Some Further Autobiographical Particulars* (New York: Vienna House, 1973), p. 407.

and musical vitality was drying up, they point rather to a full flowing stream of imagination and creativity, both in the new material that is introduced and also in the subtle reminders of what has gone before.

The restless introduction to the scene brings back the musical theme associated with Amneris' jealousy (Example 6). The setting is a hall in the Pharaoh's palace, on one side is a door leading to Radamès' cell, on the other are steps descending to the underground hall of justice, and we encounter immediately Amneris' frustration in her extended recitative. Aida has escaped her reach. Radamès faces the sentence of the judges for treason. He isn't, as Amneris assures herself, a traitor, not in his heart and intention, but he planned to flee with Aida and her father. Then they are all traitors, she decides, and deserve to die. In a more lyrical vein, she confesses that she still loves him and that her love is insane and desperate. She truly wants to save him. But how? At least she can try, and she orders the guard to bring Radamès to her. It is a mark of Verdi's skill that he has managed to convey Amneris' conflicting emotions fully and in the most concise manner conceivable.

The duet of Amneris and Radamès that follows is deceptively simple. Amneris appeals to Radamès to respond to the judges and clear his name. Then she will appeal to her father, the King, to grant him a pardon. The melody, which she sings in E-flat minor, will be repeated by Radamès in F-sharp minor.

Example 29

The shift in key is accomplished skillfully in the concluding phrases of Amneris' appeal, and somehow the repeated melody serves effectively both her appeal and Radamès' refusal. Although there was no wrongdoing in his heart, Radamès tells her, he will not defend his case before the judges.

It is a sentiment that Amneris cannot comprehend, consciously to choose death over life, and to a new theme, she begs him to live for her sake. She is prepared to give up everything in her power for him.

Example 30

Radamès responds, with the same theme, that he has already given up everything, his fatherland and his honor, for *her*. Amneris immediately understands the unstated antecedent of the pronoun, and she demands that he say no more of Aida. In a brief return of Example 30, Radamès accuses her of having slain Aida while she offers life to him. In a passage of animated *agitato*, Amneris tells him that Aida is still alive. Her father died in the military rout of the Ethiopian troops, but Aida disappeared. Radamès' gentle prayer for her is that the gods will return Aida to her homeland and that she may never know that he is dying on her behalf.

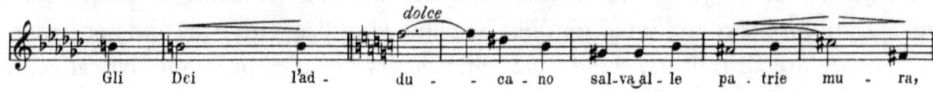

Example 31

In a passage of dramatic recitative, Amneris promises that she will save Radamès if he will renounce Aida forever. His refusal leads to the *cabaletta* of their duet, in which Amneris declares that she, who once loved Radamès, now wants only revenge.

Example 32

He, however, is ready to die for Aida. He does not fear death. It is only Amneris' pity that he fears, "tema sol la tua pietà." It is a surprisingly ambiguous farewell to Amneris. Is there at least a hint here that Radamès acknowledges the depth of Amneris' love and concern for him and recognizes in himself the possibility that he could be led to accept her help and in the process deny his devotion to Aida? If so, the music at this point hardly seems to echo his sentiment, but perhaps he truly does fear her pity.

As the guards take him away, the orchestra in a fierce, syncopated passage not only echoes Amneris' anger but also manages an effective ransposition from C minor into E major. The transposition itself tells us that this is not the occasion for an applause break and that Verdi intends the music to continue into the heart of the Judgment scene.

Given the conflict within Amneris' emotions, we are not surprised that immediately she regrets her anger and the jealousy that has condemned Radamès to death and her to eternal grief. The accompanying figure is the theme related to Ramfis and the priests first heard in the Prelude (Example 2). They cross the stage and descend into the hall of judgment.

From their subterranean room, Ramfis and the priests pray for the true spirit of justice in their decisions. Are they sincere in that prayer? Permit me to say that I believe they are. Of course, we are (unless we are sadly cold of heart) as eager as Amneris that Radamès' life be spared, but we should remember throughout this scene that Ramfis and the other priests represent law and order, the preservation of justice, and the good of the nation. I have it on good authority that had Radamès appeared before a modern American military court marshal he would have been found guilty and punished severely, although hardly with burial alive. It is the power of Verdi's music here that shapes our perception of Ramfis and his fellow priests. Although Verdi had decidedly negative opinions of oppressive governmental and ecclesiastical authority, he was no advocate of lawlessness and anarchy and, after all, the judges in this case are working to maintain the structure and organization of Egyptian society. Their music is cold and implacable not because Verdi supported a society based on lawlessness and anarchy but because his sympathy lies with the suffering individuals — Amneris, Radamès, and Aida. Some producers and directors are so intent on making the opera pertinent to the contemporary audiences that they insist on updating the setting and interpreting the opera as a single-minded attack against stern official authority, but that approach oversimplifies the opera. Perhaps what Verdi is trying to say in the music of *Aida* is that there is an inevitable ambiguity in a carefully structured, organized society, where personal desires often fall victim to the need to maintain the structure and the organization. In any case, the meaning is in the music itself, and it is no doubt better heard and grasped without a way-out contemporary "concept" production to underline it.

The drama inherent in the Judgment scene is enhanced by the contrast between the priests singing from their subterranean chamber and Amneris on stage listening and responding to their questions and decisions. The priests are accompanied off stage by four trumpets and four trombones, a combination that produces a particularly ominous sound. Three times, each a half-tone higher, Ramfis presents the charges and he and priests call on Radamès to defend himself. The first of the charges is that Radamès divulged military secrets to the enemy. The second accuses him of deserting his post the day before the battle. The third is, in effect, a summation of the other two: He has betrayed his nation, his king, and his honor. His silence in the face of each charge is emphasized by the hollow roll of the tympani, and each time the priests then condemn him as a traitor. With each condemnation, Amneris pours forth her despair and her agonized prayer for the gods to save Radamès.

Example 33

Radamès' sentence is pronounced by Ramfis

and the other priests singing in unison, accompanied only by occasional blasts from the orchestra to hammer home the severity of the punishment. (Is it possible that the quickly announced sentence sung in unison is Verdi's way of suggesting that Radamès' fate was predetermined and that his trial was essentially a sham?) Amneris' despair explodes in passionate attacks against the blood thirst of these priests, who call themselves the ministers of heaven. Her anger against the priests in general and Ramfis in particular becomes more intense as the priests return from the judgment chamber.

Example 34

They continue repeatedly to brand him a traitor who is condemned to death as they cross and leave the stage. Amneris calls down the curse of heaven on the priests.

Example 35

The fifteen bars of orchestral music that close the scene, with their snarling trills in the reeds and the brass, bring the scene to an incredibly angry conclusion. Amneris has waited a long time in this opera for her big moment, but the wait was worth it, both for her and for the audience.

Act 4, Scene 2

The second scene of the final act should begin immediately, and the early production material instructs that the Judgment scene should be played before a shallow stage setting that can be quickly removed to reveal the more elaborate scenery of the finale. What we should sense right away is the radical contrast between the two scenes. Verdi was, of course, aware that there would be applause at the conclusion of the first scene, perhaps even an extended ovation. Through the medium of modern recording, however, we are in a better position to appreciate the skill with which Verdi moves from one scene to the next, and often from one individual number within a scene to the next. Even though we can identify the more or less closed forms of much of the music in *Aida*, it is still true that Verdi almost erases many of the divisions through the subtle construction of the connecting material.

4—Words and Music

The setting takes us back to the Temple of Vulcan from the Consecration scene in Act 1 but with one important difference. We now see beneath it the subterranean burial chamber. The temple above should be, but rarely is, brightly lighted to contrast with the gloomy shadows of the burial chamber. As the scene begins, Radamès is descending the stairs while the priests secure the stone that will seal his tomb, and as we would expect his thoughts are of Aida and his hope that she is happy now and will never know of his fate. The accompaniment of his recitative is somber but suggests not so much despair as resignation.

He hears a sigh from a corner of the tomb, and his first thought is that it is a phantom spirit, but no, it is a human being. It is Aida. She is weak, close, as we discover, to the point of death. We may well wonder that she is dying so quickly after the tomb has been sealed. Mariette's original synopsis, however, reveals that she has been in the tomb four days, and we can only imagine what hardships she may have faced between the time of her flight with Amonasro and this final moment. She tells Radamès that in her heart she sensed what his sentence would be and resolved to join him in his tomb and die there in his arms.

The remainder of this short scene is essentially a duet for Radamès and Aida, who must, if the effect is to be authentic, be willing and able to sing softly, with careful attention to Verdi's dynamic and phrasing instructions. Tenors — and sopranos, too, for that matter — who shout their way through these duets should not be tolerated. The duet falls into three brief sections, each with a distinctive melody. First, Radamès laments that Aida, so pure and beautiful, should die there, destroyed by his love for her.

Example 36

Aida responds, almost in a trance now, that death, like an angel, is waiting to carry them to eternal joy, where there are no tears and only happiness abides forever.

Example 37

In the temple above the chorus of priests and priestesses call on mighty Phtha.

To Aida and Radamès it is their hymn of death, and for a moment Radamès rebels against the thought and tries to force open the stone that covers the tomb. In vain! Then they sing their own hymn of farewell to the earth, where their dream of joy was doomed to failure, and their welcome to the eternal joy ahead of them. The melody and the words are repeated three times, once by Aida, then by Radamès with Aida's complement to his song, and finally, with the sound of the chant from the temple in their ears, together.

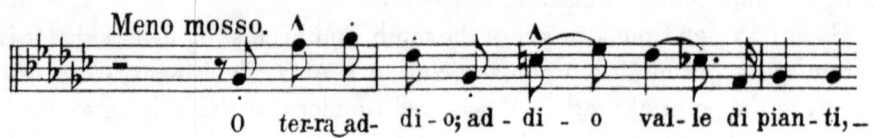

Example 38

As the duet draws to an end, Amneris, dressed in mourning, appears in the temple. She falls to her knees on the stone covering the tomb and prays to Isis for peace for Radamès. Aida dies in his arms, and the last voices we hear are those of the chorus singing to Phtha and Amneris praying for "pace ... peace." Amneris' appearance at the end of the opera was apparently Verdi's idea, and according to Philip Gossett, "a brilliant one, the supreme irony for Amneris, who remains unaware that her Requiem is also being uttered for her rival."*

She is also unaware that her prayer is being answered, for there is in the concluding portion of Aida and Radamès' duet no sense of struggle with death or the tragic circumstances that have produced it. Throughout the three parts of the final duet, the scoring is light and ethereal and the themes that the lovers sing are lyrical and gentle. This is Verdi at his most Mozartean, and the effect is of ultimate peace achieved at last. If we in the audience have given ourselves fully to the music and the drama, we can share the sense of an action that has been completed, not in grim horror, but in triumphant release.

---

*Gosset, "Verdi, Ghislanzoni, and Aida," pp. 331–332.

5

A Legacy in Sound

Although the results were not immediately obvious, 1877 was a very important year for *Aida*. The opera was conquering audiences wherever in the world there were opera houses capable of performing it effectively. What about all those people in the quiet little segments of the globe where there were no such opera houses? Would they ever have the opportunity to experience Verdi's masterpiece? The answer was born in 1877, when Charles Cros in France proposed the theory of sound reproduction and Thomas Alva Edison in the United States made it practical with the invention of the first phonograph.

Of course, it took a few years for the significance of these discoveries to bear operatic fruit. But by the final decade of the nineteenth century, the Italian military officer Gianni Bettini had persuaded singers to permit their voices to be reproduced on cylinder recordings, and Emile Berliner, a German emigrant to Philadelphia, was recording Ferruccio Giannini in operatic selections on the far more practical flat discs. The era of sound recording had arrived, and no other musical work profited from it more than *Aida*.

Sound recording has undergone periodic changes and advances throughout its history. The old acoustical process, which remained the basic recording method until 1925, was by modern standards primitive in the extreme although the results achieved were often impressive. It was based on the easily observable phenomenon that noises of different types produce vibrations. The sound was aimed toward a horn-shaped device that moved a diaphragm to which was attached a recording stylus. The vibrating stylus cut grooves in a wax disc, and from this disc copies could be made on a pressing machine. To play the resulting recording, a playback stylus reversed the process and the resulting sound emerged from another horn-shaped device. Too small a sound would not be heard, and a sound too high and too loud would blast into painful distortion. The wonder is that opera — or any other music, for that matter — could be effectively reproduced with this acoustical recording process. The result, of course, was far from the modern stereophonic, digital, super-audio standard. The voices, usually recorded with the singers standing close to the horn, tended to predominate, and often the accompanying instruments could barely be identified. Even our modern ears, however, accustomed as we are to the latest advances in sound reproduction, can adjust to the acoustical recordings and discern that real music making was taking place.

The development of the vacuum tube and other electronic discoveries made possible what is known as electrical recording. The result was far greater realism in the reproduction of instrumental and vocal sound. Application of the new technique to recorded music began in 1925 and electrical recording quickly became the standard for the entire world. An increase in the number of complete opera recordings followed even though the resulting sets included a daunting number of heavy shellac discs, each side limited to four or five minutes duration. In the years immediately after World War II, the commercial development of magnetic recording on either wire or preferably tape made possible the recording of lengthy segments of music, an advantage that proved particularly helpful for the long-playing record, which became available to the general public in 1950. The new format, at either 45 rpm or 33 rpm, made it far more convenient for the listener since, at least with the 33-rpm format, an entire opera could be included on a two- or three-disc set. The quality of the sound was further enhanced by practical application of stereophonic recording methods in 1958, and the commercial introduction of the compact disc in 1983 further increased the convenience of the listener. More recent developments in sound enhancement point to a bright future for the continued successful recording of complete operas and other musical works.

Aida, as we shall see, figures significantly in each stage of the development of recorded sound. Complete or nearly complete recordings of the opera have been available since 1906–07, when the enterprising Zonophone Company produced the first "complete" recording of *Aida*. It was soon followed in 1909–1910 by a Gramophone issue, in 1912 by the Columbia abridged version, and in 1919–20 by a set of forty discs from HMV.

Scanning the cast listings of the first four entries in the chronological discography in Appendix I reveals a significant problem with many of these early complete opera recordings. The major artists of the day, many of whom were soon recording an impressive number of individual operatic selections, were not interested in investing their time in the lengthy process of committing an entire opera to discs. After all, most opera lovers would not be able to afford to purchase the multi-disc set, and no doubt, it was far more profitable to produce a number of brief selections and reap the royalties from their sales. If the record companies had been able to lure the celebrity artists for complete recordings, they would probably have been unable or unwilling to pay the wages they would have demanded. We search thus in vain for complete recordings of any operas at all by such noted artists as Enrico Caruso, Antonio Scotti, or Louise Homer, and the reigning Aida of the acoustical period, Emmy Destinn, who made complete versions of *Faust* and

Carmen, is represented on disc only with isolated selections from her greatest role.

At the end of the nineteenth and the beginning of the twentieth centuries, however, every city or town of any size in Italy had one theatre or more presenting opera, and the demand for singers was overwhelming. Since the record producers either could not or would not engage the top echelon of artists for a complete recording, they could always draw on the army of generally competent but not outstanding secondary artists. The result is that the cast listings for the acoustical recordings of *Aida* are filled with names that aren't to be found in the standard reference sources and that are familiar only to a handful of specialists.

The 1906–07, 1910–11, and 1919–20 acoustical recordings have not been available for review, but the Columbia abridged version from 1912 has been issued on a CDR playable on home computers, and it at least gives us an impression of what we might hear on the others. "Complete" is hardly an accurate description of this considerably condensed recording. Approximately forty-five minutes of the opera are missing, and the cuts are sometimes quite painful. We do not hear the Triumphal scene ballet, and a large portion of the remainder of this scene and Act 3, the Nile scene, is seriously flawed through the omission of more than half of Aida's aria and the beautiful conclusion of the Aida/Amonasro duet. Other cuts are perhaps more judicious, and what is left gives a fair musical impression of the opera as a whole. On the other hand, some of the deletions would make it virtually impossible to follow the plot of the opera without a complete synopsis of the missing segments. This recording also perpetuates what apparently was and continued for some time to be a more or less standard omission, at least in many recordings and performances — the dialogue of Amonasro and Radamès immediately before he surrenders to Ramfis at the end of Act 3. More recent recordings, with the interesting exception of the 1954 Russian version, tend to reinstate the recitative passages.

The cast is something of a hodgepodge. Apparently not all of the singers were available every day so there are five Aidas, four Amnerises, three Radamès, and two Kings to rule over Egypt. Fortunately, two of the artists who made it almost all the way through are well worth hearing. Vincenzo Bettoni was a young basso of thirty-one at the time. His voice has the ring of authority to it, entirely appropriate for Ramfis, and he enjoyed a career that extended to at least 1950. The baritone who sang Amonasro, Cesare Formichi, was also an artist of considerable dramatic force and impressive voice. Regrettably we are denied his singing of "Pensa che un popolo" in Act 3, and Teresa Chelotti, his partner in the duet, is surely no Aida. She sounds as if Gilda from *Rigoletto* has wandered from Mantua to the banks of the Nile — and found the setting tremendously boring. Otherwise, the only familiar name in the cast is Fanny Anitua, the Mexican contralto, who justifies her generally good reputation in the Judgment scene duet with Radamès. In the trial of Radamès that follows she is replaced by the excellent Andreina Beinat. The tenors, on the whole, however, do not fare well. It's worth noting that the off-stage priestess is sung by two of the Aidas, E. Tominello and L. Remondini, a practice that was often used in staged performances to avoid the necessity of engaging an additional soprano or mezzo-soprano.

The conductor is not identified, and given the necessity of squeezing the music into the three-minute format of the ten-inch discs, it is hardly fair to complain about a few peculiarities in interpretation. Some tempi, however, are extremely rapid, and in a few cases the singers have more than they can do to keep up. On the other hand, the dance of the Nubian slaves in Act 2, Scene 1, is virtually funereal, an example perhaps of the desire to stretch the music to fill the disc.

This *Aida* was certainly no substitute for a first-rate complete performance, but there is much to enjoy in it. With occasional exceptions, the singing is acceptable and speaks well for what must have been the day-to-day level of performance in Italy's provincial opera houses. The recorded sound also holds up well almost one hundred years after it was first engraved on the discs.

The dawn of electrical recording in 1925 opened new possibilities for versions of the most popular operas, and the major recording companies were not long in taking advantage of them. It comes as no surprise that in 1928 both Columbia and HMV were eager to submit their entries into the *Aida* sweepstakes. Both employed the forces of Milan's La Scala Opera House, a decision that assured more than competent orchestral and choral contingents with the traditions of *Aida* performance in their blood. In both cases, the results were impressive then and remain so today.

The recording process for the HMV version began in October and was completed in December. When this *Aida* appeared on the market it was highly praised by the critics — and for good reason. Carlo Sabajno, the conductor, was a veteran of the recording studio. In 1907, under the composer's supervision, he had led the first complete disc version of Leoncavallo's *I Pagliacci* and had been tapped also for the 1919–20 HMV recording of *Aida*. He would continue to serve HMV well for several operatic recordings in the late 1920s and early 1930s. His approach to tempo is noticeably flexible, probably more so than most contemporary conductors would approve, sometimes faster than we expect — as in parts of "Ritorna vincitor" — and occasionally subject to sudden *retards*. Always, however, the skilled La Scala musicians are under complete control, and there is drama aplenty in the performance.

He has at his command a generally excellent cast that fails to meet the highest standards only in the two bass roles. Luigi Manfrini's dark, impressive voice is the right weight for Ramfis, but there's not much sense of dramatic involvement. He is surely no match for Tancredi Pasero in the Columbia recording. Guglielmo Masini is a lackluster King with little regal authority in his voice.

Irene Minghini-Cattaneo, however, is the real thing as Amneris, with a powerful mezzo-soprano voice that she can modulate to encompass those passages in which the Princess is neither ranting nor prevaricating. Her Judgment scene is not only forceful but also deeply moving. Some listeners will not be comfortable with her conspicuous vibrato, but she never allows it to shake her from true focus. She is fully responsive to every change in Amneris' volatile character.

Amonasro is Giovanni Inghilleri, a baritone whose long career extended from 1919 to 1953. The HMV *Aida* catches him at his appreciable best, the voice firm, secure, beautiful in timbre, and skilled in *legato*. In the Nile scene duet with Aida he traces the development from promise, through challenge and anger, to the concluding reassurance of his daughter without abandoning his vocal cool. He is one of the few Amonasros who can lose his temper without losing the note he's been assigned to sing.

It's difficult to know what to say of Aureliano Pertile's Radamès. Where there are doubts they have to do with the sometimes thick, unpleasant tone and the forceful phrase endings, particularly noticeable in an otherwise sensitive "Celeste Aida." There is ample force for the more heroic of Radamès' utterances, and unlike Lindi in the Columbia version, there is no hint of insecurity on high. Pertile is here, as often in other recordings, an interpreter of great sensitivity who has clearly thought deeply about the character. Listeners may be reminded of Jan Vickers among more recent singers. His is not a particularly beautiful voice, but he is assuredly a beautifully gifted dramatic artist.

Attention naturally falls on the Aida of Dusolina Giannini, the young American soprano whose career is remembered today primarily for this recording. She certainly has a voice appropriate for the role with ample, clear tone and breath control adequate for the long phrases Verdi has assigned to Aida. The voice, however, takes on an occasional bleak tone in the higher reaches, and phrase endings at the top can be a trifle abrupt. There is little of the *dolce* that Verdi asked on the high C at the end of "O cieli azzurri." Giannini is fully into her role dramatically if not quite as specific in response as Arangi-Lombardi in the Columbia version of the opera. All in all, her performance is better than most but not quite as good as the very best.

In November of 1928, the La Scala forces recorded a second complete *Aida*, this time for Columbia. The conductor was Lorenzo Molajoli, who became more or less a house conductor for Columbia and went on to fifteen additional opera recordings in rapid succession. He was not only conspicuously dependable, he was also a gifted musician with a good sense of dramatic values. Some of the operas he led in recordings suffer from serious casting weaknesses, but they all demonstrate his ability to shape the scores effectively, a particularly impressive achievement considering the necessity of working within the confines of the limited duration of the 78-rpm discs.

Like the HMV version, the Columbia *Aida* offered a cast of more than passing interest. The greatest weakness was Aroldo Lindi, Radamès. Swedish born, his pre-operatic name was Arnold Lindfors, but his style was thoroughly Italian. He was capable of occasional refinement without the consistent technical ability to realize all of his good intentions, as he demonstrates in the final scene of the opera, and his basic vocal sturdiness tends to fall apart on the more stentorian high notes, including the unpleasant one we hear when he surrenders to the High Priest at the end of Act 3. Over against his counterpart in the 1928 HMV recording, Lindi often sounds rather crude. One would also like a more engaging, rounded mezzo-soprano tone from Maria Capuana as Amneris. Sometimes she sounds older than her age of thirty-seven at the time of the recording. Her dramatic instincts, however, are sound, and she rises to a good Judgment scene. Amonasro, Armando Borgioli, shows a warm, dark baritone, and he is fully in the picture dramatically. His Nile scene duet with Aida is a highlight of this set.

The bass roles are filled impressively by Tancredi Pasero as Ramfis and Salvatore Baccaloni as the King. Pasero and Ezio Pinza were the outstanding Italian bassos of their day, and Pasero, who would record the role again eighteen years later, has the kind of vocal presence and authority that enable him to rank as one of the outstanding portrayers of Ramfis on any of the recordings of *Aida*. Baccaloni proves himself a surprisingly effective King, the voice somewhat lighter than Pasero's and touched with a light vibrato. His later fame as a *buffo basso* was obviously built on the foundation of a fully serviceable vocal gift and technique.

Let there be no question, however — the glory of this performance is Aida, Giannina Arangi-Lombardi. At least in this recording, the comment in *The New Grove Dictionary of Opera* that Arangi-Lombardi "lacked dramatic ability"[1] is disproved over and again. Nothing is over the top, but at every moment this is an Aida who combines both the dignity of the Princess of Ethiopia and the passion of a young woman deeply in love, and we are aware that she could hold her own against the most imperious Amneris. Then there is the voice, completely under control, beautifully produced from top to bottom, and capable of great dynamic variety, including in the Nile scene a *piano* high C that grows in volume and the ability to ring out gloriously in the ensembles of the Triumphal scene. Her technique is built on a firm *legato,* a skill in which she could give some of her partners much-needed lessons. In addition to Aida, it's not unlikely that Arangi-Lombardi also sang the off-stage priestess in Act 1, Scene 2. It's not a bad guess that Giannini had performed the same service in the HMV recording. In any case, the Columbia

---

*Harold Rosenthal [with an editorial revision in signature], "Arangi-Lombardi, Giannina," in *The New Grove Dictionary of Opera*, Stanley Sadie, ed.. (London: Macmillan Reference Limited, 1992, 1998), I, p. 161.

Priestess is more graceful and assured in the little ornamental turns included in the score than her counterpart in the HMV recording.

HMV returned to *Aida* in 1946 for a new complete recording that drew on the services of six of the most distinguished singers of the period and a conductor whose recognized ability and experience placed him near the top in his profession. Whether the all-star lineup produced a truly worthwhile version of the opera has always been open to controversy, with professional critical opinions ranging from "an electrifying performance"* to "one of the sorrier versions."† There are surely performances "sorrier" than this one, but on the whole, the electricity is turned on only sporadically.

The fabled tenor Beniamino Gigli often sang the demanding role of Radamès, although his was essentially a lyrical tenor voice. At this relatively late stage in his career (he was fifty-six at the time of the recording), Radamès' strong dramatic outbursts are not without strain, and unfortunately the warm, caressing tone that graces many of his earlier recordings is in evidence only rarely in the 1946 *Aida*. His vocal charm is almost completely absent where it is most needed in his mainly loud, four-square performance of "Celeste Aida," but there are phrases otherwise, particularly in the final scene, that remind us of what many people consider the most naturally beautiful tenor voice of the twentieth century.

His soprano partner, Maria Caniglia, was fifteen years his junior, but her voice had clearly been subject to hard use since her 1930 debut. What we admire in her performance here is dramatic conviction and vitality, not vocal poise or beauty. The pitch is occasionally doubtful, the high notes are often bleak, and the *piano* sound, which she employs only rarely, doesn't float gently to the listener's ear. Something is seriously amiss vocally, for example, when the touch is heavy in the *dolcissimo* staccati "Vedi? Di morte l'angelo" of the final scene. Caniglia's Aida, however, is fully involved in the drama, and she lets us know that she means fully every word that she sings.

We won't find much of *bel canto* vocal appeal in Gino Bechi's Amonasro, but as long as the King of Ethiopia can be interpreted as a volatile, highly excitable, and often angry person, Bechi surely gets the idea across effectively. There is more to Amonasro than he shows us, but whenever he's on the aural stage the action stirs fully into life.

For vocal excellence in the 1946 *Aida,* however, we turn instead to Ebe Stignani, who sings Amneris; Italo Tajo as the King; and once more Tancredi Pasero, whose Ramfis was one of the joys of the 1928 HMV recording. Tajo, the young

---

*Ivan March, Edward Greenfield, Robert Layton, eds., *The Penguin Guide to Compact Discs and DVDs: 2003/2004 Edition* (New York: Penguin Putnam Inc., 2003), p. 1415.
†Conrad L. Osborne, "Aida," in *The Metropolitan Opera Guide to Recorded Opera,* Paul Gruber, ed. (New York and London: W. W. Norton and Company, 1993), p. 644.

basso whose career would extend eventually to almost fifty years, is not the most commanding but is certainly a most sympathetic Pharaoh, one whose love and care for his daughter, Amneris, we can easily believe. As Ramfis, if Pasero is to any extent less authoritative and impressive than he was in the earlier version, the margin is very slight.

Stignani's Amneris is a classic, a worthy successor to the performance of Minghini-Cattaneo in 1928. The voice is dark in color, a fitting contrast with the soprano Aida, warm in hue but firm and incisive, and it is governed by a superb technique built firmly on a sound *legato*. She can open up impressively on the higher notes, but she is capable of great dynamic variety. I have heard that the visual appeal of her acting on stage was decidedly limited, but she uses her voice to great dramatic effect in communicating the complexities of Amneris' character.

Serafin was surely one of the great Italian operatic conductors, a leader who knew how to get the best from his singers and how to give them precisely the support they needed. Opinions about his conducting in this *Aida* vary a great deal. He certainly rises appropriately to the big dramatic moments, but the impression lingers that he simply allows lengthy portions of the score to play themselves and sometimes substitutes noise for true excitement. He lets his singers shout their way through much of the Nile scene, and the Triumphal scene is frankly boring until Bechi enters and brings it to life.

There is surely nothing even vaguely boring in the conducting recorded during Toscanini's concert performances in 1949.* Toscanini knew the score better than he knew almost any other opera. The only operatic work he had conducted more often than *Aida* was *Falstaff*. *Aida* was the opera that introduced him to the podium in 1886 and one of the last that he conducted. In his case, however, familiarity had bred respect and understanding, not contempt, and at no point in this performance is there reason to question the vitality, the dramatic thrust, and the musical awareness of Toscanini, a man of eighty-two years at the time. He keeps things moving, too fast for the taste of some listeners: At approximately 136 minutes, Toscanini reaches the goal up to ten minutes sooner than some of the other conductors. It is possible, however, to admire the sense of dramatic propulsion pushing forward toward the ultimate tragedy. On the whole, his artists respond well and don't seem to me unduly troubled by the rapid tempos although the singers probably have a harder time of it than the orchestra. The NBC symphony, on the other hand, is with him all the way with some wonderfully soft, *legato* passages for the strings and orchestral climaxes, particularly in the Judgment scene, that are truly cataclysmic. There's surely no danger of dozing off while Toscanini is in command.

---

*The Toscanini *Aida* has been available on video, but of course as a concert performance there was no staging involved.

Through the years, critics have managed to damn his singers with faint praise and to question why Toscanini chose many of them in the first place. Listening to the recording afresh after several years, however, we may well decide that on the whole they're not such a bad lot after all. The only conspicuous weakness in the cast is Eva Gustavson as Amneris; she simply was not ready either vocally or dramatically for one of the most challenging roles of the entire repertoire. Until the final act, she is essentially faceless and her voice suggests little of the emotional roller coaster of the character. She improves somewhat in the Judgment scene, where her tone takes on added power in the higher passages, but earlier, in the Act 2 duet with Aida, there is too little difference between her false sympathy and her flaming anger.

Herva Nelli, however, surely deserves a great deal better than critics have often given her in the past. There are a few first-string Aidas, and she is not one of them, but she's close to the top in the second string. Singing under the demanding Toscanini could not have been easy, and in 1954, before the original 1949 performance was finally issued on long-playing records, he recalled portions of both of Aida's arias and re-recorded them. Even so, in the performance as we have it in its official RCA issue, there remain occasional high notes that are not focused and there is admittedly no *dolce* high C in the Nile scene aria. The voice, however, is often very beautiful with a bright, youthful coloration, and dramatically she stays well within the picture. She is at her most engaging in a seductive "La tra foreste" in Act 3 so that one understands why Radamès so quickly agrees to flee with her. She is clearly offering something more than fragrant flowers and shady forests.

The lower male voices are fully acceptable. Amonasro, Giuseppe Valdengo, has an appealing voice and is always dramatically aware, and the two basses, Norman Scott as Ramfis and Dennis Harbour as the King, are firm and attractive in tone without revealing any particularly sensitivity to the characters or the situations. Harbour particularly sings the King's music about as well as anyone on any of the recordings. The off-stage Priestess is sung by Teresa Stich-Randall, who even at this early stage in her career — she was twenty-one at the time of the recording — demonstrates the vocal presence that would soon propel her into an outstanding international career.

Interest and praise, however, center on Richard Tucker, the young tenor to whom Toscanini entrusted the role of Radamès. The conductor's trust was fully justified, and Tucker provided one of the best recorded performances of Radamès. It would be sixteen years before Tucker would take his Radamès to the stage, by which time he had recorded the role twice, once here with Toscanini and later with Serafin on the podium. In the broadcast and recording studio, however, he was ready for his assignment with a voice attuned well to the more lyrical parts of the role but still capable of encompassing the vocal heroics of the Consecration and Triumphal scenes and the Act 3 surrender to Ramfis. At this stage of his career, he had not yet developed the abrupt consonantal emphases that intruded on some of his later performances. His singing is ardent, lyrical, fully committed, and blessedly youthful in sound. Along with most tenors, he can't manage a *morendo* on the final B-flat of "Celeste Aida," but at Toscanini's insistence he followed instead Verdi's own alternative, the note sung *forte* and then the final words repeated softly an octave below.

With the dawn of the long-playing record in 1950, the recording companies almost stumbled over each other in the attempt to provide new versions of Verdi's Egyptian opera. In a few cases they stumbled rather badly, but the seven commercially issued recordings of *Aida* between 1950 and 1956 contain more than a few performances well worth their continuing place in the catalogs. As of this writing, an enterprising collector can in fact locate all seven of them in contemporary issues.

The first of two issues from Italy's Fonit-Cetra corporation dates from 1951. That year brought a special Verdi emphasis in remembrance of the fiftieth anniversary of the composer's death, and Cetra, along with the Italian radio, set out on a major project to present all of his operas. It was a goal the company was ultimately not quite able to reach, but they earned the gratitude of opera lovers by providing versions of many of the rarely performed early operas, including *Un Giorno di Regno, I Lombardi,* and *La Battaglia di Legnano.* The recordings were made under broadcast studio conditions, which means that there are occasional live performance mishaps but not the distraction of applause or other audience noises. Any extraneous sounds apparently come from the artists themselves as they clear their throats, rattle the music stands, or shift their feet. The performances do not reflect the polish we have come to expect from the studio-made recordings of recent years: Sour notes and moments of less-than-perfect ensemble have not been removed and replaced in the recordings by the editors, and it's probable that there was little rehearsal time, particularly for those operas that were standard repertoire fare. On the other hand, in the Fonit-Cetra operas of the 1950s there is often the feel of the opera house, the sense that we are being allowed to share openly and fully and honestly in the experience itself just as it takes place.

There's no lack of drama in the 1951 Cetra *Aida*. Vittorio Gui, one of the most highly respected Italian conductors of the twentieth century, provides plenty of excitement. Some of the reasons for his fame come through in this recording, namely a sense of forceful propulsion and dramatic intensity. Everything, however, is not entirely shipshape, and there are occasional lapses in ensemble. He commands, or at least permits, the omission of all but approximately two minutes of the Triumphal scene ballet, and a more precise and demanding leader probably would not have countenanced some of the small rhythmic inaccuracies of the singers, but a more precise and demanding leader might well have missed out on some of the musical and dramatic excitement that we find in this performance.

The tenor, Mario Fillipeschi, offers a great deal of uncontrolled power and little else. He blasts away at high notes that are as penetrating and tight as a drum head stretched to the breaking point. In the quieter moments at lower altitudes, an engaging touch of warmth sometimes comes into play, but it is too often spoiled by a touch of lachrymose self-pity that is hardly compatible with a truly heroic Radamès. As Amonasro, Rolando Panerai has a basically attractive voice, but in moments of stress and strain (and those are the majority of Amonasro's moments), he will sometimes lose vocal focus. His gifts, which were many, were better employed in somewhat less strenuous baritone repertoire.

Ramfis in this recording, as in the later Fonit-Cetra version, is Giulio Neri. He commands respect with his uncommonly strong, basically uninflected voice. From the beginning of the opera, this is clearly a man of adamantine voice and character, not one who would waver under pressure. It's impossible to imagine that he would bend even a fraction of an inch under Amneris' challenges in the Judgment scene. Neri's voice is arrow straight as befits the character, but the absence of a warming vibrato makes it particularly obvious when at rare points he is not entirely in tune. Neri's may be the right voice for Ramfis, but unfortunately he isn't much fun to listen to. Antonio Massaria is considerably easier on the ears, but he is clearly a King who must bend to the power of the ancient priesthood.

On the whole, the women in the cast fare better. The young Giulietta Simionato brings more vocal glamour to Amneris than almost any other mezzo-soprano. The voice is secure from top to bottom. The chest tones boom out without growling, the middle voice is warm and full, and the high notes all the way through the B-flat are fiery and dead-on true. We appreciate particularly the way she actually finishes phrases with no hint of a parting gasp. In the second act duet with Aida, she communicates the apparently spontaneous changes in Amneris' emotions, her Judgment scene is deeply felt, and the "pace's" that conclude the opera are quiet, gentle, and moving. Her fury has been lost in the tragic grief that she is experiencing.

Aida is sung by an Italian soprano known to Westerners primarily through her recordings. Caterina Mancini is an appreciable artist with a strikingly beautiful soprano voice. There's nothing cautious either in her dramatic approach or in her employment of the voice, and as a result there are a few squally high notes and moments when the vocal line is thrown off track. She caps "O patria mia" with an inappropriately loud but entirely solid high C, but then she follows it with two beautifully placed high A's and a pure, floated high B-flat at the end of "Lá tra forreste vergini." We would like to hear more of the same in the final scene of the opera, but here she is forced to fight a losing battle with Filippeschi. Fifty years later, a soprano of her dramatic and vocal gifts would quickly have become an artist of outstanding international stature.

The next year brought three new commercially issued complete recordings, and a strikingly varied lot they are. Capitol Records 1952 entry in the *Aida* sweepstakes hardly made it past the starting line. It remains a mystery why this — and the similarly cast *Trovatore* from the same year — were actually issued for sale. Not only was the performance distressingly bad, the quality of the recorded sound was also grating and unpleasant.

Of special interest was the performance of Stella Roman as Aida. In 1950, after ten seasons at the Metropolitan Opera, the Romanian soprano had fallen victim to the house cleaning of Rudolf Bing's first season as general manager. Aida had been her debut role at the Met on January 1, 1941. On March 22 of that year, she sang for the Saturday afternoon broadcast of the opera. That performance was recorded, unofficially of course, and reveals a sizeable soprano voice governed by a generous dramatic temperament. She could produce thrilling high notes to crown the big *Aida* climaxes and still manage gently floated *pianos,* and no one could question the excitement that her performances elicited. Even in 1941, however, there were difficulties with control, with pitch, and with the failure to sing a clean Verdian line. Over the years, the problems apparently became greater, and by the 1952 recording success or failure alternated distractingly from one note to the next. Too often she swoops up to the high notes and then misses aim, and in rapid passages, she is unable to sing the notes accurately and enunciate the text clearly. She is at her best in the Nile scene duet with Radamès, but even here we hear only the remnants of what at one time was an imposing instrument.

Responsibility for the failure of this recording, however, does not fall solely on Roman. The conductor, Alberto Paoletti, adopts some strange tempis with unusual *retards* and *accelarandos* and adds lengthy pauses between the movements in the score. (Or were the pauses perhaps results of lazy, incompetent editors manipulating the tapes?) Most of the other cast members have occasional difficulties maintaining a firmly centered pitch. Ramfis, Vittorio Tatozzi, is heavy, mushy, and unsteady and Antonio Manca Serra is a strangely underpowered Amonesro. Franco Puglese offers a King of imposing vocal presence but with almost no inflection. Then there's Sylvia Sawyer, whose Amneris is the greatest of several disasters in this *Aida*. Her voice is unpleasant in the extreme, her diction hints at a too recently acquired knowledge of Italian, and her vocal face almost never changes with the situation.

That leaves Gino Sarri, the tenor. His Radamès is the best the Capitol version of the opera has to offer. His bright-toned voice is generally, but not inevitably, secure, but there are some indications particularly in the earlier acts that the role is a real stretch for him. Later there seems to be ample power for the Act 3 encounters. He tries hard to animate the big duet with Amneris in Act 4, a virtually impossible task with his stolid partner, and is similarly but fruitlessly attentive in the closing scene with Aida. It's interesting to note that he was something of a Verdi specialist in-so-far as recordings are concerned: His commercial recordings include a complete *Otello*, *Trovatore*, and *Rigoletto* and another set of excerpts from *Aida*. In none of them did he disgrace himself, but it takes more than a merely acceptable Radamès to save *Aida*.

"Acceptable" is not an unlikely word to use about the tenor in the 1952* Remington *Aida*, provided we preface it with "barely." Umberto Borsò honors Radamès with an occasional heroic ring, but otherwise his singing and vocal acting tend to be rough. Attempts to sing softly often lead to insecurity, and there's little enough of charm or sweetness in his voice outside of an honest attempt in the final scene. His wide-open Italian vowels on *i* and *e* tend to grate on the ear and wear out their welcome in a hurry.

Otherwise, however, the cast of the Remington *Aida* offers its share of qualified pleasure and in one case considerably more than that. To begin with, they are working with Franco Capuana, a conductor who clearly knows the opera, and an orchestra that plays well for him. He brings a conspicuously knowing hand to the structure of the Triumphal scene, which conductors often have difficulty pulling together into a unity. Particularly effective are the quiet entrance of the Ethiopian prisoners and the restrained development of the "Ma tu Re" ensemble.

His Aida is the American soprano, Maria Curtis Verna, who would record a second studio version of the opera in 1956. The voice is capable of some gentleness as we hear in the nicely floated high A at the end of the Act 3 aria. Unfortunately, it follows too soon after an uncomfortable high C. In general, she is at her weakest in Act 3, precisely where an Aida needs to be at her best, but "La tra foreste vergini" is poised and the final scene is engagingly voiced. Her performance would certainly give pleasure on a regular night at the opera, but there is nothing particularly distinctive about her Aida.

Both of the basses, Norman Scott and Uberto Scaglioni, sing and interpret sensitively, and Amneris, Oralia Dominguez, is impressive. Her voice is a true contralto with little evidence of register breaks — and this is a role that runs the gamut from top to bottom. The sound engineers have done her no favors, and sometimes her voice as presented here has a rather harsh, penetrating quality to it. We can tell from other recordings that she made, however, that there was more natural allure in the sound than we encounter here. In fact, all of the singers in this version of the opera often sound as if they're standing next to us and singing right in our ears. The trio in the first scene comes through mainly as an extended three-way shouting match, and there is almost no attempt to maintain the natural audio perspective of an audience in the opera house. Off-stage choruses of the priestesses in Act

---

*According to the liner notes in the recent Preiser reissue, the correct recording date should be 1952 even though apparently the actual release date was 1955.

1, Scene 2 and the crowd gathered for the victory parade in Act 2, Scene 2 are very much in the room with us.

The glory of this performance is Amonasro. Ettore Bastianini went on to a distinguished recording career before his early death, but here, close to the beginning of his career in the baritone range — he had started as a bass — he is at his best. The voice was in and of itself a superbly beautiful instrument, and in this performance he sings everything, a point of important emphasis since many baritones manage to shout and growl their way through the role. He makes his address to the King in the Triumphal scene a highlight of the entire recording, and it's difficult to imagine a more moving "Pensa che un popolo" in Act 3 than Bastianini's. Critics often complained of later performances that he was so intent on displaying his glorious voice that he forgot to sing artistically and act effectively. In this *Aida,* his only commercial recording of the role, however, he manages both admirably.

The Remington *Aida* was almost the forgotten recording before 2003, when the Preiser company resuscitated it in their "Paperback Opera" series. Other operas from the same company are beginning to resurface, and although none of them ranks high among the versions of the works performed, each one has one or more individual performances to cherish.

The third 1952 *Aida* was a product of the Decca/London company, and far from being forgotten, it has been in and out of the catalogs over and over again in the years since it was introduced. The first thing that strikes the listener is the vast improvement in the recorded sound: *Pianos* touch the ear gently and *fortes* rattle the rafters, all without distortion. The singers are closer to us than they would be in the opera house, but their voices ring clear and true. *Aida* is certainly an opera that benefits from the improved sonic quality.

Critical opinions tend to be repeated over the years until they finally solidify into unalterable concrete, and this version of the opera has been accorded relatively begrudging and hesitant approval. Coming back to it with a fresh ear, however, suggests to me that it may be time for a somewhat more favorable reevaluation. Alberto Erede was not one of the superstar conductors of the 1950s, but his leadership in this recording is entirely respectable if not precisely brilliant. In fact, many listeners may prefer a conductor who doesn't go too far in imposing a "personal" approach on Verdi's opera and who appreciates that the singers, not the orchestra or their leader, are the primary focus. To his credit, Erede shapes the orchestral score for and with his singers, and they respond effectively.

The usual complaint about Mario del Monaco is that he is too loud and too forceful too much of the time. Well, he is loud, a real *tenore di forza,* but at this relatively early stage in his recording career he also turns out to be more sensitive than we might have expected. There is a suggestion of gentleness in his final scene and at least a bit of affection comes through in "Celeste Aida." A little bit of good

Italian *portamento* would have helped soften the line of the aria, and of course he ends it with a loud B-flat. But what a resounding B-flat it is!

The lower male singers make little impression in this recording. Aldo Protti is here a run-of-the-mill, nondescript Amonasro with no glaring problems but few distinctive virtues. Both of the basses, Dario Caselli and Fernando Corena, have appealing voices but are subject to occasional attacks of unsteadiness.

Critics have also regularly lamented that Ebe Stignani, Amneris, as she was in the 1946 HMV version, has lost some of the vocal glory. Yes, six years had made a difference, but the loss is observable only in comparison with the earlier version and not in comparison with other mezzo-sopranos of the period. Her voice is better recorded here than in 1946, and it remains a tremendously exciting sound. As for interpretation, she still manages to differentiate vocally the changeable moods of the Egyptian princess.

The color and linear directness of Stignani's voice contrast effectively with the glowing, rounder tone of Renata Tebaldi as Aida. She was thirty years old at the time of this recording, and her voice was still in the fresh bloom of youth. There were a few problems on high notes, including the unpleasant, slightly off-note high C in "O patria mia." Otherwise, hers is the ideal Aida voice. She can ride powerfully over the ensembles in the Triumphal scene and provide a beautifully subdued "Numi, pietà" in the first act aria. Tebaldi's *piano* is a wonder — caressing and soft but not thin of tone. She is effective dramatically, but hardly as detailed and specific in penetrating Aida's psyche as the heroine in the 1955 EMI recording of the opera.

That, of course, was Maria Callas. She was joined in the EMI/Angel recording by a top-of-the-line cast. Richard Tucker was back for his second outing as Radamès. Amneris was sung by Fedora Barbieri in her first commercial recording of the role, and Amonasro was Tito Gobbi, all of them singing under the baton of the experienced *Aida* conductor Tullio Serafin, whose leadership had improved appreciably over the years since his first recording of the opera. He led the La Scala orchestra and chorus in a performance at its best in moments of personal reflection and emotional conflict. Serafin was a master of conducting sympathetic to the needs and abilities of individual singers. He brings out their best, particularly with Callas and Gobbi.

Nicola Zaccaria as the King and Giuseppe Modesti as Ramfis do not always suggest the authority appropriate to a ruler and a high priest, but they sing sensitively. Until the Judgment scene, Modesti seems too much the loving pastor of a faithful flock, but he becomes the stern, unmovable arbiter of justice in Act 3.

Tucker's voice retains the dramatic ring encountered in the Toscanini broadcast, and he is particularly strong and effective in his surrender to Ramfis in Act 3, one of the test moments for a tenor in this role. At the conclusion of "Celeste Aida" he sings an uncommonly forceful B-flat and fails to follow it with the softer phrase an octave below as he had in the Toscanini version. Whatever else we might say about the loud top note in his performance, Del Monaco's, or anyone else's, it fails to suggest the tender emotion Radamès feels for Aida. At other moments, however, his voice is softer and more inherently beautiful than in the earlier recordings, particularly in the final scene of the opera, and his is a first-class voice used with dramatic sensitivity.

Barbieri's Amneris is effectively shaded from gentle *pianos* to penetrating *fortes*. Hers was a classic Italian mezzo-soprano voice at the call of an equally classic Italian temperament. There is nothing subtle about her totally committed interpretation, but by the same token the listener is never in doubt about where this Amneris stands. The voice itself fills the roll fully and responds well not only at all dynamic levels but from top to bottom of the range. Although she might have denied it, she does indeed use the chest voice from time to time for emphasis, but she employs it rarely and never carries it too high in her range.

Gobbi is the most imaginative Amonasro on any of the recordings, with the keenest possible awareness of the text. Everything he sings is filled with conviction, and the tone always suggests the meaning behind the words. His is not a conventionally appealing voice. For that we may look back to Inghilleri and Bastianini and forward to Leonard Warren. The sound is indeed more interesting than beautiful. The phrasing and the *legato,* however, are so carefully considered that even the most lyrical of passages — "Pensa che un popolo," for example — possess a special beauty of their own. As Amonasro, he is the ideal partner for his equally sensitive Aida.

There isn't much that we can add to the positive praise and the negative criticism that are regularly expressed about Maria Callas. Aida was not one of the roles with which she was most frequently identified in the later years of her career. Through 1953, however, she sang the part successfully thirty-three times in a number of different venues, and she has clearly considered closely every note, every word, every phrase, and every situation. Dramatically, she is the most specific of Aidas, and musically she is also one of the most faithful in her attempt to respect Verdi's instructions. There's at least a hint of wobble on some of the sustained high notes, and the high C and the descent therefrom at the conclusion of "O patria mia" miss perfection by a mile. On the other hand, sometimes the high notes are secure and ringing, a sterling G, for example, for *giammai* when she refuses her father's request that she lead Radamès to divulge the Egyptian military strategy. Hers is not the ideal Aida voice (Whose is?), but it's difficult to imagine a fuller, more detailed, more dramatic portrayal of the role.

The duet of Amonasro and Aida in Act 3 deserves a special word of praise. It is the highlight of this performance — two supreme artists working against and with each other in the service of music drama. If the ideal *Aida* could be put together from the various recordings, this performance of the duet would win its place hands down. Verdi himself would surely have led the shouts of approval—but only, of course, at the end of the act so that nothing would break the dramatic and musical spell.

Had he been there to hear it, Verdi would no doubt have been equally pleased with the final scene in the 1955 RCA recording. This, too, is one of those moments that would fit comfortably in our hypothetical ideal *Aida*. The singers are Jussi Bjoerling and Zinka Milanov, and the control of the long-breathed line and the technical ability combined with the sensitivity to sing softly contribute to one of the classics of recorded sound. However, it is only one scene in what is among the best-sung performances of *Aida* ever committed to disc, and one that proves—just in case there are any doubters—that beautiful, polished vocalism does not preclude dramatic effectiveness.

Jonel Perlea is the conductor, and he provides a traditional performance with no eccentric tempis or distractingly strange accents. The Triumphal scene ballet is particularly well paced, but otherwise nothing in his conducting calls attention to itself. He is very much aware of his singers and lets them take their time to expand in their big moments, a particular boon probably to Milanov, who could sound uncomfortable if the pace was too much of a push. In any case, it isn't for the conducting that listeners return to this version of the opera. It is rather the highly polished quality of the singing that keeps this *Aida* high on the list of outstanding recordings.

Bjoerling is the surprise factor here. Theoretically, his *spinto* tenor was not the right voice for Radamès, but the performance itself throws the theory into question. He may have had a little assistance from the engineers, but if so there is no suggestion of it in the sound of the recording itself. The climaxes are well taken, and what he may have lacked in volume, he made up for with the radiant glow of his voice. Of course, in the quieter, more intimate portions of the score, he has everything going for him. Many tenors run into trouble with the phrase endings in "Celeste Aida," but not Bjoerling. He rises to each one with just the right amount of *portamento* and then ends it with no sense of abruptness. He doesn't deliver the requested *morendo* on the final B-flat, but the note is not shouted and it is touched with affection.

Milanov was not always the most even of singers. On stage, she could deliver some awkward high notes and some rather squally sounds as she rose to them, and things could become hectic when the tempo increased. The faults, however, are at a minimum in this recording. There is tremendous excitement in the way she can expand a note at the top of her range just when we believe she's given it all she has to give, and, of course, the *piano* notes truly are sublime. In "O patria mia" after a beautifully taken, not quite *piano* high C, she ends the aria with a phrase that lodges in the memory as something close to vocal perfection. She is adequately dramatic — not in the penetrating sense of Callas, but with a conspicuous awareness that a real character is involved in serious conflicts. What a rich time the early 1950s were with three great Aidas to choose among — Tebaldi, Callas, and Milanov.

This *Aida* was cast in depth. Barbieri is similar to her EMI/Angel recording, but her rich, vibrant tone is particularly well recorded by RCA and her performance as a whole is perhaps more vocally suave. Where mezzo-soprano power is needed, she has it to spare. When, in the Act 2 duet, she announces to Aida that "Radamès vive ... Radamès lives," we hear her overwhelming sense of triumph over her slave, and in this case Aida's rapturous response brings us one of Milanov's most impressive top A's.

Amonasro is Leonard Warren. His voice is beautiful, even in moments of anger and frustration, and he sings the notes without hedging for dramatic effect. When the recording was new, some critics complained that he didn't have the sense of fierce bravura that the role seemed to them to demand, but that was almost the same as saying that he sang too well. After all, Amonasro *is* a king in his own right, and he should be permitted to lose his temper without losing his dignity. His isn't the only way to sing the role, but it's certainly a good way.

Plinio Clabassi as the King of Egypt has a voice of ample weight and appealing tone, just the right singer to contrast with Boris Christoff's impressive Ramfis. With his strong Slavic-tinged, Boris Godunov voice, Christoff is clearly not your typical Italian basso, but he brings the strong-willed, demanding high priest fully to life. Clearly, anyone would oppose him at great personal risk.

The last of the commercially issued long-playing monophonic recordings of *Aida* appeared in 1956 on the Cetra label, at the dawn of the stereo era. Unfortunately, it takes us from the heights if not down to the depths, at least to a considerably lower plane. The conductor, Angelo Questa, leads a performance that is competent, but *Aida* calls out for stronger guidance than Questa provides. There are occasional awkward pauses and unaccountable tempo changes and at least one almost grotesque *retard* in the Triumphal scene ensemble before Radamès asks freedom for the Ethiopian prisoners. The ballet in this scene is reduced to thirty-nine seconds, less even than the truncated version in the earlier Cetra version! The segue from the preceding chorus is awkward enough to suggest that a fuller portion was included on the original tape and omitted when the recordings were actually issued.*

Giulio Neri repeats his Ramfis from the earlier Cetra recording. He remains a strong, darkly threatening high priest with only a slight reduction in the quality

---

*The recording used for review is Fonit-Cetra CDO 29, apparently issued in 1994. The omission, however, is documented for the 1956 issue in Marc Taylor Faw, *A Verdi Discography* (Norman, Oklahoma: Pilgrim Books, 1982), p. 10.

of his voice. Antonio Zerbini is a weak, relatively inexpressive King. Gian Giacomo Guelfi is an explosive Amonasro, a not-unlikely approach to the character, but he misses out on any sense of royal dignity — and once in a while on the notes as Verdi actually composed them as well.

There is much more in Amneris than Miriam Pirazzini discovered. Her darkly colored voice is essentially pleasing but not always completely steady. Primarily what she lacks is a sense of variety in expression, and the result, as is often the case in this recording, is competent but more or less ordinary.

Curtis Verna's voice has aged somewhat since the 1952 Remington recording, but she can still produce a sweet-sounding Aida most of the time. "O patria mia" shows her at her best, with a poised, if not particularly ingratiating, high C. Otherwise there are some blustery passages, a few unwieldy top notes, and brief patches of suspect pitch. We might well be happy to encounter her Aida in the opera house, but on a recording, the competition level is too high for her comfort.

When it comes to Franco Corelli's Radamès, however, we know we are hearing a significant voice used with strong verbal and dramatic strength. His is far from a spit-and-polish performance. To be certain, there are crudities, some of which the next few years of experience would refine, and he sounds then, as he often did later, as if he's forcing the words out through a mouth full of peanut butter and jelly. The color is baritonal, but, of course, there is no diminution in the high notes, which can often expand in overwhelming starbursts of sound. The B-flat at the end of "Celeste Aida" is loud but exciting. The regret, however, is that Corelli's technique would probably have enabled him to sing it softly and produce the *morendo* that Verdi wanted. When he chooses, he can soften the tone effectively, as he does at points in the Nile scene duet and in the final scene. We will encounter his Radamès in better company twelve years later, by which time some of the polish absent in 1956 had been applied.

A recording that had limited circulation and was perhaps never officially issued in complete form in the United States appeared on the Guilde Internationale du Disque label in 1958. A single disc of highlights was at one time available on the Perfect label, a budget subsidiary of the then-active Epic company, and it's on that long-playing record that these comments are based. It was probably the first officially produced stereo version of *Aida,* but it doesn't do a great deal to recommend the music recording technique. The sound is overly resonant and in common with much of the early stereo, distractingly directional.

What we hear in the highlights is a good run-of-the-mill *Aida,* the kind that might have been heard in an Italian opera house on a regular nongala evening. Collectors will probably recognize most of the names in the cast. They sang a great deal in the 1950s and 1960s, and some of their performances made their way onto recordings. Ernesto Barbini, the conductor, keeps things moving and knows how to build toward an exciting climax. Unfortunately, the Rome Opera Chorus and Orchestra are not as well disciplined as they are in some other recordings, and even in these truncated excerpts there are a few lapses in ensemble.

Aida is Anna de Cavalieri (a.k.a. Anne McKnight). Her "Ritorna vincitor" has a few hectic spots, but it is fully dramatized and the voice has a sweet sound to it here, in the last portion of "O patria mia" (all that is included on the highlights disc), and in the final duet. It's difficult to tell from the recording, but it probably was not a large voice. Aldo Bertocci, her beloved Radamès, phrases particularly well in his first-act aria, his duet with Amneris, and the death scene. His voice has a good ring to it except on the highest notes when he must strain to make it to the top.

Ira Malaniuk is tremulous of voice in her duet with Aida in the first scene of Act 2, less so when she sings with Bertocci in "Gia I sacerdotal adunansi," which has the last phrase of the Judgment scene grafted on at the end. The B-flats in the duet are not easy for her, but she caps her curse on the Egyptian priests with an exciting, firmly voiced A. As Amonasro, Scipio Colombo is anything other than subtle, but his voice has a good, solid sound to it and he makes his points dramatically with the best of them.

Like the 1956 Cetra version, the performance is far from polished, but it's fun to listen to, with plenty of vitality and excitement. There's surely enough here to make us wish that the entire opera were available in a convenient recording format.

Aida is the kind of opera that brings out the best — or in some cases perhaps the worst — in the sonic engineers who push the buttons and turn the dials on the recording devices. Obviously, Verdi's opera was just waiting for top-drawer stereo sound to bring ancient Egypt to sparkling, new life, and the 1958 attempt clearly didn't fulfill that promise. The Decca/London company, however, took their largely Italian cast to Vienna for a new recording under the distinguished conductor Herbert von Karajan, and this time there was no lack of polish or refinement in either the performance or the spectacular stereo sound.

The Vienna Philharmonic is second to none, not even Toscanini's NBC Symphony, and von Karajan draws from his players every possible subtlety he can find in the score and every conceivable gradation of dynamics. The soft passages shimmer and the *forti* shatter. What's more, it's all captured in Decca/London's overwhelming sound so that the result is truly a sonic spectacular. Listener beware: You may adjust the quiet opening bars of the Prelude to a barely audible volume level, but the orchestral climaxes in the first scene will still come as an overwhelming shock to the ears, and the Triumphal scene is still to come!

Is it just a bit too much? Some critics have thought so and have complained that on occasion the singers are almost lost in the sonic boom. It happens in this recording, but not too often, at least not in the digital remastering that is now offered on compact disc. Most of the singers on this recording can hold their own fairly well against the combined forces of the Vienna Philharmonic, Herbert von Karajan, and John Culshaw's sound recording crew.

The conducting itself has also been subjected to negative comment, primarily as a result of von Karajan's lingering tempos. He truly does take his time, and this version of *Aida,* for example, plays fourteen minutes longer than Toscanini's. At a few points, the slow tempos tend to rob the score of momentum, especially when the *andante sostenuto* of "Gia I sacerdotal a dunansi" in the first scene of Act 4 comes close to a genuine *adagio.* Von Karajan, however, not only has a cast able to project effectively over an orchestral *tutti,* he also has singers who can stay afloat through a long sustained line, as Giulietta Simionato and Carlo Bergonzi do in this duet. This is an outstanding recording and clearly deserves a place in the *Aida* honor roll.

The cast is as good as any and better than most that might have been assembled in 1958. Bergonzi was the king of Verdi tenors of that era, and he shows how he earned that title in this recording. He phrases eloquently with never a gulp at the end. His voice, although certainly not as impressive an instrument as those of Del Monaco or Corelli, is their superior in control and fully adequate to the heroic task at hand. He pays attention to Verdi's dynamic markings and caresses the appropriate phrases engagingly, particularly in the final scene. He also has that all too rare gift of singing *with* his partners rather than *against* them, a skill that he demonstrates effectively in the Nile scene duet and the two scenes of the final act. He doesn't give us a soft B-flat at the end of "Celeste Aida," which is particularly disappointing because, like Corelli, he could have done it — and in fact did on other recordings.

Renata Tebaldi's voice was not quite as fresh and youthful in 1959 as it was in 1952, but it was still probably the most beautiful soprano among all of the possible Aidas. There are a few uncomfortable top notes, a problem she would have increasingly in the years ahead, and the final A in "O patria mia" is just short enough of the pitch to be disturbing and should have been replaced with one right on the mark. Her creamy voice, however, is precisely right for the role, and she gives a performance full of open-hearted commitment.

Her father in this recording is Cornell MacNeil, a sadly under-recorded baritone who, at least at this stage of his career, had vocal gifts second to none. He isn't the fiercest Amonasro when he berates poor Aida, but for many listeners the restraint will be welcome. He sings one of the most beautiful versions of "Pensa che un popolo" on any of the recordings.

Simionato repeats her outstanding Amneris, first heard in 1952. She is secure enough in her voice and technique to communicate the complexities of Amneris' character without chewing up the scenery. She never shouts. She sings, and the truth of the role is in the voice. There were few enough rough edges in her earlier recording, but there are certainly none at all here. The chest voice, when she uses it, has force and focus, and the top notes soar just as if she were a soprano.

Fernando Corena, once more as the King, performs with very much the same results as in 1952. We would hardly suspect that there was a Don Pasquale or Dr. Bartolo hidden beneath his crown. As Ramfis, Arnold van Mill uses his beautiful voice like a *bel canto* specialist to produce an almost paternal high priest, just the opposite of Giulio Neri in the earlier recordings. I'm not certain Verdi would have approved, but it certainly does sound good to the ear.

Three years later, the first RCA (later issued on Decca/London) stereo recording of *Aida* appeared, in its own way the equal of the 1959 London version and perhaps even its superior. Georg Solti conducted Rome Opera forces and a basically North American cast in which Amneris was Belgian and only the King, the Messenger, and the Priestess were Italian. Solti is surely as much in control as von Karajan was but somewhat less intent on demonstrating his ability to highlight the quality of the orchestra. After all, the Rome Opera Orchestra is not quite the same thing as the Vienna Philharmonic. On the other hand, they acquit themselves well in this recording and surely have nothing for which to apologize. Solti is judicious in the choice of tempos. He tends to be slower, particularly in the first three scenes, but he can generate plenty of heat when it's needed. A good measure of his artistry and skill is the way he holds together and binds into a convincing unity the various contrasting elements of the Triumphal scene.

The Canadian Jon Vickers is an impressive Radamès both for the heroic quality of his voice and for his ability to modulate it to suit the demands of the score. He won't be to the taste of some listeners, primarily because he is the least Italian sounding of any of the reputable tenors on any of the recordings and he does not wrap his tone in comfortable Mediterranean warmth. For all that, however, he sings extremely well and interprets with great sensitivity. His "Celeste Aida" is one of the best with a beautiful conclusion, his soft singing in the Nile scene is ingratiating, and like the heldentenor he would soon become, he meets every challenging climax with enough power to spare. We may be glad that every Radamès doesn't sing the role quite the way he does, but we wouldn't want to be without his performance.

Robert Merrill as Amonasro is as warm and beautiful if not quite as prodigious of voice as his great predecessors — Bastianini, Warren, and MacNeil. He has been criticized by some for a lack of dramatic thrust and imagination, but he makes his points effectively, and on those occasions when Amonasro has a smooth Verdian line to sing, he surely rises to the occasion. We can be grateful for Giorgio Tozzi, an American basso in spite of his name, for a well-sung Ramfis. He manages to sound both soothing—witness his words to Amneris at the beginning of Act 3—and appropriately forbidding. Plinio Clabassi repeats his effective King from the earlier RCA recording.

Rita Gorr as Amneris, like Vickers, won't please every listener. She, too, doesn't sound like an Italian mezzo-soprano. There's none of that bright, cutting edge that Barbieri, Stignani, and occasionally even Simionato could exploit so effectively. What she does have is a vivid dramatic imagination and a strong, dark voice touched with perhaps a bit more vibrato than we'd prefer. She sounds more like a genuine contralto with a good top extension than like a typical mezzo-soprano, and that means that she has an even scale from top to bottom with almost no indication of a register break. Her interpretation suggests dignity aligned with a keen sense of royal power, but she also inspires considerably more sympathy than many of her colleagues in this role. Her laments that punctuate the opening chorus of Act 2 win our hearts almost as much as Aida's do.

Aida is Leontyne Price in the first of her two commercial recordings of the role. Her voice is in prime early condition, which means that aside from a few raw, hoarse-sounding lower tones, she can produce a beautiful, evenly produced, warmly colored tone at every dynamic level all the way up to the magnificent high C in the Nile scene aria. Aida, more than any other, was her signature role for opera houses all around the globe. Her approach certainly changed and matured through the years of her active career, and in some later performances, her singing sounded almost too studied and staid, much the way she actually appeared on stage. Here relatively early in her career, she brings understanding to the character and a remarkable ability to relate to those with whom she sings. The character of Aida is most fully revealed in a series of four great duets. She has, of course, two major arias, but beyond that, we come to know Aida primarily through Verdi's musical picture of her as she relates first to Amneris, then to Amonasro and Radamès. It is Price's ability to respond and react musically to her colleagues that produces the true highlights of this recording—a stunning Nile scene and the final duet, where she and Vickers sing with wonderful gentleness and delicacy.

In 1968, EMI added to the mix their first stereo recording of *Aida*—inevitably, we might have said, since they certainly didn't intend to let Decca/London and RCA corner the market on this most popular of operas. Like RCA, they went to the Rome Opera for their orchestra and chorus. They also followed the Decca/London and RCA example and employed a superstar conductor, in this case Zubin Mehta. Unfortunately, the resulting version, unlike the two immediate predecessors, doesn't exactly win a place among the top five or so of modern *Aida* recordings, but it has its rewards.

Mehta's conducting isn't always much of a help. He seems to be in something of a hurry. It's not so much a matter of the overall duration of the performance as it is of speedy tempis at crucial points. There are sometimes awkwardly abrupt changes of pace, particularly noticeable in the duet of Amneris and Aida in Act 2. There are also points at which the musical action seems to lose a sense of forward direction and structural unity, at the opening of the Triumphal scene, for example, where the different musical movements emerge almost like isolated, unconnected elements. Once past the rather lackadaisical opening, however, the Nile scene generates considerable excitement.

On the whole, the cast is strong. Bonaldo Gaiotti sings a firm, neatly vocalized Ramfis with ample dramatic projection. Ferruccio Mazzoli has a lighter voice that contrasts effectively with Gaiotti, but he manages to communicate authority in spite of touches of insecurity at the higher pitches. The prince of Italian comprimarios, Piero de Palma, deserves a special commendation for the sense of urgency and excitement that he brings to the brief role of the Messenger in Act 1, Scene 1.

Mario Sereni, as Amonasro, sometimes forces his basically attractive voice. He is, after all, singing with an Aida and Radamès who could easily drown him out without taking an extra breath. His is a somewhat roughshod Ethiopian King, but he brings plenty of passion to his role, particularly in the Nile scene.

It's difficult to judge Grace Bumbry in her first recorded Amneris, a role that she repeated in two further official commercial issues of the opera. In the first scenes, she sounds over parted, almost like a light lyric soprano, although at thirty-one years of age, she was already an experienced Amneris. Later the voice takes on a greater depth and she sings a powerful Judgment scene. The duet with Radamès offers special promise of things to come not only in *Aida,* but also in the other major mezzo-soprano roles. What is also obvious, however, is that she is a mezzo with decided soprano inclinations, and when she climbs to the heights she sounds surprisingly like her soprano colleague.

That colleague was Birgit Nilsson. Casting a great Brünnhilde and Isolde as Aida was a controversial decision but not an unlikely one since it was a role she sang on stage. There are times when she sounds rather like a Nordic Viking who took a wrong turn and ended up on the Nile rather than the Rhine. Like Vickers in the RCA recording, she simply does not sound Italian. She has a kind of absolute vocal security that almost never plays around with a note. The sound is not exactly cold, but it isn't rounded or shaped the way Tebaldi or Price or even their poor imitations would do. There is certainly nothing tentative about her performance, and within her basic vocal type, there is nothing she can't do with her voice — except, that is, for a soft high C for "O patria mia." There are, however, *pianos* aplenty at other points, and to hear her voice soar over the ensembles in the Triumphal scene is a glorious experience. Her "Nile" scene duet with Amonasro sizzles with excitement. Nilsson isn't precisely what most of us want to hear as Aida, but there's quite enough here to capture the attention and keep us listening.

Franco Corelli's second commercially recorded Radamès is somewhat more vocally and dramatically polished than his first, and the voice is in top condition. He tends to over emphasize words and syllables, and he can spread the emotion rather too thickly on occasion, but he's the kind of Radamès that Nilsson's Aida needs. There's not a great deal of gentleness in his "Celeste Aida" until — wonder of wonders — the last note. He attacks it loudly and then produces a beautifully modulated *morendo*. His voice is clearly functioning under uncommon technical control. Apparently, he liked the effect enough to repeat it on other occasions in the opera. It's all a bit "showy," but when Nilsson joins and equals him on their very last phrase in the final scene, we are inclined with good reason to forgive them.

In the years since its introduction to the public, RCA's 1970 recording of *Aida* has met with little enthusiasm. It's easy to imagine that once contractual agreements had transferred the Solti version to the Decca/London label, the authorities at RCA felt that they were honor bound to replace it with a new stereo recording of the opera, and it certainly didn't hurt that it could be marketed in honor of the centennial of the Cairo premiere of *Aida* in 1871. Unfortunately, the result was somewhat less than celebratory, although surely not quite as bad as some of the critics have suggested.

The conductor was Erich Leinsdorf, and he maintains high standards of execution for his musicians, soloists, orchestra, and chorus alike. In addition to some erratic tempo changes, a complaint that figured prominently in the contemporary criticism, the overall effect is rather businesslike. Even the Nile scene, which surely ought to produce a full measure of excitement, seems rather tame compared to many other recordings, and that in spite of a highly accomplished and gifted cast.

It is often commented that Leontyne Price has lost something of her earlier vocal freshness, but what remains is still one of the great Aida voices of the twentieth century. Some of the lower notes are rough going for her, particularly in the more rapid passages, and she is clearly not comfortable when the vocal line stays for an extended time at the bottom of her range as it does at more than one point in the Nile scene. The top of the voice, however, is in superb condition, and she can let it bloom safely and effectively at top volume and also hone it down to a beautiful *piano*. "O patria mia" is, if anything, more poised and polished than it was in the earlier recording with a *dolce* high C that must be the despair of other sopranos. Although Leinsdorf takes the *romanza* at a markedly slow tempo, it doesn't trouble Price in the least, and the result is virtually a lesson in the art of Verdian *bel canto*.

Therein, however, is a problem that drains some of the life from this version of *Aida* as a whole. It no doubt seems churlish to suggest that there may be too much excellent vocalism in a performance, but in this case almost everyone seems so intent on producing beautiful, rounded sounds that at some crucial points the drama suffers. Hans Sotin as the King and Ruggero Raimondi as Ramfis both have beautiful voices, although Raimondi's baritonal bass tends to fade out at the bottom of his range, but neither seems to have much to communicate about the characters they represent. In the Triumphal scene, Sherrill Milnes brings all the beauty of his gleaming baritone to "Quest'assisa ch'io vesto vi dica" and "Ma tu, Re," but there is hardly a hint of Amonasro's duplicity or his cautiously suppressed anger. On the other hand, he manages to make more of his dramatic opportunity in the Act 3 duet with Aida, although even here Leinsdorf keeps the emotional reins under rather tight control.

Grace Bumbry repeats her Amneris from the earlier EMI version, and she also brings to her role a beautiful vocal instrument, darker in color now than in 1968. She develops the character from the beginning more fully than in the earlier recording so that we don't feel that she's holding back until the Judgment scene. When she returns to the role in the 1976 Levon version, taken from live performance, both the vocalism and the drama will be considerably less restrained.

Plácido Domingo is a youthful Radamès, and in the Nile scene duet he sounds younger than Price, which indeed may be entirely appropriate for the character. He was twenty-nine at the time of the recording, and his voice has a fresh, healthy glow and spin to it. There is adequate power, but also an appealing lyricism and the ability to sing softly at the right times, for example with Price in the final scene. In the years ahead, he will take his Radamès into the recording studio three more times and sing in at least one commercially issued live performance, and his interpretation will grow, but he is well on his way here. The sense of surprise and then disappointment when he realizes that he has revealed Egypt's military secrets to Amonasro is particularly effective.

Whatever one's considered opinion of RCA's 1971 *Aida* happens to be, however, it is much preferred to the other 1971 commercial recording, a more or less depressing version originally offered by the Balkanton company and more recently available on a number of budget labels. The redeeming virtues of this recording are few indeed. They certainly do not include Aida and Radamès, Julia Viner-Chenisheva and Nikola Nikolov. An inadequate pair of lovers manages to undermine what other virtues there are in this *Aida,* and the extent of the problem is obvious well before the end of the very first scene of the opera.

Of the two, Viner-Chernisheva comes closer to being acceptable. At least an occasional *piano* on a high tone rings true, particularly in the final scene, but the lower octave is weak and poorly blended into the rest of the voice, and there's more than a hint of wobble on many sustained notes. Someone somewhere is thinking at this point, "Aren't those very much like the problems encountered in a typical Callas performance?" Well, yes, but there are two significant differences. Callas brought to her singing an inherently interesting voice, one that commanded attention in and of itself and that could on occasion be strikingly beautiful. Callas possessed unique interpretative gifts, the ability to delve into the character, find the heart there, and communicate it fully in song. Unfortunately, Viner-Chernisheva has neither the basic sound nor the imagination that illuminated Callas' performances even when her voice was far from its best.

Nikolov as Radamès is essentially a disaster. He is far too loud and clumsy to communicate the ardent reverie of "Celeste Aida." Too often the top notes are squeezed out with a throat-wrenching degree of effort, an effect that is particularly unfortunate in the Consecration scene and the duets with Amneris and Aida in Act 4. Any attempt to characterize the young Egyptian hero is fruitless with a voice that refuses to reflect either the youthful ardor or the heroic courage.

The other members of the cast are not enough to salvage the performance as a whole, although there are some bright spots along the way. Amonasro, Nikolai Smochevski, has a pleasing voice used with skill but not a great deal of dramatic thrust, a comment that can apply as well to Stefan Tsiganchev as the King. Alexandrina Milcheva, Amneris, is a far more interesting singer. Her dusky mezzo-soprano sound is under good control and she projects the drama effectively. It is easy to hear why she was able to pursue successfully an international career. She, however, shares with some of the others in this cast a tendency to darken vowel sounds enough to lose some of the color and immediacy of the tone. When singers are given those wonderful Italian vowels to sing, they surely ought to take advantage of them.

Vocally, the most satisfying performance on this recording is Nicola Ghiuselev. The voice has a solid bass sound to it—beautiful enough to charm the ear but powerful enough to summon the troops to war and pronounce the dreadful words of judgment. His Ramfis ranks with the best on any of the recordings, and it is truly only the second half of the Judgment scene that bears a second hearing in this *Aida*.

The conductor who leads these singers and the thoroughly competent Sofia National Opera Chorus and Orchestra is Ivan Marinov. Given a better Aida and Radamès, he might have made a success of this recording in spite of the slow tempos he prefers. As it is, listeners may wish at times that he'd speed things up and let us get on to another version of the opera more quickly.

Three years later, in 1974, EMI took *Aida* back to the recording studio once more and produced what for many listeners is the best of the stereo recordings of the opera. It's just possible that Verdi would not have approved. He had little regard for conductors who took upon themselves the task of "interpreting" his works, and Riccardo Muti surely "interprets" with a vengeance. Taken as a whole, however, the 1974 EMI version is one of the most convincingly conducted performances among the many recordings of *Aida*, although we add that some critics are not in agreement on that point. At a few points, Muti lets the tension sag, most noticeably in portions of the Act 3 duet of Aida and Radamès, and the opening pages of the Triumphal scene speed by in such a hurry that they make little impact. At Muti's tempo, when the priests intone their "Della vittoria," they sound as profoundly concerned as the policemen in Gilbert and Sullivan's *Pirates of Penzance*. Otherwise, however, *retards* and *accelerandi* along with frequent strong dynamic contrasts have about them a kind of dramatic logic in light of the action in the opera. The trio for Amneris, Aida, and Radamès in the first scene emerges under Muti's baton as something more than the jumble heard often in some other recordings, and he handles with special skill the rapidly changing emotional content in the first scene of Act 2. Most important, he works *with* his singers and not, as is sometimes the case, *against* them.

He has a cast worth the effort. Ramfis, in the person of Nicolai Ghiaurov, emerges as an eloquent high priest, full voiced and authoritative, one who has clearly earned the honor and power his position grants him. Luigi Roni, the King, is large enough of voice to make the appropriate impact. His basic sound is drier, less rounded than Ghiaurov's, and the contrast is effective since every time the King sings Ramfis is never far away. Piero Cappuccilli, Amonasro, has a beautiful baritone voice but, at least in this recording, truly doesn't cut a great deal of weight in this high-powered cast.

The Messenger deserves a special word of commendation. He has more voice than most singers assigned this role and he makes his important announcement sound as exciting and significant as it actually is. The singer is Nicola Martinucci, who was on his way to greater things in the dramatic tenor's repertoire. In a pinch, he could have stepped in and sung a competent Radamès.

He, however, didn't need to because Plácido Domingo was already on hand for the second of his five official commercially issued *Aidas*. His voice is the right size for the role, lyrical enough for the final scene but heroic enough for Act 2 and the conclusion of Act 3. He uses it sensitively, with keen dramatic perception and solid musical artistry. There isn't a great deal of romantic rapture in "Celeste Aida" and he still insists on a loud — but solid — high B-flat. He is another tenor who, at least at this stage of his career, could have done what Verdi wanted and provided the soft *morendo* that Verdi asked for. As a matter of fact he provides precisely that — a truly *dolcissimo* B-flat — on his penultimate note in the final duet.

The women in this *Aida* are about as good as they come and soar out literally over their gifted male colleagues. As Barbieri and Simionato drew to the end of their careers, at least in so far as the big Amneris-like roles were concerned, Fiorenza Cossotto rapidly became the leading Italian dramatic mezzo-soprano. She doesn't sound a great deal like either of her predecessors, both of whom possessed a tonal fullness that is alien to Cossotto's straight to the mark sound. She shares with them, however, the kind of inner fire that brings life to a highly dramatic character like

Amneris. She can rage with the best of them, and she can also soften her voice to a tender, beautiful *piano,* as she does at her entrance in Act 1. The two long phrases in the Judgment scene, beginning with "Voi la terra ed I Numi oltraggiate ... You are an outrage against earth and the gods," are in Cossotto's performance textbook examples of a perfect Verdian legato.

There are further lessons in the art of song from Aida, Montserrat Caballé. The display of vocal skill, however, is never an end in itself, and behind it is a clearly consistent view of the character communicated in a highly dramatic but fully controlled performance. From the beginning with an innate sadness in her first notes, Caballé lets us know that Aida is a woman doomed to grief and suffering, a thoroughly convincing view of a character who has not a single truly happy moment in the entire opera until the transcendent *Liebestod* of the final scene. (Will Verdi forgive me the implied comparison!) Other sopranos bring gifts of a different nature to the role, but in purely vocal terms, there is nothing in the role that Caballé cannot manage and manage better than any of her contemporary sopranos. The voice expands to a full, soaring *forte,* but she rather prefers opportunities for her crystalline *pianos.* Perhaps she uses them too generously, but in this case, the more we hear of them the more we enjoy. Her ability to sustain long phrases on a single breath and do amazing things with the dynamics within the phrase is cause for wonder. "O patria mia" is intensely felt and magnificently sung, and the concluding measures, with the smoothest possible ascent to a *dolce* high C and a flawless descent from it, leave the listener, but not the singer, breathless.

It's hard to imagine being satisfied with a single recording of *Aida*. The riches are simply too great. If we had to choose just one to take to the proverbial desert island, however, the 1974 EMI recording would surely be a prime candidate.

Were it not for one serious caveat, the recording that followed in 1979 might well be labelled "*Aida* light." The calorie level in the this high-quality cast is appreciably lower than in most other recordings of the opera, although the orchestra is conspicuously well fed. Too often that orchestra, the superb Vienna Philharmonic under Herbert von Karajan's leadership, dominates this version of the opera to the detriment of the cast — and, it might be added, also to the discomfort of the ears of the listener. What was sometimes a problem in his earlier Decca/London version weighs more heavily on the listener in this 1979 recording.

As audio recording technology improved, the temptation to reproduce the softest sounds and the loudest sounds was apparently too much for some conductors and engineers to resist. In this recording, for the ear to withstand safely the mammoth climaxes of the Triumphal scene, the Consecration scene, and the closing measures of the Moorish slave's dance in Act 2, Scene 1, the listener will need to turn the volume controls down to the point that the softest sounds, for example the opening of the Nile scene or the closing notes of the Prelude, will hardly be audible at all. Verdi did indeed mark the conclusion of the dance of the slaves *ff,* but the volume level here would be adequate to accompany a fight to the death by a pair of heavyweight wrestlers. Surely he intended that there would be gradations of loudness appropriate to the situation.

In the large climaxes the singers in this relatively low-powered cast are lost somewhere between the brass and the percussion, and the aural perspective is far from what we might expect to hear as audience members in an opera house. There is a reason, for example, that almost all of the photographs of various stage productions of the Triumphal scene show the six soloists lined up downstage where they can sing literally "over" the orchestra. That's probably what Verdi had in mind all along.

Once we have noticed, however, that there's something less than opera-house naturalness in the sound of this recording, we need to go ahead and admit that von Karajan's conducting here is keenly responsive to the dramatic content of the music, and although he still takes his time to make his points, the pace tends to be sharper and more natural in 1979. It is also true that the Vienna Philharmonic under von Karajan plays better than almost any other orchestra in the world.

Given their limitations in vocal amplitude, the singers in general manage quite well. José Carreras, as Radamès has a voice of warm, natural appeal. He sings ardently whether he is expressing his military valor or his romantic tenderness. In "Celeste Aida" he handles the awkward upward phrases characteristic of the aria better than most tenors, and his eagerness is almost palpable when he meets Aida in the "Nile" scene. Strain, however, is obvious on loud, high notes, and then we are aware that what was once a beautiful lyric tenor voice is being pushed beyond its limits. It was too great a price to pay just to be able to sing with the big boys.

Mirella Freni's Aida is the work of a gifted, sincere artist confronted with the difficulty of fitting her lyric voice into the wrong role. She suffers more than the others from the orchestral volume. Although she tries bravely to compensate, her voice loses its lyrical appeal when subjected to too much pressure. It is still a beautiful instrument, and she uses it with great artistry, for example in a beautifully sustained "La tra forreste," in which she isn't at all daunted by von Karajan's slow tempo. Impressive also is the conversational quality that comes through in her duets, particularly the exchanges with her father in the Nile scene. The voice is inadequate for the loud climaxes, but not since Callas and Gobbi has there been such an emotionally moving performance of these great passages in a recording. For all of Freni's conspicuous musicianship and dramatic understanding, however, hers is not a true Aida voice, and we are too often aware of the effort required to surmount the large climaxes of the role.

In the same way, Agnes Baltsa is more or less out of her milieu as Amneris, but she manages to make a virtue out of the necessity of bringing a less imposing voice than usual to the role. From the very beginning hers is a more sympathetic Amneris than we often hear so that when her jealousy of Aida boils over, we tend to understand the love for Radamès that gives rise to it. She doesn't let us forget the suffering heart that lies beneath even her curses against the priests. If we expect an Amneris who chews up the scenery, we won't be satisfied with Baltsa, but her light, captivating mezzo-soprano is more soothing to the ear than we often hear and she still manages to make her dramatic points.

The lower male singers have less difficulty filling their roles with ample sound bites, although they tend to scale back a bit given the limitations of their colleagues. Ruggero Raimondi has some difficulty making Ramfis forceful and authoritative enough, but he sings well except for some thinning on the lowest notes. Piero Cappuccilli in his second commercial outing as Amonasro never shouts and is entirely persuasive dramatically. He may well be more comfortable with a less-forceful daughter than Caballé. Then there is José van Dam, who turns out to be a prince of a King, calm and completely in control. There are other ways of singing the King, but there are no better ways.

One mark of von Karajan's importance and power as a superstar conductor was his ability to fill smaller roles with important singers. The Messenger, Thomas Moser, went on to an outstanding career that has taken him to date all the way to Wagner's Tristan, and Katia Ricciarelli, who sings the Priestess with beautiful tone, will by 1982 step into the shoes of the Princess Aida.

All in all, the second von Karajan recording of *Aida* is interesting and challenging but hardly the ideal solution to how to perform the opera. Whereas the singers tend to bring the drama down to the intensely personal human level, the conductor, with his orchestral and vocal forces, plays for all the mythic grandeur he can muster. To emphasize the intimate human relationships is a viable approach to *Aida*. Some stage productions, as we shall see when we come to consider the visual representations of the opera, move effectively in that direction. The contrast, however, reminds us a little of the house divided against itself, and in this case it is not completely convincing.

Every respectable recording company clearly wants at least one good *Aida* in its catalog, a fact that probably explains why in 1982, Deutsche Grammophon went to Milan's La Scala for a new version of the opera. They may well have hoped that it would ace von Karajan's 1982 version. The result was a recording that, in spite of a few rewards for the listener, would hardly rank among the first choices.

Among those rewards is the high quality of recorded sound fully capable of capturing the often extreme dynamic contrasts in the performance. There is power aplenty in Claudio Abbado's conducting, as there is in von Karajan's. Occasionally the singers are lost in the onslaught of the orchestral forces blowing and bowing at full power, and once more, as in von Karajan's 1979 recording, the Moorish slaves are besieged by enough orchestral armament to destroy them in a single blow. We may not like it, but the recording engineers have made it certain that we will hear it. To his credit, Abbado accompanies many of the vocal passages with a great deal of sensitivity, and the Triumphal scene has a good feel of unity and organization about it.

In general, the men out sing the women in this cast. Nicolai Ghiaurov repeats his impressive Ramfis from the 1974 EMI/Angel recording. There may be somewhat less power and authority now. In fact, his Ramfis sounds uncommonly sympathetic for the implacable high priest, but Ghiaurov's beautifully modulated bass voice falls easily on the ear. The same can be said of Ruggero Raimondi's King. His only weakness is in some relatively weak lower notes. Leo Nucci sings a vocally poised, dramatically effective Amonasro with his large, basically attractive baritone. In the Triumphal scene, the bright color of his voice sounds almost like a tenor, but he can muster the force necessary for his encounter with Aida in the third act.

Domingo, now in his third commercially recorded *Aida,* has plenty of heroic ardor and sings with admirable style in a voice at its mature prime. There's a tendency among some critics to disparage Domingo precisely because he refused to limit himself to a handful of specialties and was instead capable of performing a broad repertoire and did so regularly with a beautiful sound, a solid technique (one of the best in the business), and dependable dramatic projection. Radamès was one of the best of his many roles, and the 1982 recording stands up well against the competition. Only Vickers twenty years earlier brought a deeper psychological understanding of Radamès to his performance, and Domingo certainly has the more conventionally beautiful voice.

The women in this cast are the problem. Elena Obraztsova is in serious vocal trouble as Amneris. She apparently has a good understanding of the role and tries hard to communicate the volatile personality of the Princess of Egypt, but her voice no longer serves her good intentions responsibly. The pitch is sometimes uncertain and sustained notes are too often unsteady, particularly in loud passages at the top of her range. Amneris' last phrase in the Judgment scene is desperate for the wrong reasons. Obraztsova had probably hurled her huge voice fearlessly at too many *forte* high notes and by 1982 was paying the price for her lack of caution.

Katia Ricciarelli as Aida is, like Obraztsova, fully into her role dramatically, and when she doesn't force, she can produce a gentle, basically sweet sound in the mid range. There are ingratiating passages throughout the third act particularly, but the high *piano* tones are often pinched and thin. When the pitch and the volume rise, however, the voice loses focus, a conspicuous beat develops in the tone, and what we hear is a once-lovely lyric soprano that has been pushed beyond its natural homeland into alien *spinto* territory. Hers is very much a Mirella Freni approach to the role with a voice often similar to her colleague. In neither case, however, are the singers true Aida material although Freni pulls it off in the long run better than Ricciarelli.

It was back to La Scala for Decca/London in 1985–86 for a studio recording made in conjunction with concurrent performances at the opera house. (A video from those live performances will be discussed in the next chapter.) The recording often has about it the feel of a drama taking place on stage with the cast fully involved emotionally in the action, and with a few exceptions, the singing is admirable if not always on the very highest level.

Both the video and the sound recordings probably owe their existence to the presence of Luciano Pavarotti, the Radamès of the cast. Until 1981, when he first performed the role, he avoided Radamès in favor of generally more lyrical tenor fare, and even now the vocal demands are something of a stretch for him. His performance, however, indicates an effective compromise between the lyric and the heroic aspects of Radamès. The sound, as usual with Pavarotti, is plangent, the words are clearly projected even if occasionally rather explosively, and given the appropriate musical situation, he produces a caressing *piano* tone. Technical control enables him to provide the appropriate *morendo* after a loud B-flat in his aria, and he takes full advantage of the opportunities for a tender *dolce* in the Nile scene duet and the final scene of the opera.

His Aida is Maria Chiara, an Italian soprano who made something of a specialty of the role and who demonstrates why in this recording. Her voice is perhaps just a trifle too light for an ideal Aida, and some of the louder high notes aren't very pleasant to hear, including the strained high C in "O patria mia." Otherwise, however, the basic sound of the voice is ingratiating, the tone well rounded and secure, and she brings to Aida that special Latin temperament that never lets us forget that something important is happening in the drama at every moment. We will encounter her again, not only in the corresponding video from La Scala but also in a 1981 video from the Verona arena.

On the other hand, casting a dramatic soprano as Amneris was a questionable decision. Ghena Dimitrova has a big voice — one of her frequent roles was Turandot — and she tends to use volume to make her most striking dramatic points. Unfortunately, although there's no comparison between the size of Dimitrova's voice and Chiara's, she sounds a great deal like her Aida in terms of vocal color. When Verdi was dickering with Draneht over the cast of the first *Aida* performances in Cairo, he insisted that he needed a genuine mezzo-soprano for Amneris, not a soprano and not a contralto. He was of course absolutely right, and the point has to do with more than the ability to project the high notes and the low ones. What is needed is a difference in the basic color of the voices that will underline the contrasting characters of the two women. Singing a mezzo role doesn't alter the fact that Dimitrova is a soprano. When she uses the chest register, as she does at points in the Act 2 duet with Aida, the sound is out of kilter with the rest of the voice, and it's frankly not very pleasant to hear. In the first scene, Dimitrova seemed almost out of the picture emotionally, but her dramatic commitment seemed to increase as the opera continued, and by the Judgment scene she was fully engaged in the drama.*

As Amonasro, we have Leo Nucci. His effective performance here is not appreciably different from his assumption of the role in 1982. Luigi Roni also is much as he was when he was the King in the 1972 EMI/Angel recording, although fourteen years are bound to take a little of the impact from the voice. In the La Scala video his role is sung by Paata Burchuladze, who moves in this recording from the throne to the temple as Ramfis. The voice is large and dark and extremely impressive, the right kind of instrument for the high priest. In the first act, he doesn't sound at all like an Italian, which of course he isn't, with his deep vowel sounds that seem to come from the very back of his throat. The difference is particularly striking in contrast to the bright, open vowels in Pavarotti's singing. In the Judgment scene, however, the words come through clearly and forcefully, and he makes a good foil for Dimitrova's dramatic Amneris.

Lorin Maazel is the conductor, and he keeps everything neat and in order. In some passages there is a lack of forward thrust, and other than the ballet, the Triumphal scene moves rather slowly, but on the whole the pacing is balanced and sensible. The result is a performance that in spite of its faults gives an honest and effective aural picture of the opera.

We might almost title the 1990 recording made by the Metropolitan Opera forces under the baton of James Levine "the American *Aida*." Conductor and cast, with few exceptions, are native-born citizens of the United States, and although they don't move to first place in the *Aida* ratings, all in all they uphold the honor of their nation without quite producing the brilliant effect we may have hoped for.

The most significant exception in this "all-American" version of the opera is Plácido Domingo, earning his place as the most frequently recorded Radamès. His is a sensitive, artistically controlled performance. His voice is not as fresh as it was on the earlier recordings, but he still produces a sound to be reckoned with and particularly beautiful *pianissimos* in the final scene. The aria is sung with ardor and tenderness. He ends it with the octave descent for a quiet B-flat, just as Richard Tucker did in the Toscanini version and as Verdi himself approved for those tenors (that is, most of them) who can't handle the original note softly.

---

*This is the kind of comment that I make with some hesitation since we have no assurance that a studio recording of an opera was actually made in one clear line from the beginning of Act 1 to the end of Act 4 or that the various scenes were recorded in order. As a matter of fact, we can't be certain that a single note or phrase was committed to disc at the same time as the notes that come before or after it. It is true, however, that some artists give the impression of growing into a role from one scene to the next.

Domingo's Aida is the gifted American soprano Aprile Millo. She gets off to a rather rough, tremulous start in the first scene, where her singing fails to suggest the gentle appeal of the character. As the opera proceeds, however, she improves, and she is fully on form by the time she reaches the Nile scene. Her performance here is intensely dramatic in her encounters with both Amonasro and Radamès. One or two of the top tones are not very pleasant, but "O patria mia" is effectively interpreted and beautifully sung, complete with a *dolce* high C and a floated final note. The final scene reveals both Millo and Domingo at their best.

Dolora Zajick has given many exciting performances of Amneris in the opera house. Unfortunately, in this recording she is less impressive both vocally and dramatically. There is occasionally too much vibrato and in spite of a brilliant top, the voice tends to fade out on the lower notes. On this recording she fails to capture the many-sided character of the Egyptian princess. Perhaps it's the inhibiting environment of the recording studio that keeps Zajick from achieving what she has often accomplished in this role on stage and in recordings made from her live on-stage performances.

Amonasro is not a role that we would ordinarily think of for James Morris, and indeed he doesn't have the warm, appealing sound of the genuine Italian baritone. To a great extent, however, he compensates with a dramatic performance of the role that is both imaginative and convincing. At one important moment he is several steps ahead of most other singers of Amonasro — at that highly suggestive point in the Nile scene when he leads Aida to realize what he is asking of her. "Radamès so che qui attendi ... Ei t'ama ... et conduce gli Egizii ... Intendi? ... Radamès is coming ... He loves you ... and he commands the Egyptians ... Do you understand?" Verdi has marked the passage with a rare *ppp* to be broken only with Aida's *fortissimo* cry of "Orrore!" Both the inflection of the voice and the willingness to take the composer at his word produce exactly the right effect.

Samuel Ramey's Ramfis is one of the best — simultaneously threatening and appealing. Terry Cook as the King, however, is underpowered, at least as recorded here. The contrast when they sing back to back in the first scene and the Triumphal scene is striking and hints at an uncomfortable balance of power in old Egypt.

James Levine's conducting is hardly revelatory, but with the exception of some overly long pauses, the pacing is good and he keeps the drama moving. He's most persuasive at the same point that his singers are — in the Nile scene and the finale.

A new *Aida* appeared in 1995 on the budget Naxos label. A number of other recordings have considerably more to offer, but if budget is a primary concern, this version of the opera offers a modestly effective effort that at least strives to be faithful to the composer's intentions. Rico Saccani, the conductor, is conscientious and there are no serious mishaps along the way. He brings no special insight to the opera, and there are lengthy passages, including the entire "Ma to re" ensemble, in which although nothing bad happens, nothing much else happens either. The recorded sound is relatively subdued — not necessarily a bad change from the highly charged sonics of some other versions. For good or ill, the performance is also subdued, and from time to time there are lengthy pauses for no readily identifiable reason. One strange production decision: In the Judgment scene, Ramfis and the other priests are right in our ears and not off-stage in the subterranean justice hall.

On the whole, the cast is competent without being truly memorable. Francesco Ellero D'Artegna as Ramfis and Riccardo Ferrari as the King share voices so close in timbre and strength that they can hardly be identified by the ear alone. Both have occasional problems in security, and both tend to weaken as the vocal line descends. D'Artegna, however, improves considerably for the Judgment scene. Amonasro, Mark Rucker, demonstrates a serviceable baritone with weak low notes and some lack of power, but he understands the situation of the Ethiopian ruler and manages to communicate the changes the character must express in the Nile scene.

Kristjan Johannsson has ample power for Radamès. He strains for the high notes, and often there is more than a hint of a beat in the voice when both the volume and the pitch are reaching for the skies. Good passages alternate with the bad often enough to suggest that further work on his vocal technique might enable him to fulfill more fully the demands of Radamès, but the voice as recorded here lacks the kind of sensuous quality that we want to hear in "Celeste Aida," for example, or the more affectionate passages of the Nile scene.

Aida is, of course, a notoriously difficult role for the soprano. She must have not only a beautiful voice and keen dramatic understanding but also the kind of security and discipline to produce a solid tone from the bottom to the top of her range — and in the case of Aida, that range is extensive. Some parts of the score work quite well for Maria Dragoni. She responds to Aida's music with some tender *piano* tones in "La tra forreste" and in the closing phrase of "O patria mia," and she sings a soft, but somewhat uncomfortable, high C at the end of the aria. The louder and higher notes are not always a pleasure to hear, the B-flat, for example, at "Pietà, pietà! Padre, pietà" in her duet with Amonasro in Act III. At times, she seems fully involved dramatically, but there are also passages in which the interpretation is bland and makes little impact. It's likely that stronger leadership from the podium would have produced a more fully satisfying performance.

There is one performance here, however, that commands our attention and our admiration. Barbara Dever sings Amneris with vocal beauty and subtle interpretative skill. She doesn't bite into the notes the way many of the Italian mezzo-sopranos do, but she has an even scale and ample volume for Amneris' occasional outbursts. The Judgment scene is strongly sung, and the contrast of her control and discipline in the second-act duet with Dragoni is striking — and instructive. Hers is a performance worth remembering, and the only regret is that she is not surrounded by more fully capable and responsive colleagues.

The 2001 addition to the *Aida* discography fails to convince on several counts. It is anything other than a budget recording, either in production or in price. The performing artists and the sound engineers involved have gone as far as they possibly could to produce an outstanding version of Verdi's opera, but the entire concept was apparently flawed from the very beginning.

Nikolaus Harnoncourt, the conductor, is, of course, a noted authority and persuasive conductor of earlier music up to and including the operas of Mozart, and he brings to Verdi's score a kind of clarity and linear separation, both instrumental and vocal, that produce often surprising results. We hear things that are lost in the orchestral mass of most other performances. Listening to this recording with the full score in hand can be a learning experience into the unsuspected complexity of Verdi's compositional skill and artistry. Many of the effects, however, are achieved at the expense of forward thrust and movement. At almost 160 minutes, this is surely the slowest of all *Aida* recordings, and at a few points — for example, in the opening chorus and solos for Amneris at the beginning of Act 2 — the music almost comes to a halt. This approach works better in the Triumphal scene, where the massed choruses have the effect of an appropriate monumental grandeur. His is an often fascinating performance, but ultimately not a successful one.

His cast is decidedly a mixed bag with only one genuine standout among them. They might have produced a delightful *La Bohème,* but they simply do not have what it takes for *Aida.* Matti Salminen certainly possesses the vocal goods for Ramfis, but his singing is heavy handed and tends to lose focus and become unsteady at higher volumes. His diction is muddy enough that it is often difficult to tell what language he's singing. Some of the same problems, including the occasional unsteadiness, plague Lászlo Polgár as the King.

Thomas Hampson's Amonasro is an interesting experiment in applying the skills of an accomplished lieder singer to the meatier vocal lines of Verdi. In his initial appearance in the Triumphal scene, he presents an extraordinarily refined and quite youthful Amonasro. It's all very pleasing to the ear, particularly the *bel canto* opening to the "Ma tu re" ensemble, but it may not convey fully the character of the fiery Ethiopian leader. Much of his Nile scene is sensitively sung and interpreted, better in the more affectionate than in the angry moments, which tend to be overacted to the detriment of the purely musical content.

The problems are greater with Radamès and Aida. Both bring attractive, lightweight, essentially lyrical voices to the heavier, more dramatic vocal demands of Verdi's opera. Vincenzo La Scola manages a good measure of gentleness in "Celeste Aida" and the appropriate parts of the Nile scene. Otherwise, however, he is completely out of his element. Whenever the volume increases, particularly if the pitch goes up with it, we hear an overly forward, strained, rather nasal tone.

As Aida, Cristina Gallardo-Domâs is similarly ill cast. When her voice is not subjected to pressure, the sound is truly beautiful. Much of "O patria mia" benefits from her pure, sweet tone. As the volume increases, however, the voice takes on a distracting beat and loses focus, and what we hear is a decidedly different and not very pleasant sound. It's almost as if we had two different singers in the role. She tries hard to compensate by pumping up the dramatic emphases, but the result does not make for a convincing Aida.

The great exception in this cast is Olga Borodina, as Amneris. The voice is round, secure, and beautiful from top to bottom, and she uses it with the subtlety of a true artist. She doesn't need to impose external dramatics on the music in the Judgment scene because her vocal assurance enables her to do everything that Verdi demands without distorting either the line or the purity of the tone. Harnoncourt's slow tempos don't ruffle her, although even Borodina has trouble keeping things alive in the second act duet with Aida. Like Dever's Amneris in the Naxos recording, her performance cries out for better surroundings.

A handful of recordings of *Aida* have been professionally recorded from live staged performances and commercially issued in what appear to be official versions, that is, with the agreement of the artists and the performing groups involved. Sometimes, of course, it is almost impossible to tell from the information provided in the packaging just how "official" the recording is, and many "unofficial" versions offer valuable insight into the performing history of the opera and the artists involved. One that certainly fits the definition of an "official" recording, however, is the performance conducted by Thomas Schippers in 1976 in the ancient Roman theatre in Orange, France, and issued on long-playing records by Lèvon Records.

Let's get the bad news out of the way to start. This version suffers from most of the distractions that plague live recordings made during actual performances, including the occasional sound of movement on the stage and the tendency of singers to drift on or off mike from time to time. There is also applause, a great deal of it in fact. In this case, the difficulties were apparently multiplied because of the outdoor setting, and the sound, while always listenable, sometimes grates the ear harshly and occasionally seems to come through a minor windstorm.

The other major drawback to this version of *Aida* is the tenor, Peter Gougalov, who sings Radamès. His blunt, unmodulated tone is not a pleasure to hear, and more often than not he is blasting his voice toward the rafters—and, of course, there were no rafters in the outdoor venue. A less amorous "Celeste Aida" is hard to imagine. To his credit, he does manage some acceptable soft singing in the final scene. Otherwise, he has too much in common with Nikola Nikolov, Radamès in the 1971 Bulgarian recording.

Once we have agreed to tolerate the substandard sonics and the Radamès, however, this version of the opera has much to offer. Thomas Schippers conducts a taut, highly dramatic performance. There are a few glitches in ensemble, notably in the "fuggiam" section of the Nile scene, when Gougalov seems to have difficulty keeping up with his conductor, and there are numerous presumably unauthorized *accelerandi* and *rallentandi*. Verdi might not have approved. (As we have seen, he didn't have much patience with conductors who presumed to "interpret" his operas.) There's a great deal of excitement here and Schippers really whips things up in Act 3 and the Judgment scene of Act 4.

We might prefer a solid Italian baritone voice with less fuzz on it, but Ingvar Wixel sings a vocally plush, dramatically convincing Amonasro. Agostino Ferrin as Ramfis is firm, secure, and sufficiently weighty of voice except in the very lowest notes, and Luigi Roni maintains his record as a King to rank with the best, with full rich tone and the kind of authority to rule in ancient Egypt.

As Aida, we have the Mexican soprano Gilda Cruz-Romo. She sang frequently in the major opera houses of Europe and appeared also at the New York City and the Metropolitan Operas, but she had a limited recording career and never quite became the leading international star she deserved to be. On the basis of this performance, she was better equipped for the major Verdi roles than almost any other soprano in 1976. The voice is round, beautiful, and of ample power in the large ensembles. She manages "Ritorna vincitor" without sounding as hectic as many sopranos do in the more rapid sections, and "O patria mia" is a delight, with secure pianos on the high notes at the conclusion. What's more, she is a gifted vocal actress.

In the third of her commercially released recordings of Amneris, Grace Bumbry almost steals the show. The voice is always a joy to hear, but it is her keen dramatic involvement that marks her performance here as very special indeed. The Judgment scene rings with conviction and passion, the chest voice has real punch to it, and she sails bravely and boldly to the high A and B-flat. Surely, we can forgive her the added, non-Verdian scream when the judges announce their sentence, and the ovation she receives at the end of the scene is fully deserved.

March 22, 1979, was clearly a triumphant night at Munich's Bavarian State Opera, and we can be grateful that the performance of *Aida* that evening was preserved in recorded sound and has now been made available on the Orfeo label. In many ways this version of the opera is the *beau* ideal of live, from-the-stage recording. The stereo sound is excellent throughout, there is a minimum of stage noise, and the audience is amazingly quiet aside from their enthusiastic applause, which almost always occurs after the music has stopped. Even more important, the good sound quality brings to us an excellent performance. From the purely dramatic standpoint, it may well be the most dramatically compelling of all the recordings of *Aida,* and it certainly deserves a place beside the most successful of the studio recordings.

The conductor is Riccardo Muti, and if anything, he improves on his earlier recording for EMI. Nothing now is taken for granted. At every moment the drama is intense and the musical forces are under complete control. He upholds his reputation for rapid tempis, but at key moments — in the final scene, for example, and during Aida's Nile scene aria — he relaxes enough to let the music breathe with the singers. The large ensembles in Act 2 are clearly articulated and they hold together with an effective sense of continuity. Muti can surely whip up a dramatic storm when the action demands it, as in the red hot, angry conclusion of the duet for Radamès and Amneris in Act 4.

To a certain extent, on paper the cast looks like a rather strange combination, but the elements contrast and blend effectively. Nikolaus Hillebrand as the King makes the least impression but does nothing to spoil the overall effect, and after some rather mushy diction in the first scene, Robert Lloyd turns out to be a powerful, imposing, and decidedly threatening Ramfis. In this performance, Ramfis is clearly the power behind the throne.

As Amonasro, Siegmund Nimsgern doesn't have the rounded tone of the ideal Verdi baritone, although he manages a clear line and a good measure of eloquence at "Pensa che un popolo" in the Nile scene. Otherwise, his Amonasro is fierce, violent, a not so noble savage, for whom nothing, not even his daughter, is allowed to weaken his commitment to regain his throne and establish once more the glory of his nation. Nimsgern also does something in the Triumphal scene that seems to evade most baritones in the role — he really sounds as if he's lying.

Anna Tomowa-Sintow is a passionate, fully committed Aida. The basic vocal quality is rich and creamy with some tendency to spread, particularly under pressure, and we miss the floated soft tones that add a special dimension of gentleness to some Aidas. Her dramatic instincts, however, are right on the button, and she is particularly memorable in her four major duets, particularly the Nile scene encounter with her father. She and Domingo respond with great sensitivity to one another in the final scene.

In 1979 at the time of this recording, Plácido Domingo was at the height of his powers, and his Radamès here is arguably the best of his five official commercially issued recordings of the role. He disappoints with another loud, albeit totally steady, B-flat at the end of his aria, but leading up to that note he has addressed his "celeste Aida" with ardor and tenderness, and he has the vocal means and the emotional responsiveness to communicate all of Radamès' changing responses in the Nile scene.

The most interesting performance in this recording, however, is the Amneris of Brigitte Fassbaender. Other mezzo-sopranos, particularly those with lush Italianate voices, have produced a more beautiful sound, but none has plumbed the depths of the character as fully as Fassbaender. From the beginning, even in her first scene with Radamès, we have a sense of the character's desperation, and in the Judgment scene, her frustration, anger, and ultimate hopelessness are fully communicated.

Hers is a classic performance in a recording that will bear hearing and rehearing by every lover of the opera.

One further live performance, with considerably less auspicious casting, can be found on the D Classics label, and it turns out to be a convincing *Aida* that stacks up fairly well alongside some of the full-priced versions. Although the date is not known, this budget-priced recording, which originated in the Netherlands, was copyrighted in 1998, and it meets good contemporary standards for digital sound. It would be difficult to tell whether the performance was actually fully staged or was, rather, a concert performance, since there is the barest minimum of stage movement noise and an audience so quiet that we might doubt their presence if they did not applaud at the end—but only at the end—of Acts 2 and 4. Photographs on the album cover, however, suggest a fully staged performance.

The Württembergische Philharmonie Reutlingen and the Opera in Ahoy' Chorus are led by Roberto Paternostro, who proves himself to be a gifted interpreter. The music is always alive and the pace appropriate to the action. The orchestra falters at one or two points and at least in the "Sì: fuggiam" section of the Nile scene when Radamès agrees to flee with Aida, conductor and tenor experience a brief contretemps about the tempo. The problems, however, are few and Paternostro certainly knows his way around the score.

So does his cast of singers. The lower male voices fare least well. Riccardo Ferrari as Ramfis and Aik Martirosyan as the King have enough tremolo to undermine a clear vocal line, and Claudio Otelli as Amonasro sings with a grainy voice that develops a beat under pressure. In the excitement of performance, he more than once is noticeably sharp, and his conventional interpretation adds nothing to our knowledge of the character.

With the other singers, the situation improves noticeably. We can judge, mainly from his photograph on the album cover, that Maurizio Frusoni, who sings Radamès, is no longer in first blush of youth, and his vibrato, particularly on the higher notes, sometimes borders on a genuine tremolo. Otherwise, however, the voice is secure and has a good dramatic ring to it. Although he doesn't do so often, he is able to soften it effectively, as we hear in the final scene, and when it is needed, for example in his surrender to Ramfis in Act 3, he is able to supply ample power. Dramatically, he doesn't offer a great deal of imagination, but he makes the major points as well as most tenors, aside from the most gifted, do.

His Aida is Olga Romanko, a Russian soprano with a big, secure voice, somewhat short on the lower end of the scale. She and her partner both tend to overdo the volume, and when she sings softly the tone doesn't float the way we enjoy hearing with Caballé and Milanov, for example. The high C in "O patria mia" is sung *piano* but is not well supported. She follows it, however, with a good, clear high A at the end of the aria, and her interpretation throughout is sensitive and alert. At the big climaxes, she has all the punch she needs, and she is fully involved dramatically.

If 1998 is close to the correct date for this recording, Stefania Toczyska was drawing near the end of her international career, and we can be grateful to have a good reproduction of her Amneris, which she had taken to major opera houses all around the world. There are occasional marks of her years of experience in a frayed, unsteady tone, but they are relatively rare, and her voice serves her well all the way to the top of her range. Her interpretation of Amneris is conventional, but she makes it work, particularly in a powerful Judgment scene. If anything, this 1998 sound recording is superior to her stage performance in a 1981 video, which will be discussed in the next chapter.

Recordings abound of selections from *Aida* in languages other than the original Italian, but complete recordings are comparatively rare. Three, however, have come to my attention. One of them, a version in Hungarian from 1953, I have been unable to locate, but details, including the cast, are included in the discography. Apparently the recording had limited distribution outside of Hungary and was probably not transferred later to compact disc.

A pair of recordings by the artists involved may give us some impression of this version of the opera, although with the warning that 1953 in Hungarian may or may not have much in common with later Italian language versions of the same music. "Celeste Aida" in Italian by Josef Simandy as Radamès reveals a strong tenor voice with problems in maintaining a steady vocal line. His interesting treatment of the final B-flat swells quickly to *forte* and then there is a *diminuendo* to a very soft head tone, perhaps even a true falsetto. From 1956 there is also a version of the Act 3 duet for Aida and Amonasro, with Alexander Sved and Paula Takacs, who also sing their respective roles on the complete version. Once again the language is Italian. Takacs is given to some shrillness on loud high notes, but the voice is steady and she equals her partner in dramatic intensity. Sved, of course, had an international career, except for the six years he was not permitted to travel abroad, and his performance here confirms his reputation for a large, basically appealing baritone voice. He is fully into the role and the only thing missing is the will — surely not the ability — to lighten the volume from time to time.

The Russian language recording, released in 1954 but perhaps committed to disc earlier, calls for a certain measure of aural adjustment for any of us accustomed to Italian language performances recorded in up-to-date sound. Given the rather harsh acoustics typical of Russian recordings at the time, we can expect some stridency in the higher voices. (I have to remind myself that in the opera house they probably sounded considerably better.) Then there's the adjustment to the language itself. There are simply too many consonants, exotic and otherwise, for a comfortable line in the nineteenth-century Italian operas. Approach this recording with patience and tolerance, however, and we discover a challenging, deeply felt, and musically satisfying performance of *Aida.*

The conductor, Alexander Melik-Pashayev, is occasionally somewhat business like in his approach, but generally the tempos and the decisions about when to hurry and when to slow down are well judged. He works *with* his singers, not *against* them, and the performance deserves credit for unusual care in observing Verdi's own interpretative markings in the score.

Natalia Sokolova as Aida has a voice on the decidedly bright side, with high notes sometimes shrill and sometimes strained. In the first scene, she sounds almost girlish, but as she proceeds the voice takes on greater depth, the soft tones open up to a certain extent, and the interpretation grows in sensitivity.

We might say much the same for Vera Davydova as Amneris, but her voice is often tight, as if the notes are being squeezed out, and the result can be unpleasant. The combination with Sokolova in the second act duet with Aida is something of a trial to the ear. In the first scene, there is little attempt at characterization, but the interpretation improves as she goes along, and she is full of passion by the time she arrives at the Judgment scene.

The men in the cast are better. The King, Igor Mikhailov, is strong of voice with a rather hard, blunt tone. He is decidedly the most un-Italianate among the singers. On the other hand, Ivan Petrov is an outstanding Ramfis; his voice is absolutely straight and steady and his interpretation is appropriately stern, unyielding, and commanding. Petrov was, of course, an outstanding Boris in Mussorgsky's opera and was noted for being a "singing" Boris rather than one who indulged in a great deal of *parlando,* off-the-note declamation. It is that skill, the ability to project a strong characterization without distorting the voice or the vocal line, that he demonstrates as Ramfis.

Listening to Georgy Nelepp can be an exhausting process. So much bright, ringing, loud "tenorizing" can wear on the ears after the first few minutes. His voice, however, is the real thing, and after all, Radamès doesn't sing all the time. He offers a neat, affectionate "Celeste Aida" until the expected loud B-flat at the end, and he is always alive and awake to what's happening in the opera. We would like a little more vocal sensitivity, but his is clearly a Radamès voice.

We've saved the best to last — Pavel Lisitsian as Amonasro. He alone makes the Russian language sound right in this opera. His tone is always luscious, rounded, and well supported. He phrases eloquently and limns perfectly the changing emotions of the Nile scene. His Amonasro is a classic performance that fully justifies his reputation as one of the finest baritones of the twentieth century.

From Russia in the 1950s to Great Britain at the dawn of the twenty-first century is indeed something of a leap, but we can assume that the 2001 recording had much the same purpose in mind as the Russian language predecessor — namely, to bring *Aida* to the audience in the language they could most readily understand. Whether English works any better than Russian in this opera is a matter of personal taste, but we need to make clear from the outset that the Chandos recording uses a generally excellent translation by Edmond Tracey that the singers only intermittently manage to communicate. Italian opera in English, it would seem, still needs a printed libretto, which Chandos has graciously provided, if the listener is to follow the text.

The conductor, David Parry, leads his troops effectively. His reading of the score is sometimes fast but never seems rushed, and at all points but particularly in the Judgment scene he brings the drama vividly to life. The Triumphal scene ballet is reduced to a mere minute and fifty-five seconds, but a note in the accompanying booklet tells that what is performed here is Verdi's original ballet music without the additions made for the Paris Opéra premiere. The recorded sound is excellent throughout although Ramfis and priests have a judgment chamber so highly resonant that their words are barely decipherable.

Jane Eaglen sings the role of Aida. Her voice is enormous, warmly plush, very imposing, and often of great beauty. Along with many other full-blown dramatic sopranos, rapid movement from one note to the next is not easy for her and sometimes finds her slightly under the pitch, and she apparently has difficulty scaling her opulent tone down for a true, floated *piano*. She handles the Nile scene aria better than we might have thought possible, but much of her impressive singing is simply too loud. It is certainly too loud for her Radamès, Dennis O'Neill, and even for Gregory Yurisich, Amonasro. We get the feeling that she could have sent either of them scurrying off in terror with a single "Ho-jo-to-ho!" She seems to be fully involved emotionally, but her muddy English diction doesn't tell us a great deal about the character.

There, however, is character aplenty in Rosalind Plowright's Amneris. Hers is a highly specific, extremely thoughtful interpretation, responsive at every point to the situation of the Princess of Egypt. The words are not always clear, and in the Judgment scene they tend to get in the way of her vocalizing, but she goes well beyond Eaglen in communicating the text. The voice is weakest at the bottom with very little effective use of the chest tones, and in all candor it shows the signs of much past experience — too much past experience in fact.

Radamès, Dennis O'Neill, also sounds older than the dashing young Egyptian military leader should. His voice is not without strain, and loud high notes from time to time develop a conspicuous beat. He is, however, a keen interpreter. His aria in praise of Aida is tender and quietly subdued with a good soft ending, and the opening passages of the final scene bring a hushed acceptance of his fate. The dramatics of the Nile scene are less effective for O'Neill, in part because of the contrast with his super-charged Aida. His English can generally be understood clearly even if it does occasionally remind us of a proper British Sunday afternoon oratorio, but the effect may not be entirely inappropriate for the character of this uptight, upright young man.

Gregory Yurisich as Amonasro makes perhaps the best case for opera in English. He communicates the text clearly but without engaging in a stuffily precise enunciation. His vocal tone is relatively grainy, but he's a good technician who phrases eloquently, for example in his eloquent statement at the end of the Nile scene duet. Unfortunately, he is underpowered in the duet. It truly would take an Ettore Bastianini or a Leonard Warren to subdue this Aida. Both of the bass roles are well taken, with Alastair Miles as an impressive, dark-voiced Ramfis and Peter Rose as an authoritative King. Rose is particularly convincing in the Triumphal scene, a point at which many basses demonstrate their vocal weakness.

If these comments about the Chandos *Aida* seem unduly negative, it's not because this recording is in any sense a complete washout. The quality of the conducting is first rate, the drama is truly communicated, and much of the singing, even of Eaglen's over-powering Aida, is impressive and well worth hearing. The questions that arise have more to do with the overall problem of recording the standard foreign-language operas in English translation. First of all, the best candidates for the roles are often either unwilling or unable to learn and then actually to sing the English text, and just as often, singers who are native to the language simply have not mastered the art of communicating the words in song. What's more, Verdi was a master of capturing just the right musical sound for the individual words, and even the best translations can't duplicate his skill and artistry. That's why I find myself listening to this recording and yearning all the while for "Celeste Aida" and "Pensa che un popolo" and "Empia razza" and "O terra, addio."

Aida has of course been represented on disc in many different guises other than complete performances. The major arias and ensembles are available in multiple versions sung by almost all of the major vocal artists of the last one hundred years, occasionally without any particular appropriateness for the individual type of voice. Recordings of extensive highlights have appeared frequently, many of them derived from the complete versions discussed in this chapter. Two condensed or abridged versions of the opera, however, deserve special comment.

One, which appeared in 1952, earns its fame not from any special virtues in the performance but rather from the conspicuous absence of them. The orchestra and chorus of the Maggio Musicale Fiorentino are conducted with some skill by Emidio Tieri, and they play and sing adequately. A little more than one-third of the opera is included (at least that is the case in the version available to me for review), after "Celeste Aida" and "Ritorna vincitor," we have the duet of Aida and Amneris in Act 2, Scene 1, a large portion of the Triumphal scene beginning with the King's initial address to Radamès and continuing to the end, Aida's duet with her father in the Nile scene, the Judgment scene from the exit of Radamès through the end, and the final portion of the closing duet in the opera. There are enough abrupt track endings to suggest that more than appears on the disc was actually recorded, perhaps the entire opera.

Radamès, Gino Sarri, sang for other labels in a variety of operas, and he was Stella Roman's partner on the complete Capitol recording. He knows what to do with his role and can do it as long as it's loud. Unfortunately, as he sings the role, it usually is, and the resulting sound at the top of the voice is often crude and unpleasant. The unidentified Ramfis and King are competent vocalists, the King actually a bit more than that, and by far the best performance is by Amonasro, who has a vibrant voice guided by solid technique and good dramatic understanding. The star, however, is Vasilka Petrova, and it is her performance that has made this recording something of a "party" record for those who can find nothing better about which to laugh. The voice is out of focus, the top notes often shouted, and the sound unpleasant enough to deny completely any possibility of a "*Celeste* Aida." Unfortunately, Elisabeth Wysor as Amneris isn't much of an improvement. Frankly, I prefer not to laugh. Rumor has it that Petrova paid to have her recordings made. Whether the rumor is true or not, I cannot say, but if it is, then to me there is something sad about a singer, obviously without adequate natural gifts, so in love with the opera that she is willing to pay for the opportunity to sing it. How many of us who couldn't afford to hire colleagues and orchestra have sung along with recordings of Bjoerling or Domingo or Milanov, or intoned a few wavery bars of "Celeste Aida" in the shower!

The other abridged version offers more of value and is particularly interesting to those interested in mid-twentieth-century performances of the Metropolitan Opera. During the 1950s, the Met initiated, on a subscription basis, recordings of excerpts from famous operas made by the in-house singers, conductors, orchestra, and chorus. The attempts to condense the operas to the length of one or two-long playing recordings were variously successful. In the case of *Aida,* however, most of the omissions involved the deletion of repeated passages along with all of the Triumphal scene ballet and all of the Judgment scene after Amneris and Radamès' duet.

Many of the major Metropolitan artists were bound by contract limitations that made their participation in these issues impossible.* As a result, many of these Metropolitan Opera Record Club recordings document the voices of those singers who had little opportunity to visit the studios of the major record companies. Such is the case in this 1956 abridged *Aida,* and therein is its particular value.

---

*Among the notable exceptions were Richard Tucker, who recorded for this series selections from *Andrea Chenier* and *Eugene Onegin,* and Dorothy Kirsten, who committed to disc almost complete performances of *Madama Butterfly* and *Tosca.*

Only Radamès, Albert da Costa, was never given the opportunity to sing his role on the stage at the Met. He had a secure, brightly hued voice, of more than adequate volume — some of his useful Metropolitan service was in the Wagner roles — and he uses it with a great deal of skill. He is loud most of the time, and he comes through as more effective in battlefield heroics than in romance. Frank Guarrera is a somewhat gruff, blustery Amonasro, but he is fully in character. It is interesting to hear Louis Sgarro's smooth bass as the King, and of course, Giorgio Tozzi's Ramfis was soon to become familiar both on stage and in the 1962 RCA recording of the opera. It's worth noting also the sturdy messenger who brings the news of the Ethiopian uprising in the first scene. He would return to the Met later as Otello, and in 1966, the good messenger was elevated to the rank of Egyptian General to sing Radamès.

Aida was Lucine Amara, sweet and secure of tone almost throughout without the unsteadiness that developed in her overworked voice later in her career. It is engaging to hear an Aida who sounds like a young girl, not like a mature dramatic soprano. Vocally, the biggest disappointment is the way she rushes over the climactic phrase of her Nile scene aria as if she wants to get past an uncomfortable high C as quickly as she can. She sang the role on stage at the Met a few times, but at this early stage of her career, her voice truly is too light for Aida's more dramatic outbursts. For all that, however, she is well matched with Rosalind Elias as Amneris, another singer who was out of her natural *fach* in the large Verdi mezzo-soprano roles. For a few years in the 1950s, the Metropolitan Opera and apparently the RCA Victor recording company tried to make her into their own Giulietta Simionato, but it was not a comfortable role for her. Elias' appealing voice handles the more lyrical portions of the role effectively, but the heavy vocal dramatics put her under considerable strain.

This is the kind of performance that often must have been presented on the stage at the Metropolitan's old student matinees, and for all of its shortcomings, it needs to be said that if students had heard and seen this version of *Aida,* they would not have been short changed. The Met could, and often did, give solid performances without sending a single expensive super star onto the stage. None of the singers was less than adequate, the orchestra and chorus were impressive, and Fausto Cleva, the conductor, knew just about everything there was to know about the opera.

And there we have it — thirty-three complete official, commercially issued recordings of *Aida,* two abridged performances, and one condensed acoustical version thrown in for good measure. It's a remarkable record, and no other opera can quite equal it. Recording company executives and the owners of shops that sell sound recordings should surely bow down before Verdi in humble gratitude and thank him for lining their pockets with precious Egyptian gold.

6

Linking Sight to Sound

It was, no doubt, inevitable that an opera with the visual appeal of massed crowd scenes, triumphal marches, and exotic rituals, all set amid the majesty and mystery of ancient Egypt, would find its way onto the screen with the advent of motion pictures. Much as the development of sound recording in the closing years of the nineteenth and the opening years of the twentieth centuries brought *Aida* to a vast new public, the simultaneous advances in projecting moving images offered wonderful new possibilities for bringing the visual wonders of the opera to thousands who would never have the opportunity to venture inside an opera house to see a live performance.

The success of Eadweard Muybridge during the 1870s in demonstrating animal movement through a series of rapidly shot still photographs of a horse in motion led other scientists to experiment with the reproduction of continuous motion. One of those scientists was Thomas Edison, who created and offered to the public in 1894 his Kinetoscope, a device that enabled an individual viewer to see a brief "moving picture" imprinted on a celluloid film that had been developed by George Eastman.

The long-range commercial potential of the new medium, however, depended on the ability to project an image onto a screen so that not one but many people could see it at the same time. That was the achievement of Auguste and Louis Lumière, who in December of 1895 demonstrated their Cinématograph for the first time to a group of people who had paid for the privilege. From then on, the potential of the motion picture was virtually unlimited.

The early motion pictures were, of course, silent, and attempts to coordinate sight and sound through the use of separate sound recording devices were of small success. The limitation for the presentation of a musical work like an opera must have seemed obvious, but the producers of films were not discouraged and moved forward with ingenious attempts to provide sound from outside sources or to present operatic plots without the music. In 1911, Edison produced a fifteen-minute abridgment of *Aida* with live musicians providing the accompaniment, and in the same year an Italian company presented an abbreviated version of the opera as a silent film.* Even Ethel Barrymore got into the act with her 1914 film *The Nightingale,* in which the young heroine makes her way from singing songs in the streets to singing Aida at the Metropolitan Opera, one of the first of what would eventually become a long series of films that depict the rise of potential stars from obscurity to operatic fame and fortune.

The development of sound-on-film in the mid-nineteen twenties not only brought Al Jolson in *The Jazz Singer* but also music from *Aida* and other operas to the screen with ever increasing frequency. Vitaphone produced a number of operatic short subjects in which great singers performed their operatic specialties, among them Giovanni Martinelli, who appeared singing not only "Celeste Aida" but also the third-act duet with Ina Bourskaya as his Amneris. Through the years, when the screenplay called for an operatic segment to enhance the story, often the work chosen was *Aida,* and when in 1952 the producers wanted to demonstrate the wonders of the new three-screen Cinerama process, one of the segments of *This Is Cinerama* included two ballet sequences — the dance of the Nubian slaves in Act 2 and the triumphal ballet from Act 3 — filmed on the stage of the La Scala Opera House in Milan and led by the dean of Italian conductors, Victor Da Sabata.

In 1953, *Aida* as a whole — or at least approximately two-thirds of the whole — appeared on screen in a spectacular production. It was promoted noisily and distributed widely by Sol Hurok as a kind of special road-show presentation and, at least on the billboards, it promised a performance to fulfill the wildest dreams of opera lovers.

To begin with, this *Aida* truly was spectacular. Taking the opera away from the stage and into the vast outdoors and the elaborately equipped motion picture studio presents a special opportunity, and a few special challenges as well. There were elaborate settings to depict the ancient Egypt of mythological imagination , thousands of extras for the Triumphal scene and the battle scenes that were added to the scenario, colorful costumes with a penchant for brightly hued feather adornment, and a cast of 1950-style "beautiful people." Beautiful they surely were. There on the giant screen were Lois Maxwell as an Amneris seductive enough to turn the head of any Radamès; Sophia Loren as the Aida whose charms were more than adequate to overcome the attractions of the Egyptian princess; as Radamès, youthful, strikingly handsome Luciano della Marra; and Afro Poli as an appropriately wild, wooly, and fierce Amonasro. What's more, they and their colleagues acted their roles effectively for the camera under the direction of Clemente Fracassi, with particular credit to Sophia Loren, who made an entirely convincing Aida. Only della

---

*For much of the information about the history of *Aida* on film, I am indebted to Ken Wlaschin's *Encyclopedia of Opera on Screen: A Guide to More than 100 Years of Opera Films, Videos, and DVDs* (New Haven: Yale University Press, 2004), pp. 8–12.

Marra as a faceless, uninvolved Radamès, whose expression never seemed to change for either joy sorrow, let us down seriously. Margherita Waldmann's choreography was no more distracting than most of the ballets one sees in *Aida* on stage.

The quality of the music making was high indeed. The singers behind the faces of most of the cast members were an outstanding group. Renata Tebaldi sang for Aida, Ebe Stignani for Amneris, Giuseppe Campora for Radamès, Gino Bechi for Amanasro, and Giulio Neri for Ramfis, the role acted by Antonio Cassinelli. Enrico Formichi as the King and Paolo Caroli as the Messenger apparently both sang and acted, and of course Giovanna Russo, as the off-stage Priestess in Act 1, Scene 2 remained an invisible presence. The orchestra and chorus of RAI Rome were led with adequate dramatic sense by Giuseppe Morelli.

The performances of Tebaldi and Stignani are as satisfactory on the sound track as they were in the 1952 Decca/London recording, and the result is vocalism that ranks with the best. Gino Bechi is remembered from the HMV version, and he is still the rough, rowdy, warrior king that he was in 1946. It's something of a surprise here that he sings on the sound track while Afro Poli, another baritone of considerable experience, acts the role on the screen. Giulio Neri remains the coldest, most implacable Ramfis of all. The other singers are all capable, Giuseppe Campora somewhat more than that as Radamès. Campora made his international career primarily in lyrical roles, and in a staged performance he might have found Radamès too heavy for comfort. The voice is not particularly distinctive, but he manages some real ring and ping here when it's demanded, and his phrasing, particularly in the aria, is easy and ingratiating in spite of an eardrum-blasting final B-flat. In other words, the quality of the singing in the 1953 film holds up quite well against other recorded versions of the opera.

Why, then, is the film essentially a failure? Why does it leave us with the impression of a wonderful opportunity that went unhappily astray? For one thing, the cuts in the score are destructive to both musical and dramatic continuity. Large chunks are absent from the Nile scene at key points in the duets of Aida with her father and later with Radamès, and the action of the Triumphal scene simply does not make sense when everything in the score after Amonasro's entrance is severely truncated. As if by way of compensation, a little bit of battle music was stitched together by unknown hands from various themes to accompany the battle sequence that was not, of course, part of the original. Verdi's musical structure in *Aida* was remarkably neat and tight, and almost any change in it or omission from it tends to destroy the artistic effect.

Then there is the problem of making the plot itself clear to an audience with no knowledge of the Italian language. A narrator speaks over the music from time to time to fill in the gaps in the story, but how much more effective would have been the use of subtitles at the bottom of the screen or a brief summary perhaps before the beginning of each scene.

There are, of course, other problems that appear to be inherent in the process of filming an opera with one cast on screen and another on the sound track. In this case, the lip-synching has been done with considerable accuracy, but those of us familiar with opera in live performance will notice immediately that although the mouths move at the right time, the actors are clearly not singing. Only Afro Poli really looks as if he's actually voicing his role, and it's a fair guess that he actually was even though the sounds that we hear came from Gino Bechi. The others whose roles are dubbed don't open their mouths wide enough for the loud tones, and they show none of the effort that real singers truly must exert. The resulting effect is artificial in the extreme — as if singing in an opera were as easy as everyday speaking. It isn't, as any genuine opera singer will confirm. If actors are to lip-synch opera scores, they simply must perfect the art of looking like real opera singers in the process.

Is the ideal solution to film opera always with real singers who actually sing their roles? That's an issue that we'll have to confront more fully as we look at the twelve generally available video versions made from actual stage performances, but it's clear that the 1953 film would have had an entirely different look to it if Tebaldi had acted the Aida or Stignani had actually appeared as Amneris. For one thing, Tebaldi, attractive though she certainly was, could easily have grabbed this Egyptian lover by the arm and dragged him off to Ethiopia, and with Stignani, Amneris would have had only her voice and not the more visible feminine charms to appeal to Radamès.

Apparently the 1987 Swedish film of *Aida* used singers that with one exception (Radamès was acted by Niklas Ek and sung by Robert Grundin) also acted their roles. This version has not been available for review, but the impression from published notices suggests that it was both visually stunning and dramatically convincing. Without either seeing or hearing the film it is impossible to comment on the quality of the music making, but unlike the 1953 version, the reported length of one hour and thirty-five minutes promises a complete or nearly complete performance. The film was shot in the natural setting of the Canary Islands, and one feature that was noted at the time of its release was the costuming — or lack thereof: Some critics referred to it as "the topless *Aida*." Other cast members included Ingrid Tomasson as Amneris, Jan van Der Schaaf as Amonasro, and Alf Håggstam as Ramfis, with the Swedish Folk Opera Orchestra and Chorus conducted by Kerstin Nerbe. The director was Claes Fellbom. A conveniently available DVD issue would certainly be of interest to all fans of the opera, but an *Aida* sung in Swedish will hardly replace versions in the authentic Italian.

The other twelve performances of *Aida* under consideration here were filmed from actual stage performances primarily for viewing on home television screens. The difference is obvious immediately in the 1961 version from Tokyo. Franco

Capuana, the first-rate conductor, enters the orchestra pit and bows to the audience, after the brief prelude the curtain rises (literally in this case), and we see Radamès and Ramfis standing stiffly at center stage waiting for their cue to begin doing what they're there to do — and that is to sing.

That is more or less what happens throughout the remainder of the performance. The singers move downstage toward the audience and sing, very much as if they were participating in a concert. Even the Messenger addresses the paying customers instead of the characters on stage to deliver his warning about the military actions of the Ethiopians. The primary exceptions are Aida and Amonasro in the Nile scene, where they turn up the dramatics and relate to one another. The scenery is nondescript. The Triumphal scene is big and crowded, and the other settings have little character and do not present a unified visual concept. The costuming is varying degrees of disastrous. Notice, for example, the strange get-up of the dancers in the major ballet in Act 2. There is nothing at all flattering about the gowns that Aida is required to wear, and Amonasro's makeup and costume when he appears in Act 2 are truly alarming. What's more, the quality of the video is substandard with frequent changes from light to dark, and at least in the copy that I watched, a good measure of fuzzy, poorly focused images.

The audience loves it. It must be something other than what they see that gives rise to their thunderous applause and resonating *bravos, bravas,* and *bravis*. As a matter of fact it's precisely what it should be in an opera: It's the quality of the music making. The Japanese orchestra and chorus perform well for Capuana. Only the trumpeters in the Triumphal scene let us down badly. Aida makes one false entrance in the Nile scene, but she catches it immediately and is back on track. Admittedly, Capuana tends to give the singers their way, and there are a few unduly extended notes apparently just to show off the impressive voices. Amonasro holds on for a lengthy acknowledgement that he truly is "Suo padre" to Aida, and Radamès takes his time with the high A's when he surrenders to Ramfis in Act 3, but they are good notes and exciting to hear.

As Radamès, Mario Del Monaco doesn't actually sing very well. The voice is sturdy and certainly more than adequate for the role, but it is not as appealing as it would have been ten years or so earlier. He is loud. At the beginning of "Celeste Aida," there's a hint that he may temper the volume as he thinks of his beautiful Aida, but he moves relentlessly toward the high B-flat at the end, and it must be one of the loudest tenor notes ever recorded. In spite of it all, he manages an effective final scene. Unfortunately, his acting is rudimentary and mainly consists of raising his arms in preparation for another loud high note. It is, however, still an impressive voice, and it's good to hear it in a staged performance where he can truly let in ring out into the opera house.

Aldo Protti, as Amonasro sounds and interprets a great deal better than he often did in his Decca/London studio performance of the opera. Apparently a live audience inspired extra intensity in his performance. He has a loud, firm baritone with an attractive spin to it. He also shares a problem with many another Amonasro: When the temperature rises and his anger boils over, he has a tendency to bolt away from the notes that Verdi actually wrote. Paolo Washington is a firm, forceful, rather frightening Ramfis, but Silvano Pagliuca, in spite of singing well, lacks the power to rule Egypt effectively.

Giulietta Simionato is the impressive Amneris. Her voice is more inherently beautiful than either Cossotto's or Stignanis and is more cleanly focused than Barbieri's. In some of her studio recordings, she seems to lack dramatic involvement, but with an audience in front of her, she uses her voice with keen dramatic perception. She colors the tone to suit the situation, and she is a sovereign mistress of phrasing. On the video, her two curtain calls at the end of the Judgment scene offer a fascinating example of an artist so fully in control of herself and her audience that she can maintain the character while she is acknowledging the applause and cheers.

Gabriella Tucci proves herself an Aida of true quality. We miss a voice that is full in the mid range, and there are certainly singers, Tebaldi for example, who bring more velvet to the tone. Tucci, however, is an artist of great sensitivity, and her technical control makes up for a great deal of what is lacking in sheer voice. The Nile scene aria is beautifully sung, and her soft high notes, including the *dolce* high C, come gently and float engagingly out into the audience. She recorded far too little in the studio, and this *Aida* is a particularly valuable addition to our knowledge of her art.

This version of the opera is, in short, well worth hearing, even if it's a rather dreary performance to watch.*

In contrast, there was a great deal to see with plenty of opulence and more than ample space on the mammoth stage of the Verona arena on the evening of August 9, 1966. There is, in fact, too much space cluttered with too much scenery, and the director, Herbert Graf, obviously had a problem trying to fill it with something, occasionally with just about anything. The Triumphal scene is overwhelming. It looks as if the entire population of ancient Memphis has turned out to wave palm branches in celebration. The Egyptian army marches down en masse from high in the background. Poor Radamès must take a long down hill hike to arrive at stage center after he dismounts from his horse-drawn chariot, and the entry of the Ethiopian prisoners brings on what must be half of the population of that defeated nation. The ballet is danced by the full ensemble of the Kirov Ballet from St. Petersburg, and it so enchants the audience that they demand, and receive, a

---

*The soundtrack from the performance included on the video can be heard on Gala GL 100–507 for those who would rather hear than see this *Aida*.

complete encore. The eye simply can't take it all in, and the relatively primitive camera work doesn't help us to isolate the various fields of action.

In truth there are a great many things wrong with this production. The arena stage has too many steps. It must have been treacherous for the singers trying to maneuver and sing at the same time. The size of the stage keeps the principal singers almost constantly on the run from one side to the other and back again, and often they are singing straight out to the audience instead of to one another. The costumes for Aida and Amneris are acceptable, but most of the men, including the unfortunate Radamès, are clothed in attire awkward enough to be almost laughable. Then there's the acting. The challenge to communicate human emotion to an audience of thousands in an outdoor arena leads to tremendously exaggerated motions and a great deal of windmill arm waving, and most of the time Carlo Bergonzi as Radamès to all appearances doesn't act at all.

So why does this performance turn out to be tremendously exciting and moving in spite of all the problems? The answer is simple. The artists are singing their hearts out, and the drama is exactly where it belongs — in the voices. Bergonzi was the classic Verdi tenor. He sings here with a steady line, he communicates the text precisely, and the voice is full and resounding. The B-flat at the end of the aria is too loud, but at other points in the Nile scene and later in the tomb, he modulates the tone effectively. When in Act 3 he surrenders to Ramfis, he takes his time and lets the notes — they are high A's — ring out with total conviction and commitment. He isn't the world's loudest Radamès (Mario del Monaco offers a good number of extra decibels), but he is at that moment by far the most heroic.

Leyla Gencer, who sings Aida, is far from a perfect vocalist, and she's the boldest arm-waver of all in this cast. There's a loud, grating high C at the end of the Nile scene aria, and in the heat of the moment she can sometimes let the notes slip slightly below pitch. She sings softly, however, at most of the appropriate times, and there is never the slightest doubt that she means every word and every note of what she sings. In many of her largely unofficial recordings, she sounds vocally stretched, dramatically over the top, and somewhat mannered, but on that August night in 1966, she was right up there with the most exciting Aidas.

Fiorenza Cossotto's voice is more appealing and beautiful in her commercial studio recordings. At the Verona arena, she may be pushing a bit too much to reach the distant audience members, and the rather harsh quality of the recorded sound is surely no help. Her tone, however, is sure, incisive, and steady, even though as recorded here it has a rather sharp cutting edge to it. She, however, was often an artist who responded to opera as a competitive sport, and in this high-powered company she gives it her all. As often with her colleague Bergonzi, it's the completeness of the phrasing, the way she carries the line through to the end, that impresses. We don't hear as much affection for Radamès as we'd like, but she surely knows how to let the priests feel the full weight of her anger and frustration in the Judgment scene.

Bonaldo Gaiotti as Ramfis and Franco Pugliese as the King make less of an impression than the others in this cast, but Anselmo Colzani is a powerful and convincing Amonasro. His approach is primarily to belt it out and leave the *bel canto* niceties to the others, but he makes some good points. In the Nile scene, he is particularly keen in interpretation as he leads Aida to realize that he wants her to lure Radamès to reveal his military secrets. He is also the best actor from the visual standpoint in this cast, primitive and wild but fully motivated at every moment.

Musically, there are some lapses from the orchestra, and there's a particularly unpleasant High Priestess with a conspicuous wobble in the voice. Franco Capuana, however, remains a knowing conductor who paces the score quite well. There's nothing subtle in his leading, just as there's nothing subtle in the performance, but at the end we know we've experienced the real *Aida*.

A performance from the arena fifteen years later also made its way onto a commercially issued video. The visual quality of the color video is quite good, and Brian Large, who directed the video, varies camera angles and distances to good effect. The cast is not quite so highly charged as their 1966 counterparts, but for an all-around presentation of *Aida,* Verona had somewhat more to offer in 1981. All of the scenic clutter has been removed and the opera is staged now in a relatively austere, basic setting that is varied effectively for the different scenes of the opera. Lighting is used in striking ways to reflect the changing mood, and the cast, particularly the men, are costumed more simply and appropriately. The action throughout is blocked for maximum dramatic effect, the motivation is always made clear, and the singers are convincing in their roles. Giancarlo Sbragia, the producer, was apparently responsible for the skillful stage direction, particularly helpful in clarifying the action at the end of Act 3 although Amonasro's apparent slaying at the hands of the Egyptian soldiers flies in the face of the libretto.

The excellent King of Egypt, Alfredo Zanazzo, is powerful and secure enough to rule a restless nation. His high priest, Ramfis, as sung by Carlo Zardo, shares the power but falls short on security. Amonasro is frequently portrayed as a primitive, and Giuseppe Scandola fits that description to a fault. His singing is rough, occasionally uncertain of pitch, and almost always blustery. In all candor, he finds himself in better vocal company than he deserves.

Nicola Martinucci's Radamès is enough of a success to make us wonder why he didn't have a far more extensive recording career. He just might have been able to spell one of the Three Tenors occasionally. The voice is firm and well produced, but he has little of Bergonzi's elegance or ability to phrase both musically and dramatically. His primary fault is a tendency to sing loudly most of the time, but he manages to temper the volume appropriately in the final scene. He isn't much of an actor on stage, but he's still several steps ahead of Bergonzi, and he looks as if he might be a dashing young Egyptian military officer.

As Aida, Maria Chiara performs what would soon become her signature role with vocal skill and polish and an ingratiating voice that tends to thin just a bit on the top. She doesn't have the *dolce* high C that Verdi wanted for the Nile scene aria, but she manages the note better here than she does in the later sound recording and video. Otherwise the aria is eloquent in sound and expression, as is her "Ritorna vincitor" in Act 1. She looks beautiful and she acts with a great deal of dramatic reserve and subtlety.

Fiorenza Cossotto is still an arm-waver as she was in 1966, but she waves here to great dramatic purpose. Her voice is much better recorded so that the tenderness shows through where appropriate. She paces the stage like a wounded tiger in the Judgment scene, and there is nothing vocally in this score that she can't handle. Her voice is wonderfully secure, with not a wobble to be heard, from the top to the powerful chest tones. Her Amneris is a classic performance, and she certainly deserves the overwhelming ovation she receives at the end of her big scene. It's rather heartwarming to see her rise from the floor to acknowledge the applause, then bow deeply to her knees and throw a few kisses to the audience, a time-honored tradition of great Italian singers.

Some of the other films and videos of the opera have a great deal to offer, visually and vocally, but as an overall performance of *Aida* for home viewing, the 1981 Verona video ranks among the best.

Also from 1981 comes a performance from the San Francisco Opera. The production values are high and stage settings and costumes are attractive even if a bit cumbersome for the artists. Sam Wanamaker's direction clarifies the plot effectively, and García Navarro conducts with youthful enthusiasm and dramatic thrust. All of this is brought vividly to colorful life in an excellently produced DVD.

Interest centers first of all on Luciano Pavarotti's first Radamès. Time and experience will add a little more polish to his interpretation, but in 1981 the voice was at its mature prime, and he sings with warm, rounded tone throughout. He suffers from a common problem in "Celeste Aida," the failure to maintain a gentle, caressing touch for the rise to F and F-sharp in the opening phrases, but time after time he is far more attentive than many of his tenor colleagues to Verdi's expression markings in the score. After a few bars of almost unvocalized crooning, he is excellent in the final scene and, with his soprano partner, produces a truly ethereal effect at the conclusion. Some viewers might insist on a little more voice for the big climaxes and a little less Pavarotti for the effective portrayal of a romantic hero. Brian Large, the excellent video director, has aimed his cameras wherever possible on Pavarotti's highly expressive face, and the result is a performance as appealing visually as it is vocally.

Large's cameras also tend to focus on Margaret Price's face as she sings Aida. In spite of her ample form, she is a beautiful woman and her face reflects Aida's emotional states almost as effectively as Pavarotti's. Hers is not a typical Aida voice, perhaps a shade too small to fill out all of Verdi's soaring phrases. The tone, however, is wonderfully pure, the scale even and balanced, and she uses the chest voice only rarely and with great caution. All that is lacking vocally is the ability to float the soft high notes. Her interpretation is always alive and aware, not only in the two arias but also and particularly in her Nile scene duets.

Stefania Toczyska is a visually stunning Amneris. Her acting, however, smacks of standard opera house routine although she makes her mark with it in the Judgment scene and receives an excited ovation from the audience. She pushes her voice beyond its natural capacity so that the vibrato and often the strain are excessive. In short, we yearn for Stignani, Barbieri, Simionato, or Cossotto.

Simon Estes suffers from some of the same problems as Amonasro, and he apparently tries to compensate with an explosive overemphasis on the words. We miss a true *legato* in "Ma tu Re" and "Rivedrai le foreste imbalsamate," and in both cases it remains for Margaret Price to show him the way to do it. The King, Kevin Langan, does not have a voice adequately impressive for the role, and Kurt Rydl, who sings Ramfis, is sometimes shaky of tone, particularly in the early scenes. One suspects in his case that he has strayed into the wrong role.

The San Francisco version of the opera is valuable primarily for its impressive visual qualities and for the interesting and often appealing performances of Pavarotti and Price. Pavarotti, however, we will encounter later in a preferable version of the opera from La Scala.

In 1986 at Parma, Chiara is once more Aida and Martinucci again sings Radamès. The video recording of this performance turns out to be thoroughly frustrating. When the stage is adequately lighted, the color reproduction is quite good, but in scene after scene there are extended periods in which we can see virtually nothing. The stage is divided throughout into two levels, and action on the lower level is often lost in the shadows. The problem is particularly damaging in the Nile scene, and here, since there are no summaries of the action or subtitles, anyone not already familiar with the opera will end up both literally and figuratively in the dark.

What we are able to see of the stage, however, is not much of an improvement. The upper level is occupied mainly by a large stairway that remains virtually unchanged and serves primarily as a platform for the priests. In the first act and the Consecration and Triumphal scenes, the priests or other court attendants stand there in concert formation, and the other Egyptians present are lined up in similar fashion on the lower level. The chorus sings the praises of the Egyptian armies and the trumpets blare out the familiar march, but no conquering forces enter, and as far as the viewer can tell, Radamès slips in almost unnoticed. Until the final two acts, what we are seeing is essentially an oratorio set to the music of Verdi's *Aida,* not an opera, The ballets, which are interestingly choreographed in a rather "primitive" style, relieve the dramatic tedium somewhat. The human action of Acts 3 and 4, however, is played out with some intensity, but all of it on the lower level and much of it virtually invisible to us.

The performers deserved better, and musically they give us a better than average *Aida.* Chiara is still a good heroine. There are more thin and unpleasant notes at the top of her range, but after a somewhat hectic "Ritorna vincitor," she sings her Nile scene aria even better than in 1981 with a high C that comes closer to meeting Verdi's challenging demand. Dramatically, she is convincing and responsive, much as she was seven years earlier.

Martinucci is, if anything, even louder than he was at Verona, but the voice still has a good ring to it and ample heft for the role's dramatics. From time to time he appears to be nervous, and his acting, when we can see him, suffers for it. A botched phrase with a high B-flat in the "Si Fugiam" portion of his Nile scene duet with Aida sends him plunging an octave below the score pitch, but he recovers quickly. After all, this recording comes from a live staged performance, and mistakes are almost inevitable. He seems even more nervous during the final curtain calls when the stage is being bombarded with enough bouquets to empty all of Parma's flower shops.

Elena Obraztsova is Amneris with a vengeance. She was always a high-powered vocalist, and she can and does still turn the volume up too high too often. Combined with the volume, the tendency to sit heavily on the lower chest tones has apparently done damage to vocal security, and she has some problems with pitch. When she sings softly, however, much of the vocal beauty is still there, and she performs with passionate intensity in the Judgment scene.

Bruno Pola is equally passionate and has power aplenty as Amonasro. He doesn't demonstrate a great deal of affection for his daughter so that his interpretation is essentially one dimensional, but he sings a strong, eloquent, well phrased "Pensa che un popolo" in the Nile scene. Franco Federici as the King is firm voiced and authoritative as a King should be.

Completing the major roles in this cast is Cesare Siepi as Ramfis. According to the notes in the Bel Canto Society video edition, these Parma performances marked Siepi's farewell to the opera stage. At first, it seems that he might have a little trouble with vocal security, but he soon hits his stride. His was always one of the most beautiful bass voices warmed with a velvety vibrato, and he sings the text knowingly. Very few basses are able to make as much of the questions in the Judgment scene as this sixty-five year old veteran.

Donato Renzetti is the able conductor. He can't quite conceal the fact that the

Orchester Sinfonia dell Emilia Romano is not one of the world's greatest instrumental ensembles, but aside from occasional and inevitable ensemble lapses everything holds together well.

We may wonder if the frequent bows of the artists within the acts are a local custom in Parma. There is a certain quaintness about them, for example, when Obraztsova must rise somewhat uncomfortably from her kneeling position to acknowledge the applause at the end of the Judgment scene. Even stranger: At the end of Act 2, Scene 1, after Aida has fallen to her knees appealing to the gods for "pietà," Amneris returns to the scene and gives her a hand to help her to her feet. Then together they bow to the appreciative audience. Come to think of it, opera may be more fun in Italy than it is in more sedate societies.

Also from 1986 is the La Scala *Aida,* this time pairing Chiara with Luciano Pavarotti. The production, well captured on the video, is oppressively monumental, so much so that in the Triumphal scene the stage setting almost overwhelms the dramatic action. Giant monoliths and mammoth heads carved of stone move about the stage propelled by whip-driven slaves, a multi-layered wooden prison holding the Ethiopian prisoners is pushed onto the scene, and the Egyptian royals from their safe position on high toss down bread to the hungry peasants, who dance the ballet in response to their largesse. It's almost like an indoor version of the Verona amphitheatre. Throughout the first two acts, it seems that almost anything to avoid the traditional is thrown into the mix, including topless maidens and almost naked Moorish children cavorting in a pool in Amneris' boudoir. The geography of the Judgment scene makes it a bit hard to figure how everyone manages to end up where they didn't start out, but the Nile scene is quite atmospheric and the final scene, created almost entirely with the subdued lighting, conveys fully the radical loneliness and isolation of the tomb.

What happens musically and dramatically in this setting is often impressive. Chiara is much as she was in Parma. She is a gifted actress, and she brings the character vividly to life. Her voice is generally in good condition although there are a few more raw notes in the higher pitches and the Nile scene aria isn't as neatly polished as it was in Parma. All in all, however, she is a thoroughly respectable Aida.

Pavarotti retains much of his vocal glamour. Things don't go quite as well for him as they did in Decca studio recording from the same period. For example, the *morendo* at the conclusion of his aria is not in evidence here, but he shapes phrases carefully, and as always the voice is just about as beautiful as they come. Dramatically he is off form and he moves awkwardly on the stage — or perhaps it's just that we miss the many close-ups of his face that Brian Large provided in the 1981 San Francisco performance.

A soprano Amneris would not have met with Verdi's approval, but that's precisely what we have here. Ghena Dimitrova has enough power to shake the obelisks of ancient Egypt, but the voice itself is often harsh and unpleasant, and the chest tones are not only loud, they're also abrasive to the ear. She, however, generates a great deal of dramatic excitement and is highly specific in communicating the emotional content of her encounters both with Aida in Act 2 and with Radamès in Act 4.

The lower voiced men really shine in this performance. Paata Burchuladze, now the King rather than the High Priest of the sound recording, is a dark-voiced, impressive ruler, better perhaps in royal robes than in priestly vestments. For Ramfis, we have Nicolai Ghiaurov. He's not quite the powerhouse basso that he was a few years earlier, but the voice retains its basic, warm quality, and there is good contrast with Burchuladze. Juan Pons turns in an excellent Amonasro, fiercely determined but capable also of affectionate concern for Aida. It isn't the world's most beautiful baritone voice, but he handles it well. In the Nile scene, it's good to have an Amonasro who sings to Aida and not either to the audience or into the theatre wings.

Lorin Maazel was the controversial conductor. Some critics found his performance unduly slow and mannered, but the La Scala orchestra and chorus perform well for him, the drama comes through in the performance, and there's no particular reason why a conductor should need to race through *Aida*. After all, compared to many operas, it's surely not unduly long.

The 1989 video of a Metropolitan Opera performance will appeal primarily to those who prefer a traditional production that is also well sung. The cast is largely familiar from various sound recordings of the opera, and on the whole they acquit themselves well here. The massive stage settings consist primarily of large, solid, architectural units; the costumes are conventional and attractive; and the stage direction clarifies the action for the audience, particularly in the Nile scene with such touches as having Amneris oversee and overhear enough of the action to make her charge of "Traitor!" convincing. In an age of way out "concept" productions of standard repertoire operas, it's reassuring to discover that the old, traditional virtues of faithfulness to the composer and the librettist have not been completely forgotten.

James Levine conducts the excellent orchestra and choral forces of the Metropolitan Opera. He tends to take his time, but there is adequate excitement in the playing and even in the brief prelude he lets us know that there is high drama ahead.

As Radamès, Plácido Domingo is his familiar self. His voice is not as fresh as it would have been a few years earlier, but he sings with a great deal of sensitivity and produces firm, heroic tone when it's needed. He is also keenly aware that he is performing not alone but with a cast of colleagues. He listens and reacts effectively. His aria concludes with the alternative ending that Verdi provided — a loud high

B-flat followed by "vicino al sol" sung softly an octave lower — and with Millo in the final scene he provides the true *dolcissimo* that Verdi requested. He may be a better Radamès on other recorded versions, but even late in his career he belongs with the best.

Aida is one of the most demanding soprano roles in the repertoire, both musically and dramatically. Aprile Millo doesn't give us the full dimension of a character who is far more complex than some commentators will allow. There is more of sweetness and light than sound and fury in her performance. In the opening scene, she sounds thin and rather metallic, but her voice warms up as the performance continues. By the time she comes to the Nile scene she is fully in command, with ringing *fortes* produced with no tonal harshness, and she sings an eloquent "O patria mia" capped with a good high C.

Dolora Zajick is unfortunately a rather distracting actress on the stage. Anger — and Amneris has a great deal of it — is expressed primarily by huffing and puffing, and she often seems more peeved than furious and despairing. She is not, however, the first Amneris to do most her acting with the voice (we think for example of Stignani), and she is an inherently dramatic *singer*. She has a warm ample voice touched with an appealing light vibrato, and she colors it appropriately to express Amneris' rapidly changing emotions. On the whole, her performance works better in the theatre than it did in the recording studio.

Sherrill Milnes is a more sympathetic Amonasro than we often encounter. We sense the love for his daughter in his demeanor even after he has disowned her as a "schiava" of the Pharaoh. He isn't afraid to sing softly, but he can rant and rave with the best of them. When the musical phrase will permit it, as in "Ma tu re" and "Rivedrai la foreste imbalsamate," he produces a smooth *legato*, occasionally so conspicuously liquid as to throw the pitch momentarily into question. Paata Burchuladze is again Ramfis, as he was in the 1986 Decca studio recording, a figure both powerful and threatening, but Dimitri Kavrakos makes a poor showing as the King with occasional pitch problems and some rather mushy Italian diction.

We travel from New York to London for a 1994 performance from Covent Garden. Michael Yeargen designed what might well be called a minimalist production. Other than the performers themselves the stage is kept virtually empty, and effects, often very impressive, are achieved primarily with lighting, varying from subdued dark blue for the Nile scene to blazing sun-bathed orange for the Triumphal scene. The costumes blend effectively with the stage settings, but we're hard put to decide what historical time and place these more or less exotic designs are meant to represent. Elijah Moshinsky's direction is persuasive in clarifying action and motivation, and only the decision to make Radamès attempt what appears to be an unsuccessful attempt to escape at the end of Act 3 before surrendering is questionable. The most striking visual effect in the performance is the Act 2 ballet with its violent martial arts maneuvers. If you're inclined to complain that it isn't authentically ancient Egyptian, remember that most *Aida* ballets have nothing to do with the findings of historical research.

Edward Downes conducts effectively and also unobtrusively. There is nothing distinctive about his interpretation of Verdi's score, which means that he's willing to do what Verdi asks of him without imposing anything personal on top of it.

At some key points, however, his singers let him down. Cheryl Studer as Aida apparently has some clear ideas about the character of the Ethiopian princess, and Brian Large's expert camera gives us close-ups of her effective reactions to her father and her lover in Act 3. Her voice, however, is at considerably less than its best. As we would expect in a live performance, she warms up as the opera proceeds so that what began as rather narrow, wiry tone takes on more color by the Nile scene. She sings a secure high C at the end of her Act 3 aria, but it is thin and inadequately related to the rest of her voice, and from time to time top notes are marginally under pitch. Her performance is far from a disaster, but it isn't going to replace our memories of the great Aidas.

Dennis O'Neill sings Radamès, a role he will repeat seven years later in the English language compact disc recording on the Chandos label. There is not much sensuous appeal in his voice, and he sounds here, as he does in the later recording, like a surprisingly mature military hero with loud, strained high notes. He matches the sound with aging appearance in Act 3 when, after sporting brown hair in the earlier scenes, he shows up with a conspicuous gray mane. Was Moshinsky trying to tell us something, or is it something only his hairdresser knows? O'Neill, however, is an effective actor, particularly strong in his realization of his betrayal in Act 3.

Luciana d'Intino isn't a perfect vocalist, and her acting is more conventional than revelatory. She is none-the-less a powerful Amneris with the insight and ability to turn from cajoling to loving and then to anger, and let the changes be heard in her voice and seen in her actions. She can handle the soaring vocal line of this mezzo-soprano role with ease, although she has somewhat less to offer at the bottom of her range.

Mark Beesley makes little impression as the King, but Robert Lloyd is a force of stern, implacable nature as Ramfis. His full and secure voice and his towering appearance in his unusual orange-colored robe make him a formidable enemy for the despairing Amneris in the Judgment scene.

Best of all is Alexandru Agache as Amonasro. He gives us a multi-layered picture of the Ethiopian King, clearly torn between his love for Aida and his desire for military revenge against Egypt, and he lets us know vocally the difference between lying to the Pharaoh and speaking the absolute truth to his daughter. What's more, he manages a well-controlled *legato* where appropriate, and he rings out movingly in a soaring "Pensa che un popolo."

The 1999 performance from the San Carlo Theatre in Naples is anything other than minimalist in design. Costumes by Zaira De Vincentus and scenic designs by Aldo De Lorenzo take us back to the style of the nineteenth century, and were we not in a much larger theatre than the little Cairo Opera House, we might well imagine ourselves sitting in for the 1871 premiere. We could call this the "historicizing" approach, and it is certainly a legitimate way to present the opera. Better the 1870s than the far-out restaging of some recent productions. Whether the acting style duplicates the nineteenth-century approach is impossible to tell, but I have a feeling that our contemporary singers are both more subdued and probably less effective than their counterparts from one hundred forty or more years ago. In any case Naples in 1999 offers us no startling new insights into the characters.

Dramatically and musically speaking the performance moves slowly and not without a degree of tedium. In the Triumphal scene, for example, scores of Egyptian soldiers march onto the stage with nowhere to go so that they circle the stage and exit the same place they entered. Conductor Daniel Oren keeps the pace slow too much of the time, but in the more meditative, reflective moments like Aida's "Ritorna vincitor," he allows the singers ample time to make their points effectively. There are a few problems in ensemble with singers and orchestra, but they do not occur often enough to mar the effect of a rather stately performance of the opera.

The singers are a mixed lot. Fiorenza Cedolins brings a basically attractive voice to Aida. When pitch and volume go up simultaneously she works too hard and the result is strain and a tendency to produce decidedly uncomfortable high notes. She's at her best when she's not fighting against a full orchestral *forte*. "O patria mia" is a highlight of her performance, sung sensitively with a beautiful *dolce* high C at its climax. Her acting is conventionally effective, but the camera has not done her any favors. Her makeup, which was no doubt planned with the effect on the audience in the auditorium in mind, often makes her look at times as if she has two black eyes, and close-up shots make us all too aware of the effort involved in producing the voice.

Radamès, Walter Faccaro, makes a favorable impression with a sensitively phrased "Celeste Aida" until he blasts our ears with a shattering B-flat. Top notes, as a matter of fact, are often tight and unpleasant, but he holds on to them for all he's worth none the less. The final scene shows him in a better light with the right touch of gentle, concerned tenderness for Aida. Sad to tell, he's simply not much of an actor and often moves awkwardly on the stage.

The only readily familiar name in this cast is Dolora Zajick, whose performance we have already encountered in the Metropolitan Opera sound recording and video. Her costumes, like many others in this production, are unfortunate, and she is here no more effective as an actress than she was in 1989. For Zajick, the drama remains in the voice, which is still as fresh and vital as it was ten years earlier. If she generates somewhat less vocal excitement here, the difficulty may have been the relatively uninspiring production in which she found herself.

Both of the basses, Giacomo Prestia as Ramfis and Carlo Striuli as the King, are entirely acceptable, although we need more sheer sonic power for a ruler of Egypt. The best performance in this production, however, comes from Vittorio Vitelli as Amonasro. Once or twice in lower passages, he is drowned out by the orchestra. Otherwise, however, his voice is firm, secure, appealing, and used with great skill and his dramatic presence brings things to vivid life when he appears both in the Triumphal scene and Act 3. He's the kind of artist from whom we would enjoy hearing more in the future.

It's interesting to speculate on the importance of the audience in a live operatic performance. The Naples audience shows their approval rarely and without a great deal of obvious enthusiasm. Applause after arias and major ensembles is either reluctant or virtually nonexistent. Even during the final curtain calls, the reception is relatively subdued and large portions of the audience are heading toward the exits as soon as the last "pace" has faded away. Would a more responsive audience have produced a more exciting evening at the opera?

On January 26, 2001, the centennial of Verdi's death, *Aida* was performed at Busetto, the composer's home town, in the theatre dedicated to him. We can only guess how Verdi would have reacted to the occasion. He had very little patience with strictly formal affairs, and only reluctantly had he permitted the Teatro Giuseppe Verdi, which opened in 1868 in his absence, to bear his name. Given the amount of attention he paid to the production details of the early performances of *Aida* and his frequent refusals to permit changes in his score, he might well have protested the omission of the dances of the Moorish slaves and the major ballet in the Triumphal scene. It's entirely possible, however, that once he experienced the commemorative performance, he just might have smiled his approval. After all, it is a performance of sterling qualities.

Franco Zeffirelli, the distinguished Italian director and designer, is generally identified with complicated, elaborate, and *expensive* productions peopled by hundreds of dancers, singers, extras, and occasional animals. How he would deal with an opera like *Aida,* with its reputation for overwhelming, monumental productions in the Teatro Verdi, a small-scale jewel box opera house with limited stage space and an auditorium that seats a mere three hundred fifty, was very much the question. The answer, as it turned out, was also a jewel with beautiful, evocative scenery and costumes that looked good and told us something important about the characters who wore them. Most impressive of all, however, was the depth of the insight that Zeffirelli brought to the characters and their motivation and the skill with which he communicated that insight to his cast of young singers.

All of the artists were young, primarily in their mid-twenties, and obviously close to the beginning of their careers, but there is no hint of uncertainty or immaturity in their performances. (Look for the ageless Carla Fracci, the famous Italian ballerina and actress, in the Temple of Vulcan.) The documentary that accompanies the DVD issue of this performance shows us Zeffirelli rehearsing his cast, giving them a detailed understanding of the characters and their actions, and encouraging them to think "outside the box" about their roles. No doubt, one of the advantages of youth was that on the whole they'd never yet been *inside* the box in so far as *Aida* is concerned, and they had little or nothing to unlearn. The documentary that accompanies the DVD of this performance shows us Zeffirelli at work with his cast, and it is, in and of itself, an exciting, stimulating introduction to the opera.

Aida, Adina Aaron, is a beautiful young woman with a supremely expressive face that reveals every one of Aida's shifting emotions. She is the only Aida in any of these video versions of the opera who is dressed like a slave, not like a princess. Hers is certainly the most seductive approach to Radamès in the Nile scene, and all of the ambiguities of her situation are mirrored perfectly in her face. From the visual standpoint, it is bar none the best-acted Aida in any of the performances. She handles the role with a great deal of vocal polish, and like the other singers in this cast, her voice is blessedly free of wobble and insecurity. Of course, these young artists have one great advantage: They do not have to project into a vast opera house with two or three thousand in the audience.

Her Radamès, Scott Piper, is similarly gifted. How he would fare in a larger house, we can't say, but at the Teatro Verdi he sings a superb "Celeste Aida" with a clear understanding of when to be heroic and when to be tender, and his high B-flat would surely have brought a happy smile to Verdi's face. He, too, is a gifted actor who has learned well from Zeffirelli's instruction. We notice particularly the sense of boyish joy in his choice as the general to lead the Egyptian forces in Act 1, and his shame for his own failure when he encounters Amneris in Act 3, Scene 1. Zeffirelli has also helped his cast to make clear from the very beginning that the relationship with Amneris was already well on its way before love for Aida entered the picture, and what a telling touch it is to have him kiss Amneris gently on the forehead before his final departure from her in the Judgment scene.

Kate Aldrich is almost as good in the role of Amneris, which is in some ways the most difficult role in the opera. She, like Aaron, is beautiful enough to have attracted the attention of Radamès, and she makes it clear that she is honestly and seriously in love with him. There is far more than angry jealousy in her emotional makeup. She has a voice of ample size for this small theatre, and she doesn't hesitate to release its full force in the Judgment scene. Aldrich uses her chest register a great deal frequently at the highest volume levels. The effect is admittedly exciting, but we may wonder if it's really a healthy approach for a young singer still in her vocal formative years.

As Amonasro, Giuseppe Garra reveals an sizeable baritone of good quality and he acts convincingly, although it isn't clear why he appears to be so angry with Aida at the opening of their duet in Act 3. It makes the real anger later in their encounter somewhat less impressive. Enricco Giuseppe Iori sings well as Ramfis, as does Paolo Pecchioli as the King. Both of them, however, have some difficulty looking old enough for these austere characters, and Pecchioli particularly sounds like a surprisingly young fellow to be the father of Amneris.

The conductor, Maximilliano Stefanelli, manages to make his ensemble sound larger than it actually is, a great help in the Triumphal scene, but he never allows the orchestra to overwhelm the singers. His musical leadership along with the vocal coaching provided by Carlo Bergonzi assures a performance that is careful in the observation of Verdi's indications in the score.

Is this performance perfect? Of course not. We really do want a little more spectacle than the Teatro Verdi's limited stage can provide. We miss the two omitted ballet passages, and the singers, for all of their many gifts and superior discipline, are not quite Caballe or Cossotto or Domingo or even Bergonzi himself. The performance, however, rings true with conviction and imagination, and it is the most challenging and interesting interpretation of the opera on any recording. Only Gobbi and Callas can equal it from that standpoint, but then we can only *hear* them, and in this case, it's seeing that is believing.

Seeing is the major attraction of the video of a 2001 performance at Barcelona's Gran Teatre del Liceu. The stage settings were designed and painted from 1936 to 1945 by Josep Mestres Cabanes and were restored by Jordi Castells for this production. They were painted on paper — cheap paper, the commentary informs us — stretched over wooden forms and then suspended from the fly loft of the theatre to be lowered onto the stage at the proper time. Seen in combination with Franca Squarclapino's period-inspired costumes, they are filled with color and a special type of visual excitement, created in part by superbly controlled theatre lighting. Aside from the impressive settings and costumes, this performance of *Aida* is musically acceptable but not precisely outstanding.

The conductor, Miguel Anagel Gomez Martinez, keeps everything in order and underlines the drama effectively. He is particularly good at marshalling his forces in the Triumphal scene so that we can follow clearly the contributions of the various groups and individuals. Dramatically, the performance offers nothing new, and it certainly pales in contrast to Zeffirelli's inspired direction in the Busetto *Aida*. Best is the final scene, which ends as Aida leads Radamès away from the tomb and toward the gleam of a distant light — a graphic realization of what they have sung. "A noi si schiude il ciel e l'alme erranti/Volano al raggio dell'eterno di ... To us the heavens open and our wandering souls rise to the glowing light of eternal day."

Aida is Daniela Dessì. She knows the traditions of the role, and her acting is conventionally old-fashioned but highly emotional and sympathetic. Her voice is not quite large enough to fill out the climaxes in the role, but she has a warm, inviting tone, and she sings well aside from a few squally high notes and some occasional insecurity. Her costuming is the one serious blot on the engaging visual aspect of this production. In Act 3, as she wraps and unwraps her large stole, she looks like the Queen of England complete with what could pass as a tiara on her head. On the whole, however, hers is an endearing performance.

Fabio Armiliato offers a loud, rather stentorian Radamès. To his credit, the voice is steady and secure, the tone forward and bright almost all the time, and frequently tight as if the sound is being forced from his throat. In small doses, his singing works well, but over the long haul it's a bit exhausting for the ears of the listener. As an actor, he is fully involved without being very imaginative, but he's certainly a few steps ahead of those tenors who view the role primarily as a vocal recital in costume.

Ramfis, Roberto Scandiuzzi, is large of voice with a big, hollow, forbidding sound that is no doubt appropriate for the character. Stefano Palatchi passes muster as the King, although his voice is not always steady and secure. As Amonasro, Juan Pons is a less-effective singer and interpreter than he was at La Scala in 1986. The voice is still an impressive instrument, but it is used here explosively in a style that too often breaks the Verdian line.

I'm afraid we listen in vain for something positive to say of Elisabetta Fiorillo's Amneris. Well, she is loud enough and angry enough to communicate the vindictive aspect of the character. Otherwise, however, she is an unfortunate throwback to the arm-waving Amneris of the past. As a singer, the voice can sound pleasant enough when it's not under pressure. Unfortunately, it's usually under pressure, and a distracting tremolo develops. The audience, however, loves her and gives her quite an ovation at the end of the Judgment scene.

Taken as a whole, this *Aida* surely doesn't challenge any of the front runners, but the opportunity to see Cabanes' beautifully restored stage settings in glowing color may well be worth the price. This version of the opera occupies two DVD discs and includes an interesting documentary on the origin and restoration of the scenery.

The DVD catalogs list a 1997 *Aida* from the St. Marghareten Festival in Austria. It turns out to include approximately half of the opera in frustrating selections that more often than not come to an abrupt end before the actual conclusion of either the aria or the ensemble involved.* The production is set in a vast ancient

---

*A later and apparently complete performance of the opera from St. Margarethen has been released in Europe and the United States (EuroArts 2054058). The conductor is Ernst Marzendorfer,

Roman stone quarry, which is declared on the DVD box to be "the biggest Open-Air Stage in Europe." Big it certainly is. The none-too-polished orchestra sits on the stage area itself, but there is ample room left for great numbers of chorus members, stage extras, horses, and even three elephants. The pachyderms cross the stage in the Triumphal scene, and two of them come back for no discernible reason during the ensemble with the Ethiopian prisoners.

Elephants, however, do not an *Aida* make, and what is missing in this performance, at least in the portion we are permitted to see, is the one thing without which the opera cannot hope to succeed — a cast of gifted singers. We really do not hear enough of Walter Donati as Amonasro, Aleksander Teliga as Ramfis, or Ivan Tomasev as the King to pass judgment. They apparently have appreciable voices, although Donati tends to push his voice slightly above pitch in the Triumphal scene. What he may have accomplished in the Nile scene is neither seen nor heard on this DVD. Adriana Nicolai as Amneris has a large, blowsy voice with a heavy vibrato. Bruno Sebastian as Radamès is a disaster. His voice is unpleasant in timbre and out of focus a great deal of the time, and his acting is rudimentary. It would have been an interesting but not particularly happy experience to hear him in a performance with Vasilka Petrova, the Aida of the notorious abridged Ace sound recording mentioned in Chapter 5.

Pauletta de Vaughn, who sings Aida, however, has real promise. She is an effective actress with perhaps more emphasis on the abject slave than the proud Princess of Ethiopia, and her voice, substantial enough for the role, is under good control and has a well-rounded, tonally beautiful sound. We get most of her "Ritorna vincitor" and the final scene, in which she far out sings Sebastian, and snippets of other parts of her role. Hers is the one performance in this *Aida* that we would enjoy seeing and hearing in a complete version and with better company.

Aida on film and video it seems is very much a mixed bag, and no single version offers everything we want in a performance. Perhaps the best all-round choices are the Metropolitan opera in 1989 and the 1986 La Scala performance. We can add to them for sheer spectacle the Verona arena in 1981 and for a special kind of vocal excitement the 1966 version from the same venue. However, for a penetrating understanding of the drama nothing can quite equal Zeffirelli's 2001 production from Busetto even without the ballets.

[*continued*] and cast members include Eszter Sumegi, Kostadin Andreev, Cornelia Helfricht, Pier Dalas, and Janusz Monarcha. A 2003 *Aida* video (Icestorm Entertainment, Direct Video Distribution DVDG2007) reproduces a production from the Basel football stadium, with Marko Letonja as conductor and 1,000 people in the company. Cast members include Ines Salazar as Aida, Keith Olsen as Radamès, Hermine May as Amneris, Johannes Von Duisburg as Amonasro, Ivan Urbas as Ramfis, and Stefano Rinaldi-Miliani as the King. It is not available in the NTSC format for viewing in the United States.

Appendix I — Discography

(The original label of release is indicated beside the date. On the last line, the language, if other than the original Italian, is listed. At the end of the artist listing a current or recent compact disc recording, if such exists, is listed by label and number. Sources for discographical information include the resources listed in Appendix III along with various catalogues and the notes included with recordings.)

1906–07	**Green Zonophone**
Aida	Teresa Chelotti, Elvira Magliulo
Amneris	Vittoria Colombati
Priestess	Unlisted
Radamès	Orazio Cosentino
Amonasro	Giovanni Novelli
Ramfis	Alfredo Brondi
King	Unlisted
Messenger	Unlisted
Conductor	Unlisted
Orchestra	La Scala, Milan
Chorus	La Scala, Milan

1909	**Gramophone**
Aida	Celestina Boninsegna, Adalgisa Rossi-Murino, Elena Ruszkowska, Giulia Fabris
Amneris	Maria Cappiello, Carolina Pietrszewska, Bianca Lavin de Casas
Priestess	Unlisted
Radamès	Egidio Cunego, Carlo Giovanni Davi
Amonasro	Giuseppe Maggi, Ernesto Badini
Ramfis	Arturo Rizzo di Sant'Elia
King	Giuseppe Quinzi Tapergi
Messenger	Unlisted
Conductor	Carlo Sabajno
Orchestra	La Scala, Milan
Chorus	La Scala, Milan

1912 Columbia	**(Abridged Recording)**
Aida	Lya Remondini, Ester Toninello, Lia Moglia, Teresa Chelotti, De Perez
Amneris	Andreina Beinat, Eugenia Lopez-Nuñes, Fanny Anitua, Dolores Julia Frau
Priestess	Unlisted
Radamès	Giuseppe Armanini, Gaetano Tommasini, Egidio Cunego
Amonasro	Cesare Formichi
Ramfis	Vincenzo Bettoni, Giovanni Martino
King	Luigi Baldassarri
Messenger	Unlisted
Conductor	Unlisted
Orchestra	Unlisted
Chorus	Unlisted

"House of Opera" CD-R AE 301, "From Which We Came"

Appendix 1

1919–20 HMV
Aida	Valentina Bartolomasi
Amneris	Rosita Pagini
Priestess	Valentina Bartolomasi
Radamès	Enrico Trentini
Amonasro	Adolfo Pacini
Ramfis	Guido Fernandez
King	Pietro Brilli
Messenger	Gaetano Mazzanti
Conductor	Carlo Sabajno
Orchestra	La Scala, Milan
Chorus	La Scala, Milan

1928 HMV
Aida	Dusolina Giannini
Amneris	Irene Minghini-Cattaneo
Priestess	Unlisted
Radamès	Aureliano Pertile
Amonasro	Giovanni Inghilleri
Ramfis	Luisi Manfrini
King	Guglielmo Masini
Messenger	Giuseppe Nessi
Conductor	Carlo Sabajno
Orchestra	La Scala, Milan
Chorus	La Scala, Milan

Romophone 89004–2

1928 Columbia
Aida	Giannina Arangi-Lombardi
Amneris	Maria Capuana
Priestess	Unlisted
Radamès	Aroldo Lindi
Amonasro	Armando Borgioli
Ramfis	Tancredi Pasero
King	Salvatore Baccaloni
Messenger	Giuseppe Nessi
Conductor	Lorenzo Molajoli
Orchestra	La Scala, Milan
Chorus	La Scala, Milan

VAI Audio VAIA 1083–2

1946 HMV
Aida	Maria Caniglia
Amneris	Ebe Stignani
Priestess	Maria Huder
Radamès	Beniamino Gigli
Amonasro	Gino Bechi
Ramfis	Tancredi Pasero
King	Italo Tajo
Messenger	Adelio Zagonara
Conductor	Tullio Serafin
Orchestra	Rome Opera
Chorus	Rome Opera

Naxos 8.110156–57

1949 RCA
Aida	Herva Nelli
Amneris	Eva Gustavson
Priestess	Teresa Stich-Randall
Radamès	Richard Tucker
Amonasro	Giuseppe Valdengo
Ramfis	Norman Scott
King	Dennis Harbour
Messenger	Virginio Assandri
Conductor	Arturo Toscanini
Orchestra	NBC Symphony
Chorus	Robert Shaw Chorale

BMG 60300-2-RG

1951 Fonit Cetra
Aida	Caterina Mancini
Amneris	Giulietta Simionato
Priestess	Unlisted
Radamès	Mario Filippeschi
Amonasro	Rolando Panerai
Ramfis	Giulio Neri
King	Antonio Massaria
Messenger	Salvatore Di Tommasso
Conductor	Vittorio Gui
Orchestra	RAI, Rome
Chorus	RAI, Rome

Warner Fonit 8573 83010–2

1951(?) Melodiya
Aida	Natalia Sokolova
Amneris	Vera Davidova
Priestess	Anna Ivanova
Radamès	Georgi Nelepp
Amonasro	Pavel Lisitsian
Ramfis	Ivan Petrov
King	I. Mikhailov
Messenger	A Sirovatko-Zolotariov
Conductor	Alexander Melik-Pashaev

Orchestra   Bolshoi Theatre
Chorus   Bolshoi Theatre
Computer disc AE 207 "Opera Russe"
Russian language

1951   Ace (abridged recording)
Aida   Vassilka Petrova
Amneris   Elizabeth Wysor
Radamès   Gino Sarri
Amonasro   A. Manca-Sera [?]
Conductor   Emilio Tieri
Orchestra   Maggio Musicale Fiorentino
Chorus   Maggio Musicale Fiorentino
House of Opera CD 928

1952 (?)   Capitol
Aida   Stella Roman
Amneris   Sylvia Sawyer
Priestess   Anna Marcangeli
Radamès   Gino Sarri
Amonasro   A. Manca Serra
Ramfis   Vittorio Tatozzi
King   Franco Puglese
Messenger   Paolo Caroli
Conductor   Alberto Paoletti
Orchestra   Rome Opera
Chorus   Rome Opera
House of Opera CD846

1952   Decca/London
Aida   Renata Tebaldi
Amneris   Ebe Stignani
Priestess   Unlisted
Radamès   Mario del Monaco
Amonasro   Aldo Protti
Ramfis   Dario Caselli
King   Fernando Corena
Messenger   Piero de Palma
Conductor   Alberto Erede
Orchestra   Academia di Santa Cecilia, Rome
Chorus   Academia di Santa Cecilia, Rome
Decca 440 239–2

1952 (?)   Remington
Aida   Mary Curtis Verna
Amneris   Oralia Dominguez
Priestess   Unlisted

Radamès   Umberto Borsò
Amonasro   Ettore Bastianini
Ramfis   Norman Scott
King   Enzo Felicitati
Messenger   Uberto Scaglioni
Conductor   Franco Capuana
Orchestra   Teatro La Fenice, Venice
Chorus   Teatro La Fenice Venice
Preiser "Paperback Opera" 20027

1953   Radioton
Aida   Paula Takacs
Amneris   Klara Palánkay
Priestess   Judith Sandor
Radamès   Josef Simandy
Amonasro   Alexander Sved
Ramfis   Giorgy Littasy
King   Pal Rissay
Messenger   Josef Reti
Conductor   Viktor Vaszy
Orchestra   Hungarian Radio-Television Symphony
Chorus   Hungarian Radio-Television
Hungarian language

1955   RCA
Aida   Zinka Milanov
Amneris   Fedora Barbieri
Priestess   Bruna Rizzoli
Radamès   Jussi Bjoerling
Amnonasro   Leonard Warren
Ramfis   Boris Christoff
King   Plinio Clabassi
Messenger   Mario Carlin
Conductor   Jonel Perlea
Orchestra   Rome Opera
Chorus   Rome Opera
BMG 6652–2–RG

1955   EMI
Aida   Maria Callas
Amneris   Fedora Barbieri
Priestess   Elvira Galassi
Radamès   Richard Tucker
Amonasro   Tito Gobbi

Ramfis	Giuseppe Modesti	**1959 Decca**	
King	Nicola Zaccaria	Aida	Renata Tebaldi
Messenger	Franco Ricciardi	Amneris	Giulietta Simionato
Conductor	Tullio Serafin	Priestess	Eugenia Ratti
Orchestra	La Scala, Milan	Radamès	Carlo Bergonzi
Chorus	La Scala, Milan	Amonasro	Cornell MacNeil

EMI 5 56316 2 6

1956 Fonit Cetra

Aida	Mary Curtis Verna
Amneris	Miriam Pirazzini
Priestess	Unlisted
Amonasro	Gian Giacomo Guelfi
Ramfis	Giulio Neri
King	Antonio Zerbini
Messenger	Athos Cesarini
Conductor	Angelo Questa
Orchestra	Orchestra Sinfonica, Turin RAI
Chorus	Chorus, Turin RAI

Warner Fonit 8573 82642–2

1956 Metropolitan Opera Record Club (abridged recording)

Aida	Lucine Amara
Amneris	Rosalind Elias
Priestess	Shakeh Vartenissian
Radamès	Albert Da Costa
Amonasro	Frank Guarrera
Ramfis	Giorgio Tozzi
King	Louis Sgarro
Messenger	James McCracken
Conductor	Fausto Cleva
Orchestra	Metropolitan Opera
Chorus	Metropolitan Opera

1958 Orpheus/Guilde International du Disque

Aida	Anna de Cavalieri
Amneris	Ira Malaniuk
Priestess	Unlisted
Radamès	Aldo Bertocci
Amonasro	Scipio Colombo
Ramfis	Paolo Dari
King	Ugo Trama
Messenger	Walter Bertelli
Conductor	Ernesto Barbini
Orchestra	Rome Opera
Chorus	Rome Opera

1959 Decca (continued)

Ramfis	Arnold van Mill
King	Fernando Corena
Messenger	Piero de Palma
Conductor	Herbert von Karajan
Orchestra	Vienna Philharmonic
Chorus	Singverein der Gesellschaft der Musikfreunde

Decca 289 460 078–2

1961 RCA

Aida	Leontyne Price
Amneris	Rita Gorr
Priestess	Mietta Sighele
Radamès	Jon Vickers
Amonasro	Robert Merrill
Ramfis	Giorgio Tozzi
King	Plinio Clabassi
Messenger	Franco Ricciardi
Conductor	Georg Solti
Orchestra	Rome Opera
Chorus	Rome Opera

Decca 417 416–2

1966 EMI

Aida	Birgit Nilsson
Amneris	Grace Bumbry
Priestess	Mirella Fiorentini
Radamès	Franco Corelli
Amonasro	Mario Sereni
Ramfis	Bonaldo Giaiotti
King	Ferruccio Mazzoli
Messenger	Piero de Palma
Conductor	Zubin Mehta
Orchestra	Rome Opera
Chorus	Rome Opera

EMI CMS 63 229–2

1970 RCA

Aida	Leontyne Price
Amneris	Grace Bumbry
Priestess	Joyce Mathis

Radamès	Plácido Domingo
Amonasro	Sherrill Milnes
Ramfis	Ruggero Raimondi
Messenger	Bruce Brewer
Conductor	Erich Leinsdorf
Orchestra	London Symphony
Chorus	John Alldis Choir

BMG 74321-39498-2

1970-71 Balkanton
Aida	Julia Viner-Chenisheva
Amneris	Alexandrina Milcheva
Priestess	Maria Dimchewska
Radamès	Nikola Nikolov
Amonasro	Nikolai Smochevski
Ramfis	Nikola Ghiuselev
King	Stefan Tsiganchev
Messenger	Verter Vrachovski
Conductor	Ivan Marinov
Orchestra	Sofia National Opera Orchestra
Chorus	Sofia National Opera Chorus

Laserlight Classics LC 24421

1974 EMI
Aida	Montserrat Caballé
Amneris	Fiorenza Cossotto
Priestess	Esther Casas
Radamès	Plácido Domingo
Amonasro	Piero Cappuccilli
Ramfis	Nicolai Ghiaurov
King	Luigi Roni
Messenger	Nicola Martinucci
Conductor	Riccardo Muti
Orchestra	New Philharmonia
Chorus	Royal Opera House Covent Garden

EMI 7243 5 56246 2 8

1976 Levon
Aida	Gilda Cruz-Romo
Amneris	Grace Bumbry
Priestess	Mirella Fiorentini
Radamès	Peter Gougalov
Amonasro	Ingvar Wixel
Ramfis	Agostino Ferrin
King	Luigi Roni
Messenger	Gerard Friedmann
Conductor	Thomas Schippers
Orchestra	Lirico di Torino
Chorus	Lirico di Torino

1979 EMI
Aida	Mirella Freni
Amneris	Agnes Baltsa
Priestess	Katia Ricciarelli
Radamès	José Carreras
Amonasro	Piero Cappuccilli
Ramfis	Ruggero Raimondi
King	José van Dam
Messenger	Thomas Moser
Conductor	Herbert von Karajan
Orchestra	Vienna Philharmonic
Chorus	Vienna State Opera

EMI 7 69300 2

1979 Orfeo
Aida	Anna Tomowa-Sintow
Amneris	Brigitte Fassbaender
Priestess	Marianne Seibel
Radamès	Plácido Domingo
Amonasro	Siegmund Nimsgern
Ramfis	Robert Lloyd
King	Nikolaus Hillebrand
Messenger	Norbert Orth
Conductor	Riccardo Muti
Orchestra	Bavarian State
Chorus	Bavarian State Opera

Orfeo C 583 022 I

1981 Deutsche Grammophon
Aida	Katia Ricciarelli
Amneris	Elena Obraztsova
Priestess	Lucia Valentini Terrani
Radamès	Plácido Domingo
Amonasro	Leo Nucci
Ramfis	Nicolai Ghiaurov
King	Ruggero Raimondi
Messenger	Piero de Palma
Conductor	Claudio Abbado
Orchestra	La Scala, Milan
Chorus	La Scala, Milan

DGG 410 092-2

1985 Decca
Aida	Maria Chiara
Amneris	Ghena Dimitrova

Priestess   Madelyn Renée
Radamès   Luciano Pavarotti
Amonasro   Leo Nucci
Ramfis   Paata Burchuladze
King   Luigi Roni
Messenger   Ernesto Gavazzi
Conductor   Lorin Maazel
Orchestra   La Scala, Milan
Chorus   La Scala, Milan
Decca 417 439–2

1990   Sony
Aida   Aprile Millo
Amneris   Dolora Zajick
Priestess   Hei-Kyung Hong
Radamès   Plácido Domingo
Amonasro   James Morris
Ramfis   Samuel Ramey
King   Terry Cook
Messenger   Charles Anthony
Conductor   James Levine
Orchestra   Metropolitan Opera
Chorus   Metropolitan Opera
Sony S3K 45973

1994   Naxos
Aida   Maria Dragoni
Amneris   Barbara Dever
Priestess   Monica Trini
Radamès   Kristjan Johannsson
Amonasro   Mark Rucker
Ramfis   Francesco Ellero D'Artegna
King   Riccardo Ferrari
Messenger   Antonio Marceno
Conductor   Rico Saccani
Orchestra   National Symphony
                Orchestra of Ireland
Chorus   RTE Philharmonic Choir;
                Culwick Choral Society,
                Bray Choral Society;
                Dublin County Choir;
                Dun Laoghaire Choral
                Society, Cantabile Singers,
                Goethe Institut Choir,
                Musica Sacra,
                Phoenix Singers
Naxos 8.660033–4

1998   Companions Classics
Aida   Olga Romanko
Amneris   Stefania Toczyska
Priestess   Janny Zomer
Radamès   Maurizio Frusoni
Amonasro   Claudio Otelli
Ramfis   Riccardo Ferrari
King   Aik Martirosyan
Messenger   Alexei Grigorev
Conductor   Roberto Paternostro
Orchestra   Wüttembergische
                Philharmonie Reutlingen
Chorus   Opera in Ahoy' Chorus
D Classics DCL 704072

2001   Teldec
Aida   Cristina Gallardo-Domás
Amneris   Olga Borodina
Priestess   Dorothea Reichmann
Radamès   Vincenzo La Scola
Amonasro   Thomas Hampson
Ramfis   Matti Salminen
King   Laszlo Polar
Messenger   Kurt Streit
Conductor   Nicolaus Harnoncourt
Orchestra   Vienna Philharmonic
Chorus   Arnold Schoenberg
                Chorus
Teldec 6 8573–85402–2 8

2001   Chandos
Aida   Jane Eaglen
Amneris   Rosalind Plowright
Priestess   Susan Gritton
Radamès   Dennis O'Neill
Amonasro   Gregory Yurisich
Ramfis   Alastair Miles
King   Peter Rose
Messenger   Alfred Roe
Conductor   David Parry
Orchestra   Philharmonia
Chorus   Geoffrey Mitchell Choir
Chandos CHAN 3074
English language

Appendix II — Videography

(With the exception of the first item in the videography, the date at the heading of each entry is the date of the performance itself rather than the issue date. The final line in each entry includes the format—either VHS or DVD—and the label name and issue number.)

1953 original motion picture film
Aida   Sophia Loren
   (sung by Renata Tebaldi)
Amneris   Patricia Morrison
   (sung by Ebe Stignani)
Priestess   Giovanna Russo
Radamès   Luciano della Mora
   (sung by Giuseppe Campora)
Amonasro   Afro Poli
   (sung by Gino Bechi)
Ramfis   Antonio Cassinelli
   (sung by Giulio Neri)
King   Enrico Formichi
Messenger   Paolo Coroli
Conductor   Giuseppe Morelli
Orchestra   RAI Rome
Chorus   RAI Rome
Director   Clemente Fracassi
VHS   Bel Canto Society BCS-0553

1961 live opera house performance
Aida   Gabriella Tucci
Amneris   Giulietta Simionato
Priestess   Unlisted
Radamès   Mario del Monaco
Amonasro   Aldo Protti
Ramfis   Paolo Washington
King   Silvano Pagliuca
Messenger   Unlisted
Conductor   Franco Capuana
Orchestra   NHK Radio Symphony
Chorus   Nikikai and Fujiwara
                   Opera Chorus
Director   Carlo Piccinato
DVD   House of Opera   5070

1966 live outdoor performance
Aida   Leyla Gencer
Amneris   Fiorenza Cossotto
Priestess   Adalina Grigolato
Radamès   Carlo Bergonzi
Amonasro   Anselmo Colzani
Ramfis   Bonaldo Giaiotti
King   Franco Pugliese
Messenger   Ottorino Begali
Conductor   Franco Capuana
Orchestra   Arena di Verona
Chorus   Arena di Verona
Director   Herbert Graf
DVD   Hardy Classic Video   HCD 4010

1981 live outdoor performance
Aida   Maria Chiara
Amneris   Fiorenza Cossotto
Priestess   Maria Gabriella Onesti
Radamès   Nicola Martinucci
Amonasro   Giuseppe Scandola
Ramfis   Carlo Zardo
King   Alfredo Zanazzo
Messenger   Gian Paolo Corradi

Conductor	Anton Guadagno	Conductor	Donato Renzetti
Orchestra	Arena di Verona	Orchestra	Sinfonia Del Emilia Romano "Arturo Toscanini"
Chorus	Arena di Verona		
Director	Giancarlo Sbragia		
Director (TV)	Brian Large	Chorus	Teatro Regio Di Parma, Coro D'Parma
VHS	Thorn EMI TVE 2790		
		Director	Mauro Bulognini
		Director (TV)	Pierpaolo Pessini
		VHS	Bel Canto Society BC-0694

1981 live opera house performance

Aida	Margaret Price
Amneris	Stefania Toczyska
Priestess	Susan Quittmeyer
Radamés	Luciano Pavarotti
Amonasro	Simon Estes
Ramfis	Kurt Rydl
King	Kevin Langan
Messenger	Colenton Freeman
Conductor	Garcia Navarro
Orchestra	San Francisco Opera
Chorus	San Francisco Opera
Director	Sam Wanamaker
Director (TV)	Brian Large
DVD Kultur	D2251

1989 live opera house performance

Aida	Aprile Millo
Amneris	Dolora Zajick
Priestess	Margaret Jane Wray
Radamés	Plácido Domingo
Amonasro	Sherrill Milnes
Ramfis	Paata Burchuladze
King	Dimitri Kavrakos
Messenger	Mark Baker
Conductor	James Levine
Orchestra	Metropolitan Opera
Chorus	Metropolitan Opera
Director	Sonia Frisell
Director (TV)	Brian Large
DVD	Deutsche Grammophon 073 001–9

1985 live opera house performance

Aida	Maria Chiara
Amneris	Ghena Dimitrova
Priestess	Francesca Garbi
Radamés	Luciano Pavarotti
Amonasro	Juan Pons
Ramfis	Nicolai Ghiaurov
King	Paata Burchuladze
Messenger	Ernesto Gavazzi
Conductor	Lorin Maazel
Orchestra	La Scala, Milan
Chorus	La Scala, Milan
Director	Luca Ronconi
Director (TV)	Derek Bailey
VHS	Home Vision 58

1994 live opera house performance

Aida	Cheryl Studer
Amneris	Luciana d'Intino
Priestess	Yvonne Barclay
Radamés	Dennis O'Neill
Amonasro	Alexandru Agache
Ramfis	Robert Lloyd
King	Mark Beesley
Messenger	John Marsden
Conductor	Edward Downes
Orchestra	Royal Opera House
Chorus	Royal Opera House
Director	Elijah Moshinsky
Director (TV)	Brian Large
DVD	Kultur D1487

1988 live opera house performance

Aida	Maria Chiara
Amneris	Elena Obraztsova
Priestess	Wilma Colla
Radamés	Nicola Martinucci
Amonasro	Bruno Pola
Ramfis	Cesare Siepi
King	Franco Federici
Messenger	Gianfranco Manganotti

1997 live outdoor performance (abridged)

Aida	Pauletta de Vaughn
Amneris	Adriana Nicolai
Priestess	Francesca Lauri
Radamés	Bruno Sebastian

Amonasro	Walter Donati
Ramfis	Alexander Teliga
King	Ivan Tomasev
Messenger	Franco Traverso
Conductor	Giorgio Croci
Orchestra	Stagione d'Opera Italiana
Chorus	Stagione d'Opera Italiana, Bolschoi Don Kosaken
Director	Wolfgang Werner
DVD	Classic World CWP-1373

1999   live opera house performance

Aida	Fiorenza Cedolins
Amneris	Dolora Zajick
Priestess	Antonella Trevisan
Radamés	Walter Fraccaro
Amonasro	Vittorio Vitelli
Ramfis	Giacomo Prestia
King	Carlo Striuli
Messenger	Angelo Casertano
Conductor	Daniel Oren
Orchestra	San Carlo, Naples
Chorus	San Carlo, Naples
Director	Gianfrano De Bosio
Director (TV)	Elisabetta Brusa
DVD	Image Entertainment ID1514ERDVD

2001   live opera house performance

Aida	Adina Aaron
Amneris	Kate Aldrich
Priestess	Micaela Carosi
Radamés	Scott Piper
Amonasro	Giuseppe Garra
Ramfis	Enrico Giuseppe Iori
King	Paolo Pecchioli
Messenger	Stefano Pisani
Conductor	Massimiliano Stefanelli
Orchestra	Fondazione Arturo Toscanini
Chorus	Fondazione Arturo Toscanini
Director	Franco Zeffirelli
Director (TV)	Valentino Buriol
DVD	TDK DVUS-AIDDB1–2

2003   live opera house performance

Aida	Deniela Dessi
Amneris	Elisabetta Fiorella
Priestess	Ana Nebot
Radamés	Fabio Armiliato
Amonasro	Juan Pons
Ramfis	Roberto Scandiuzzi
King	Stefano Palatchi
Messenger	Josep Fadó
Conductor	Miguel Angel Gómez Martinez
Orchestra	Gran Teatre del Liceu
Chorus	Gran Teatre del Liceu
Director	José Antonio Guitiérrez
Director (TV)	Toni Bargallo
DVD	Opus Arte OA 0894 D

2004   live opera house performance

Aida	Eszter Sümegi
Amneris	Cornelia Helfricht
Priestess	Sewan Salmasi
Radamés	Kostadin Andreev
Amonasro	Igor Morosow
Ramfis	Pièr Dalàs
King	Janusz Monarcha
Messenger	Martin Fournier
Conductor	Ernst Märzendorfer
Director	Robert Herzl
Directors (TV)	Rudi Dolezal, Hannes Rossächer
DVD	EuroArts 2054058

Appendix III — Additional Resources

Biography

At first glance, the story of Verdi's life seems simple and straight forward — he struggled to prepare himself, he suffered tragedy in the death of his first wife and their two children, he triumphed, he married happily a second time, then he died as the most honored and respected Italian of his age. The more we read, however, the more complicated the issues become. The problem stems in part from Verdi himself. He was a very private man, and he often kept his secrets from his own family members and closest friends. There are, alas, a few occasions in his own comments about his life when he either suffered from a faulty memory or chose to compress events into a neater, more dramatic framework. Biographers have their work cut out for them, and if you read more than one biography, you will no doubt notice areas of disagreement about what was actually going on in Verdi's life at some key moments.

The various strands of his life are woven together most persuasively in **Mary Jane Phillips-Matz's** *Verdi: A Biography* (Oxford University Press, reprint of 1993 edition, 1996), a detailed account based on extensive original research on and off the Italian field. It is a lengthy, fully documented study, the standard work in English on the composer's life, but it just may offer more than you really want to know about Verdi. **George Martin's** *Verdi: His Music, Life and Times* (Dodd, Mead, 1963; reprint, Limelight Edition, 1992) is a good, briefer biography. It includes sensitive critical analyses of Verdi's operas. Another readable and accurate modern biography is *Verdi: A Life in the Theatre* by **Charles Osborne** (Alfred A. Knopf, 1987). A standard Italian work, *Verdi: The Man and His Music* by **Carlo Gatti**, was abridged and translated for English language readers (Dutton, 1955), but you'll need to search the used book stores or the shelves of a library to find it. *Verdi* by **Joseph Wechsberg** (Putnam, 1974) offers a comprehensive, well-written summary of Verdi's life and a wealth of interesting illustrations. **Francis Toye's** *Giuseppe Verdi: His Life and Works* (reprint, Alfred A. Knopf, 1970) appeared first in 1930 and was one of the earliest scholarly attempts in the English language to survey Verdi's life and the entire body of his works. Toye, of course, did not have available the latest critical and scholarly studies and in many cases he had not had an opportunity to see or even to hear the operas. For Verdi's life story we will turn to more recent scholarship, but his perceptions concerning the operas are keen and always of interest.

More specialized than the general biographies is **Frank Walker's** *The Man Verdi* (Alfred A. Knopf, 1962). It is not a biography in the regular sense but rather a series of scholarly essays centering on some of the more highly controversial periods and relationships in the composer's life. Walker's book is highly respected and has proved itself particularly valuable to students of Verdi since its publication in 1962.

If you would like to dig into the original sources that the biographers use in preparing their books, take a good, long look at **William Weaver's** *Verdi: A Documentary Study* (Thames and Hudson, 1997). Here you will find reproductions of original sources — letters, reviews, comments, and illustrations — from throughout Verdi's life and career, and you'll be encouraged to do the interpreting for yourself. Verdi's correspondence is often interesting and challenging, and much of it centers on his compositions. A good selection is available in *Letters of Giuseppe Verdi,* **translated and edited by Charles Osborne** (Holt, Rinehart, and Winston, 1972). An earlier selection of letters was published in *Verdi: The Man in His Letters,* **edited by Franz Werfel and Paul Stefan** (L. B. Fischer, 1942; reprint, Vienna House, 1972). This volume includes Werfel's sensitive essay on the life and work of the composer. We still wait, however, for an English translation of Verdi's complete correspondence.

The easy way out in surveying Verdi's biography is the televised mini-series, *The Life of Verdi*, available from Kultur in a four CD set. Watch it carefully and you'll have a good general summary of the facts, a beautiful interpretation of Verdi's second wife, Giuseppina, by Carla Fracci, and a convincing Verdi portrayal from a young man to his final years by Ronald Young — and you'll also hear some good music.

For all matters relating to Verdi, his life and his operas, and all other operatic subjects, the essential reference work in English is *The New Grove Dictionary of Opera* (Macmillan, 1992), a four volume set, **edited by Stanley Sadie.**

The Opera Itself

For those of you who want to follow through on the whole picture of the origin and early life of *Aida*, the absolutely essential reference source is **Hans Busch's** *Verdi's Aida: The History of an Opera in Letters and Documents* (University of Minnesota Press, 1978). It's all here in this remarkable volume, from the first hint of Verdi's interest in Egypt in 1868 through his comments on the origins of the idea as late as 1891.

Background and critical analysis of Verdi's compositions are the subjects of *The Complete Operas of Verdi* **by Charles Osborne** (Alfred A. Knopf, 1970). Chapter 24 is devoted to *Aida* and packs an incredible amount of detail and commentary into twenty-five decidedly readable pages. For the real *Aida* connoisseur, however, nothing can replace the extended study in **Julian Budden's** *The Operas of Verdi: From* **Don Carlos** *to* **Falstaff** (Oxford University Press, 1981). *Aida* is treated to detailed and careful dramatic and musical analysis by Budden. Be warned, however; his discussion of the opera is much more technical than Osborne's and may prove somewhat daunting to those without a musical background.

A considerably more popularized approach to Verdi's life and work, as the title of the volume surely suggests, is available in **William Berger's *Verdi with a Vengeance*** (Vintage, 2000). Berger includes a brief essay on each of Verdi's operas along with a discussion of recordings, films, production styles, and other books and a glossary of operatic terminology. ***The Verdi Companion*, edited by William Weaver and Martin Chusid** (W. W. Norton, 1979) is a collection of essays on Verdi's art by a distinguished group of scholars, musicians, and Verdi specialists, and ***The Cambridge Companion to Verdi*, edited by Scott L. Balthazar** (Cambridge University Press, 2004) offers a similar series of essays on the life and career of the composer. **Frank Martin** has collected an assortment of his writings in ***Aspects of Verdi*** (Dodd, Mead, 1987), but there is not an essay on *Aida* as such nor are there many references to the opera.

A fascinating volume entitled ***Aida in Cairo*** was published by the Banca Nazionale del Lavoro in 1982 to mark the opening of their Egyptian office. Essays by Italian musicians, conductors, and scholars, all in English translation, are accompanied with magnificent illustrations of designs from productions of *Aida* over the years.

Of course, the most important source for *Aida* is the opera itself. If you are able to read music, you may well want to see a copy of the *Aida* score. The piano-vocal score, that is the vocal lines with accompaniment arranged for piano, is available from G. Schirmer and no doubt from other publishers as well. The Schirmer score includes the Italian text and an English translation. A full orchestral score can be purchased in an inexpensive edition from Dover Publications. It includes only the Italian text.

If you do not have a score that includes an English translation or a recording that prints the text in the annotations, you will probably also want and need a copy of the libretto with parallel Italian and English lines. Many, but not all, of the audio recordings include an Italian-English libretto along with the liner notes, and most — but again not all — visual recordings will include subtitles with the English translation. Otherwise, copies of the libretto with both original text and translation are available in several different formats. **The English National Opera** (John Calder, 1980) has published a series of opera guides compact enough to accompany you to the opera house. The volume devoted to *Aida* includes essays on the opera and a complete libretto in Italian and an English language translation by Edmund Tracey. The same translation is used in the 2001 recording on the Chandos label. The translation included in the **Opera Classics Library introduction to *Aida*, edited by Burton D. Fisher** (Opera Journeys Publishing, 2001), is less poetic than the performance version in the English National Opera volume, but it is also a more literal version of the Italian text. It is, of course, designed to be read and not sung.

If, however, you're headed to the opera house to see a performance of *Aida* on stage, chances are there will be either "super titles" projected above the stage or — as in the case of the Metropolitan Opera — a little screen on the back of the seat in front of you. In either case, a translation of the text will appear line by line, and you simply won't have to worry about handling a book and a flashlight during the performance.

Discography

Over the years since its publication in 1982, I have had frequent occasion to refer to **Marc Taylor Faw's** *A Verdi Discography* (Pilgrim Books, 1992). He referred to it as "a preliminary discography," but in reality every discography is decidedly temporary. We simply do not know what recordings from the past will be discovered the next day and what new recordings will appear when next Tuesday rolls around. For *Aida,* the best current discography that I have found is the one on Carlo Marinelli's Opera Discography Encyclopædia Web site (carlomarinelli.it). He gives detailed information about each recording of the opera and includes scores of unofficial, non-commercially made performances. Other helpful lists can be found on the Web sites of House of Opera and Premiere Opera, both of which are listed in the section that follows.

Audio and Visual Recordings

For additional information about *Aida* and most other operas and operettas in the various visual formats, **Ken Wlaschin's** *Opera on Screen: A Guide to More Than 100 of Opera Films, Videos, and DVDs* (Yale University Press, 2004) is an up to date source with over eight hundred pages of fascinating material. *The Metropolitan Opera Guide to Opera on Video,* **edited by Paul Gruber** (W.W. Norton, 1997), reviews videos of *Aida* and many other operas in often stimulating essays by a variety of critics, but it appeared slightly too early to include DVDs.

The three volumes of **Opera on Record,** **edited by Alan Blythe** (Hutchinson, 1979–1984), are much loved by opera fans and collectors. Individual critics deal with the different operas, not only the complete versions but also individual selections. *Aida* is covered in the first volume, published in 1979. **Paul Gruber also edited** *The Metropolitan Opera Guide to Recorded Opera* (W.W. Norton, 1993), similar in its approach and coverage to the corresponding volume on video. The critics deal only with complete, commercially issued recordings beginning with the electrical recording era and ending with the 1993 publishing date. Conrad Osborne contributed the delightfully controversial section on *Aida.*

As an inveterate collector of operatic recordings, I know the frustration of searching in vain for just the right performance. Just in case Chapters 5 and 6 whet your appetite for audio and visual recordings of *Aida* (and I hope they will), you may find helpful a few comments on how to locate the material. Rest assured, my suggestions are based on personal experience.

Many of the compact discs, DVDs, and VHS tapes mentioned in this book are still available and can easily be purchased or ordered from your favorite local or on-line sources. Some that are temporarily unavailable will return to the catalogues, and the general word of advice is patience, and then more patience. For those that prove elusive, you may want to try one of the more specialized dealers that offer out of print and other rare audio and visual recordings. In some cases these dealers produce their own recordings that will not be available through your regular commercial sources.

Here are two that specialize in operatic CDs, DVDs, and VHS tapes: Premiere Opera, 163 Amsterdam Ave., New York, NY 10023–5001 (premiereopera.com; telephone 212–769–0897), and House of Opera, P.O. Box 3992, Duluth, GA 30096 (operapassion.com; telephone 999–495–9742 or 678–584–5909). For sound recordings of opera and other vocal music, you will also want to try Norbeck, Peters, and Ford, P.O. Box 210, Swanton, VT 05488–0210 (norpete.com; telephone 800–654–5302 or 802–868–9300). In addition to some of the material mentioned in this book, these dealers also carry extensive catalogues of live, from-the-stage recordings. All three have Web sites, and I can vouch from experience for their good service and helpful attention to your needs.

For long-playing records (known among dealers and collectors as "vinyl"), there are many dealers. Here are two good ones from which I have ordered successfully and pleasantly. Ars Antiqua/Microcosmos, 314 Churchill Ave., Toronto, Ontario, M2R 1EV Canada (mikro@interlog.com; telephone 416–224–1956), and Irvington Music, 9580 NW Cornell Rd., Portland, OR 97729 (irvmusic.com; telephone 503–985–7335). For used compact discs, a good source is Parnassus, 51 Goat Hill Road, Saugerties, NY 12477–3008 (Parnassus records.com; telephone 845–246–3332) And if you are budget conscious — and who isn't? — check out the discounted offerings at Berkshire Record Outlet, 461 Pleasant St., Lee, MA 01238 (berkshirerecordoutlet.com; telephone, for orders only, 800–992–1200). Once again, all of these stores have Web sites and on-line catalogues.

In some cases, what you can't find in the United States will be available abroad. There are certainly many British and other European dealers who will be happy to help you. Check the advertisements in the monthly *Gramophone* magazine for names and addresses. One of my favorite dealers *anywhere* in the world is Crotchet Ltd., P. O. Box 5435, Birmingham B 388DZ, UK (crotchet.co.uk; telephone +44 121 459 55 66). Their excellent Web site includes listings not only of currently available material but of recordings scheduled for release in the future.

Index

Aaron, Adina 168
Abbado, Claudio 75, 133–134
Adler, Dankmar 56
Agache, Alexandru 165
Aldrich, Kate 168
Allievi, Marietta 42
Amara, Lucine 149
Amato, Anthony (Tony) 56–57
Anderson, Marian 66
Andrews, Carol 18
Anitua, Fanny 105
Anna 66
Arangi-Lombardi, Giannina 107, 108–109
Aristotle 72–73
Armiliato, Fabio 170
Arrivabene, Opprandino 25
Arroyo, Martina 66
Auber, Daniel-François-Esprit, *La Muette de Portici* 69, 70

Baccaloni, Salvatore 108
Baltsa, Agnes 132–133
Bampton, Rose 63
Barbieri, Fedora 117–118, 120, 125, 130, 160
Barezzi, Antonio 12, 13, 25
Barrymore, Ethel 152
Bastianini, Ettore 116, 118, 124, 147
Baum, Kurt 64
Bechi, Gino 109, 153–154
Beesley, Mark 165
Beinat, Andreina 106
Bellini, Vincenzo, *Norma* 2, 45, 68–69
Bergonzi, Carlo 77, 123–124, 157, 158, 159, 169
Berliner, Emile 103
Bertani, Prospero 51
Bertocci, Aldo 122
Besanzoni, Gabriella 55
Bettoni, Vincenzo 105
Bing, Rudolf 66
Bizet, Georges, *Carmen* 1, 14, 54, 105
Bjoerling, Jussi 119, 148
Borgioli, Armando 108

Borodina, Olga 140
Borso, Umberto 115
Bottesini, Giovanni 41–42; *Cristoforo Colombo* 41
Bourskaya, Ina 152
Brandt, Marianne 51
Budden, Julian 6, 32, 35–36, 72, 80
Bumbry, Grace 63–64, 126, 128, 141
Burchuladze, Paata 136, 163, 164
Busch, Hans 6, 28

Caballé, Montserrat 131, 169
Cabanes, Josep Mestres 169
Callas, Maria 2, 54, 64, 117–118, 120, 128–129, 132, 169
Cammarano, Salvatore 69
Campanini, Italo 51
Campora, Giuseppe 153
Caniglia, Maria 109
Capponi, Giuseppe 49, 77
Cappuccilli, Piero 130, 133
Capuana, Franco 115, 154–155, 158
Capuana, Maria 108
Carey, Annie Louise 51
Caroli, Paolo 153
Carreras, José 132
Caruso, Enrico 1, 55, 61, 66, 104
Caselli, Dario 117
Cassinelli, Antonio 153
Castagna, Bruna 63
Castells, Jordi 169
Cazara-Campos, Antonio 64
Cedolins, Fiorenza 166
Celletti, Rodolfo 77
Chelotti, Teresa 105
Chiara, Maria 135, 159, 160–161, 162
Christoff, Boris 120
Clabassi, Plinio 120, 125
Cleva, Fausto 149
Coates, Edith 62
Coleridge, Samuel Taylor 29
Collins, Janet 66

Index

Colombo, Scipio 122
Colzani, Anselmo 158
Cook, Terry 137
Cooper, Emil 2
Corelli, Franco 5, 121, 123, 127
Corena, Fernando 117, 124
Cossotto, Fiorenza 130–131, 156, 157–158, 159, 160, 169
Costa, Tommasso 42
Cros, Charles 103
Cruz-Romo, Gilda 141
Culshaw, John 123
Curtis Verna, Mary 115, 121

Da Costa, Albert 149
Dal Monte, Toti 54
Danise, Giuseppe 54
D'Artegna, Francesco Ellero 138
Da Sabata, Victor 152
Davy, Gloria 59, 66
Davydova, Vera 145
De Baillou, Luigi 45
De Cavalieri, Anna (Anne McKnight) 122
De Giuli, Giuseppina 47
De la Vega, L. Pèrez 18
De Lesseps, Ferdinand 8
De Leuven, Adolph 14
Della Mara, Luciano 152–153
Del Monaco, Mario 64, 116–117, 123, 155, 157
De Lorenzo, Aldo 166
Del Rivera, Josè 55
De Reszke, Jan 52
Dessi, Daniela 170
Destinn, Emmy (Ema Kittl) 36, 61, 65, 104–105
De Vaughn, Paoletta 171
Dever, Barbara 138, 140
De Vincentus, Zaira 166
Didur, Adamo 61
Di Giosa, Nicola 39
Dillard, William 59
Dimitrova, Ghena 63, 135, 162–163
D'Intino, Luciana 165
Domingo, Plácido 128, 130, 134, 135, 142, 148, 163–164, 169
Dominguez, Oralia 115
Donati, Walter 171
Donizetti, Gaetano 7, 45–46, 68–69; *Lucia di Lammermoor* 54
Downes, Edward 165
Dragoni, Maria 138
Draneht, Paul 11, 16, 33–41, 135
Dubrow, Betty 59
Du Locle, Camille 6, 13–15, 17–18, 21–22, 26–28, 37, 67

Eaglen, Jane 146
Eastman, George 151
Edison, Thomas Alva 103, 151
Ek, Niklas 154
Elias, Rosalind 149
Erede, Alberto 166
Estes, Simon 160
Eugénie, Empress 8, 13

Faccaro, Walter 166
Faccio, Franco 38, 50
Fancelli, Giuseppe 49
Fassbaender, Brigitte 142–143
Federici, Franco 161
Fellbom, Claes 154
Ferrari, Riccardo 138, 143
Ferrin, Agostino 141
Fétis, François Joseph 32
Filippi, Filippo 43, 53
Fillipeschi, Mario 113
Fiorillo, Elisabetta 170
Fischer, Emil 51
Flagstad, Kirsten 65
Formichi, Cesare 105
Formichi, Enrico 153
Fracassi, Clemente 152
Fracci, Carla 168
Fraschini, Gaetano 35
Freni, Mirella 132, 134–135
Fricci, Antoinette (Frietsche) 47
Frusoni, Maurizio 143

Gaiotti, Bonaldo 126, 158
Gallardo-Domâs, Cristina 139–140
Garra, Giuseppe 169
Gatti-Casazza, Giulio 61
Gavazzeni, Gianandrea 88
Gay, Maria 54
Gencer, Leyla 157
Ghiaurov, Nicolai 130, 134, 163
Ghislanzoni, Antonio 3, 6, 26–32, 46, 67
Ghiuselev, Nicola 129
Giannini, Dusolina 107, 108
Giannini, Feruccio 103
Gianoli, Isabella Galletti 34
Gigli, Beniamino 54, 66, 109
Gobbi, Tito 117–118, 132, 169
Gomes, Carlos 28
Gorr, Rita 125
Gossett, Philip 68, 83, 102
Gougalov, Peter 140–141
Gounod, Charles 22; *Faust* 104
Graf, Herbert 156
Grossi, Eleonora 37–38, 42
Grundin, Robert 154
Guarrera, Frank 2, 149

Index

Gueymard-Lauters, Pauline 35
Gui, Vittorio 112
Gustavson, Eva 111

Håggstam, Alf 154
Halevy, Fromental 70; *La Juive* 69
Hampson, Thomas 139
Harbour, Dennis 111
Harnoncourt, Nikolaus 139
Harshaw, Margaret 2
Heliodorus, *Aethiopica* 19
Henderson, W. J. 52
Herbert, Victor 51–52
Herbert-Föster, Theresa 51–52
Hillebrand, Nikolaus 142
Hines, Jerome 2
Homer, Louise 61, 104
Hopf, Hans 62
Hurok, Sol 152

Inghilleri, Giovanni 107, 118
Iori, Enrico Giuseppe 169
Ismail Pasha 8–9, 11, 14, 16–17, 22, 42–43

Jagel, Frederic 2
Jarratt, Howard 59
Johannsson, Kristjan 138
John, Elton, *Aida* 60
Jolson, Al 152
Jones, Spike 59

Karajan, Herbert von 122–123, 131–132
Kavrakos, Dimitri 164
Kerman, Joseph 18
Kinsman, Philip 2
Klein, Herman 65
Kraus, Gabrielle 35

Lampugnani, Giovanni 35, 39
Langan, Kevin 160
Large, Brian 158, 159–160, 162, 165
La Scola, Vincenzo 139
Lauri-Volpi, Giacomo 62
Lawrence, Marjorie 55, 63
Lehmann, Lily 52
Leinsdorf, Erich 127–128
Leoncavallo, Ruggero, *I Pagliacci* 36
Levine, James 136–137, 163
Lindi, Aroldo (Arnold Lindfors) 108
Lisitsian, Pavel 145
Lloyd, Robert 142, 165
Loren, Sophia 152
Lucca, Francesca 26
Lumière, August and Louis 151
Luzio, Alessandro 28

Maazel, Lorin 136, 163
MacNeil, Cornell 123, 124
Maini, Armando 49
Malaniuk, Ira 122
Malbin, Elaine 59
Mancini, Caterina 113
Manfrini, Luigi 106
Mapleson, J. H. 56
Marchiso, Barbara 35
Marchiso, Carlotta 35
Maré, Giovanni 34
Mariani, Angelo 39–41, 47–48, 50
Mariette, Auguste (Bey) 6, 14–22, 25, 27, 30, 32, 33–37, 42, 53, 58, 67
Mariette, Edouard 16
Marinov, Ivan 129
Martin, George 67–68
Martinelli, Giovanni 1, 152
Martinez, Miguel Anagel Gomez 169
Martinucci, Nicola 79, 130, 158–159, 161
Martirosyan, Aik 143
Masini, Guglielmo 106
Massaria, Antonio 113
Massenet, Jules 49
Maurel, Victor 36, 51
Maxwell, Lois 152
Mayer, Simone 46
Maynard, Olga 58–59
Mazzoleni, Ester 54
Mazzoli, Ferruccio 126
McCracken, James 79, 149
Medini, Paolo 34, 42
Mehta, Zubin 125–126
Melba, Nellie 65
Melchior, Lauritz 65
Melik-Pashayev, Alexander 145
Mercadante, Saverio 46
Merrill, Robert 62, 124
Méry, Joseph 14
Metastasio, Pietro 18–19
Meyerbeer, Giacomo 46, 70; *L'Africaine* 34, 69, 70; *Les Huguenots* 69; *Le Prophète* 69; *Robert le Diable* 69
Mikhailov, Igor 145
Milanov, Zinka 5, 63, 65, 119–120, 148
Milcheva, Alexandrina 129
Miles, Alastair 147
Millo, Aprile 137, 164
Milnes, Sherrill 128, 164
Minghini-Cattaneo, Irene 106–107
Modesti, Giuseppe 117
Molajoli, Lorenzo 107
Molinari, Bernadino 75
Mongini, Pietro 35–36, 42
Morelli, Giuseppe 153
Morris, James 137

Moser, Thomas 133
Moshinsky, Elijah 164, 165
Mozart, Wolfgang Amadeus 1, 139; *Le Nozze di Figaro* 1; *Die Zauberflöte* 33
Muhammad Ali 7–8
Mussolini, Benito 54, 75
Mussorgsky, Modest, *Boris Godunov* 145
Muti, Riccardo 129–130, 141–142
Muybridge, Eadweard 151
Muzio, Emmanuelle 9, 10, 33–34, 39, 51

Napoleon III, Emperor 8
Naudin, Emilio 34
Navarro, Garcia 159
Nelepp, Georgy 145
Nelli, Herva 111
Nerbe, Kerstin 154
Neri, Giulio 113, 120–121, 124, 153
Nicolai, Adriana 171
Nicolini, Ernesto 35, 77
Nikolov, Nikola 128–129, 140
Nilsson, Birgit 65, 66, 126
Nimsgern, Siegmund 142
Nucci, Leo 134, 136

Obrasztsova, Elena 134, 161
Olvis, William 59
O'Neill, Dennis 146–147, 165
Oren, Daniel 166
Osborne, Charles 18–19
Otelli, Claudio 143

Pacetti, Iva 62
Pagliuca, Silvano 156
Palatchi, Stefano 170
Pandolfini, Francesco 49
Panerai, Rolando 113
Paoletti, Alberto 164
Paralta, Angela 64
Parry, David 146
Pasero, Tancredi 5, 108, 109–110
Pasquale, A. 1
Paternostro, Roberto 143
Patti, Adelina 35, 56, 65
Pavarotti, Luciano 135–136, 159–160
Pecchioli, Paolo 169
Peerce, Jan 61–62
Perlea, Jonel 119
Perrin, Emile 14
Pertile, Aureliano 1, 107
Petrella, Erico 28
Petrov, Ivan 145
Petrova, Vasilka 148
Phillips, Harvey 54
Phillips-Matz, Mary Jane 6, 16, 17, 19, 41
Piave, Francesco Maria 11, 13, 25, 46

Pinza, Ezio 108
Piper, Scott 168
Pirazzini, Miriam 121
Plowright, Rosalind 146
Pola, Bruno 161
Polgár, László 139
Poli, Afro 152–154
Ponchielli, Amilcare 28; *La Gioconda* 54
Pons, Juan 163, 170
Porter, Andrew 48
Povoleri, Paride 49
Pozzoni, Antonietta 35, 36, 42, 47
Prestia, Giacomo 167
Price, Leontyne 65, 66, 125, 126, 127–128
Price, Margaret 160
Protti, Aldo 117, 155–156
Puccini, Giacomo: *La Bohème* 52, 139; *Tosca* 54; *Turandot* 54, 135
Pugliese, Franco 158

Questa, Angelo 120

Racine, Jean 19
Raimondi, Ruggero 128, 133, 134
Ramey, Samuel 137
Rankin, Nell 2
Remondini, L. 106
Renzetti, Donato 161–162
Rethberg, Elisabeth 1, 5, 65
Reyer, Ernest 43
Rhea, La Julia 66
Ricciarelli, Katia 133, 134–135
Rice, Tim 60
Ricordi, Giovanni 26
Ricordi, Giulio 26–27, 32, 34, 40, 47, 49, 50, 68; *La Secchia Repita* 27
Ricordi, Tito 26–27
Rivista, Minima 28
Robinson, Adolf 51
Roman, Stella 114, 148
Romanko, Olga 143–144
Roni, Luigi 130, 136, 141
Rose, Peter 147
Rossi, Giulio 61
Rossini, Gioacchino 7, 68–69; *Messa per Rossini* (mass in memory of Rossini) 40; *Il Turco in Italia* 45
Rothstein, Edward 57
Rovato, Ottone 54
Rucker, Mark 138
Russo, Giovanna 153
Rydl, Kurt 160

Sabajno, Carlo 106
Saccani, Rico 137–138
Said Pasha 9, 14

Index

Saint-Saëns, Camille 55, 59
Salieri, Antonio, *L'Europa Riconosciuto* 45
Salminen, Matti 139
Sardou, Victorien 14
Sarri, Gino 114–115, 148
Sass, Marie 35, 36
Sawyer, Sylvia 114
Sbraglia, Giancarlo 158
Scaglioni, Uberto 115
Scandiuzzi, Roberto 170
Scandola, Giuseppe 158
Schauler, Eileen 59
Schiller, Friedrich von 71
Schippers, Thomas 140–141
Scott, Michael 55
Scott, Norman 111, 115
Scotti, Antonio 61, 104
Sebastian, Bruno 171
Seidl, Anton 52
Serafin, Tullio 110–111, 117
Sereni, Mario 126
Serra, Antonio Manca 114
Sgarro, Louis 149
Shaw, George Bernard 96–97
Short, Ramsay 56
Siepi, Cesare 161
Sills, Beverly 65
Simandy, Josef 144
Simionato, Giulietta 113, 123–124, 125, 130, 149, 156, 160
Singher, Martial 77
Slonimsky, Nicolas 66
Smochevski, Nikola 129
Sokolova, Natalia 145
Solera, Temistocle 9–10, 17, 25; *Hymn for the Celebration of Ismaila* 10, 11
Solti, Georg 124
Sotin, Hans 128
Squarclapino, Franca 169
Stecchi-Bottardi, Luigi 42
Stefanelli, Maximilliano 169
Stella, Antonietta 2
Steller, Francesco 36, 42
Stich-Randall, Teresa 111
Stignani, Ebe 109–110, 117, 125, 153, 156, 160, 164
Stolz, Teresa 40, 47–48, 63
Striuli, Carlo 169
Studer, Cheryl 165
Sullivan, Louis 56
Sved, Alexander 144

Tajo, Italo 109–110
Takacs, Paula 144
Talbert, Florence Cole 65
Tatozzi, Vittorio 114
Tebaldi, Renata 65, 117, 120, 123, 126, 153, 156
Teliga, Aleksander 171
Thénard Louis-Jacques 33
Tiberini, Mario 47
Toczyska, Stefania 144, 160
Tomasev, Ivan 171
Tomasson, Ingrid 154
Tominello, E. 106
Tomowa-Sintow, Anna 142
Toriani, Ostavia 51
Toscanini, Arturo 5, 61, 75, 77, 110–111, 122, 136
Tozzi, Giorgio 124–125, 149
Tracey, Edmond 146
Traubel, Helen 2
Tsiganchev, Stefan 129
Tucci, Gabriella 156
Tucker, Richard 62, 77, 111–112, 117–118

Usiglio, Emilio 75

Valdengo, Giuseppe 111
Valentino, Rudolf 66
Van Dam, José 133
Van Der Schaaf, Jan 154
Van Mill, Arnold 124
Varnay, Astrid 62
Verdi, Carlo 13
Verdi, Giuseppe: *Aroldo* 39; *Attila* 10, 25, 26; *Un Ballo in Maschera* 11, 13, 55, 66; *La Battaglia di Legnano* 112; *Il Corsaro* 26; *Don Carlos (Don Carlo)* 13, 14, 15, 23, 25–26, 29, 70, 71–72; *I Due Foscari* 46; *Ernani* 11, 28; *Falstaff* 27, 68, 110; *Forza del Destino* 11, 13–14, 26, 28–29, 40, 46–47, 53; *Un Giorno di Regno* 12, 46, 112; *Giovanna D'Arco* 46; *Jerusalem* 70; *I Lombardi* 46, 70, 112; *I Masnadieri* 26; *Messa de Requiem* 34, 49; as *My Darlin' Aida* 59; *Nabucco* 10, 13, 46; *Oberto, Conte di Bonifacio* 10–11, 12, 26, 46; *Otello* 1, 14, 27, 36, 68, 115; *Rigoletto* 9, 11, 13, 68, 69; *Rocester* 12; *Simon Boccanegra* 36; *Stiffelio* 13, 39; *La Traviata* 11, 53–54, 68; *Il Trovatore* 11, 21, 68, 69, 114; *Les Vêpres Siciliennes (I Vespri Siciliani)* 70
Verdi, Giuseppina 10, 13, 39, 40, 48
Verdi, Icilio 12
Verdi, Margherita (Barezzi) 12
Verdi, Virginia 12
Verrett, Shirley 63–64
Vickers, Jon 124, 134
Viner-Chenishova, Julia 128–129
Vitali, Giuseppina 34
Vitelli, Vittorio 167
Von Bülow, Hans 50

Wagner, Richard 22, 68; *Lohengrin* 40–41;
  Die Walküre 51
Waldmann, Margherita 153
Waldmann, Maria (Massari) 48–49
Walker, Frank 39
Walters, Jess 62–63
Wanamaker, Sam 159
Warren, Leonard 118, 120, 124, 147
Washington, Paolo 156
Welitsch, Ljuba 2
Wixel, Ingvar 141
Wysor, Elisabeth 148

Yeargen, Michael 164
Yurisich, Gregory 146–147

Zaccaria, Nicola 117
Zacchi, Ginevra Giovannoni 34
Zajick, Dolora 137, 164, 166–167
Zanazzo, Alfredo 158
Zardo, Carlo 158
Zeffirelli, Franco 167–168, 169, 171
Zenatello, Giovanni 54
Zerbini, Antonio 121
Zobel, Carl 51

www.ingramcontent.com/pod-product-compliance
Lightning Source LLC
Chambersburg PA
CBHW081558300426
44116CB00015B/2932